THE POEMS OF
ARTHUR HUGH CLOUGH

Oxford University Press, Ely House, London W.1

GLASGOW NEW YORK TORONTO MELBOURNE WELLINGTON
CAPE TOWN SALISBURY IBADAN NAIROBI LUSAKA ADDIS ABABA
BOMBAY CALCUTTA MADRAS KARACHI LAHORE DACCA
KUALA LUMPUR HONG KONG TOKYO

THE POEMS OF
ARTHUR HUGH CLOUGH

EDITED BY
A. L. P. NORRINGTON

LONDON
OXFORD UNIVERSITY PRESS
NEW YORK TORONTO
1968

ARTHUR HUGH CLOUGH

Born, Liverpool, 1 January 1819
Died, Florence, 13 November 1861

This Oxford Standard Authors edition of The Poems of
Arthur Hugh Clough, *edited by A. L. P. Norrington
from the Oxford English Texts edition (Clarendon Press,
1951), was first published in 1967*

REPRINTED LITHOGRAPHICALLY IN GREAT BRITAIN
AT THE UNIVERSITY PRESS, OXFORD
BY VIVIAN RIDLER
PRINTER TO THE UNIVERSITY

INTRODUCTION

I

ARTHUR HUGH CLOUGH was born on New Year's Day 1819, in the same year as Ruskin, George Eliot, Walt Whitman, and Queen Victoria. His father, James Butler Clough, came of a well-to-do family long established in North Wales; his mother, born Anne Perfect, was the daughter of a Yorkshire banker. They had three sons, of whom Arthur was the second, and one daughter, Anne Jemima, who became the first Principal of Newnham College, Cambridge.

Clough's father went into business in Liverpool as a cotton merchant, and in 1823 took his wife and young family out to Charleston, South Carolina, in order to attend to the American end of the trade, and there he made his home for the next thirteen years. Arthur and his elder brother were sent back to England to be educated, and in 1829 were both entered at Rugby School, where Dr. Thomas Arnold had just become headmaster. Arthur won a scholarship to Balliol and went up to Oxford in 1837. He surprised his friends by only obtaining a second class in 1841, but was elected to a Fellowship at Oriel in 1842. Six years later he resigned his Fellowship, and in 1849 was appointed Principal of University Hall, London, a new hostel for students, founded by Presbyterians and Unitarians. At the end of 1851 he resigned this post too. In the following year he became engaged to Blanche Smith, a cousin of Florence Nightingale, and he had to find a way of earning enough to marry on. He set sail for America in October to seek his fortune, but nothing came of it, and he returned to England next year to take up a post as examiner in the Education Office. In 1854 he and Blanche were married.

Clough's responsibilities and salary were at first moderate, but the family income was augmented by Blanche's father. Clough had 'settled down' at last, but he was not to enjoy his marriage long. By 1859 his health began to fail, and in 1861, after months of sick leave spent wandering in search of health in Europe, he died in Florence on 13 November, aged 42.

v

II

Clough was thought by many of his contemporaries, indeed by most of those who came to know him, to be a man of uncommon distinction. He had been Arnold's most brilliant pupil at Rugby. He made a deep impression at Oxford, as undergraduate and as young don. It was the same later in London and New England. Matthew Arnold, Carlyle, Thackeray, and Tennyson, Emerson, Lowell, and C. E. Norton, and many other leading men on both sides of the Atlantic, knew and admired him, and were in no doubt about his character and his ability. J. A. Symonds was going to a tutorial with Jowett on the day the news of Clough's death reached Oxford. 'I cannot hear your essay this evening, Mr. Symonds,' said Jowett, 'I have just heard that Clough is dead.'

It was the man himself who so much impressed these eminent Victorians. It cannot have been his career. He had resigned from two educational appointments by the time he was thirty-two, and the post in the Education Office that he accepted two years later was a minor one. As for his poetry, there was little for them to judge by in his lifetime, and there were other poets to hold their attraction. Between 1837, when Clough went up to Oxford and Victoria came to the throne, and 1861, when he died, Browning was producing a new volume almost every other year. Most of Matthew Arnold's poetry was published during those twenty-four years, and a great deal of Longfellow's. Wordsworth's *Prelude* appeared (posthumously) in 1851, and Tennyson, who succeeded him as Poet Laureate in 1850, published *The Princess* in 1847, *In Memoriam* in 1850, *Maud* in 1855, and *Idylls of the King* in 1859.

Clough made the briefest of appearances on this copious scene. Just before his thirtieth birthday, in December 1848, he published a long poem of some 1,700 lines, *The Bothie of Toper-na-Fuosich* (reprinted after his death as *The Bothie of Tober-na-Vuolich*). A few weeks later, in January 1849, appeared *Ambarvalia*, a joint production with a clergyman friend, Thomas Burbidge. The book attracted little attention at the time and was not reprinted, though the sheets of Clough's section—forty short poems—were reissued, bound as a separate volume, in 1850. The rest was silence until, in 1858, another long poem, *Amours de Voyage*, was published serially in the newly founded American *Atlantic Monthly*. The bulk of his mature poetic output—in total almost as large as Matthew Arnold's—was still in manuscript when he died, and was known, if at all, only to his wife and a few friends.

One of these friends, C. E. Norton, had been encouraging him, ever since they had met in Boston in 1853, to publish a volume of poetry in America. The project seems to have been well advanced by the summer of 1855, when Clough, who had been sending material to Norton, wrote (14 September) that he thought the book might be called 'The Bothie, Roman Hexameters, and Other Poems —chiefly reprinted'. But before the work of selection and revision had been completed, the 'Roman Hexameters', which would have formed the bulk of the new material, were published as *Amours de Voyage* in the Atlantic Monthly: 'a great event to me', wrote Clough to Norton, 'this is the first money I ever received for verse-making. ... I should be very glad if next year a volume of my verse should be published.' That was in 1858. By the end of 1860 all the copy for the volume must have been in Norton's hands, for Clough wrote, in February 1861, assuring him that he was not disappointed by 'the postponement of my republication by Ticknor and Fields' (the Boston publishers). It was almost the last letter he wrote to Norton. He died before the American 'republication' could take place.

It was only after his death, therefore, that the products of his 'verse-making' were made available to the public in a collected volume. Two editions appeared simultaneously in 1862, one in London, published by Macmillan with a memoir by F. T. Palgrave (whose *Golden Treasury* had come out in 1861), the other in Boston, published by Ticknor and Fields with a memoir by Norton. The American edition contained one extra poem, but otherwise the material in the two books was identical, as Mrs. Clough and Norton intended. A second English edition in 1863 contained a few more short poems, and in 1869 Mrs. Clough brought out a much enlarged edition (Vol. II of *The Poems and Prose Remains*), containing 'all such additional matter as, after careful consideration, has been deemed worthy to be given to the public'. This remained the standard collection for many years until the last edition (in Macmillan's 'Globe' series) went out of print in 1932.

A new and fuller edition of the poems appeared in 1951 in the *Oxford English Texts* series. This was based on a re-examination of Clough's own manuscript drafts and fair copies, used by Mrs. Clough a century before and preserved by the family.[1] It restores to the canon several *Ambarvalia* poems omitted, according to Clough's instructions, from the previous posthumous volumes, adds a few poems not previously printed, and presents fuller versions of *Dipsychus* and *Mari Magno* than Mrs. Clough saw fit to print. The present *Oxford Standard Authors* edition is a reprint of the poems in the 1951 edition, omitting *Dipsychus Continued*, *Mari Magno*, and the groups there called Unfinished Poems and Miscellaneous Poems.

III

If Clough had, perforce, few readers in his lifetime, he became a much-read poet after his death. There were those who thought him overrated. Swinburne, not unexpectedly, admired him not at all. 'There was a bad poet named Clough', he wrote in 1875, 'whom his friends found it useless to puff; for the public, if dull, has not quite such a skull as belongs to believers in Clough.' But the collected poems were reprinted many times before the end of the century, and selections appeared in due course in such popular series as *The Canterbury Poets* (Walter Scott), *The Muses' Library* (Routledge), and Macmillan's *Golden Treasury Series*. The public, it seems, did believe in Clough. He was among the favourite poets of the last forty years of the Victorian era.

Soon after the turn of the century, however, his popularity began to decline rapidly. The decline was hastened by Lytton Strachey's allusions to him in *Eminent Victorians* (1918), '*vignettes dessinées avec un subtil mélange d'apitoiement et de dérision narquoise*', as M. Paul Veyriras describes them. A new selection of the poems edited by Humphrey Milford (*Oxford Library of Prose and Poetry*, 1910) took

---

[1] They were deposited in the Bodleian Library by Clough's grandniece, Miss Katherine Duff, in 1953.

some twenty years to sell out. The major edition was last reprinted by Macmillan in 1920. There came a time when, for nearly twenty years, Clough's poetical works could only be bought in second-hand bookshops.

The new edition published by the Clarendon Press in 1951 co-incided with a revival of interest and provided the means for a reappraisal. Four recent studies, British, American, and French, are evidence of this renewed attention: Lady Chorley's *Arthur Hugh Clough: The Uncommitted Mind* (Oxford, 1962), Walter E. Hough-ton's *The Poetry of Clough: An Essay in Revaluation* (Yale, 1963), Paul Veyriras's *Arthur Hugh Clough, 1819–1861* (Paris, Didier, 1964), and Michael Timko's *Innocent Victorian* (Ohio, 1966). An extensive selection of his letters, more than half of them printed for the first time, was provided in the two-volume *Correspondence* edited by Frederick A. Mulhauser (Oxford, 1957), and the *Selected Prose Works* edited by Buckner B. Trawick (University of Alabama Press, 1964) also contains some hitherto unpublished matter. There is thus ample material now available for the student and the scholar, and it is hoped that the present edition may help to satisfy a wider public.

IV

Clough's first published poem, the *Bothie*, is written in hexameters—'Anglo-savage hexameters', as he called them—and he used the same metre in *Amours de Voyage*. It was a popular metre in the nineteenth century, Longfellow's *Evangeline* (1847) being perhaps the best-known example, though no other poet used it with such freedom and gusto as Clough. But it is unfamiliar to many modern readers, and some account of Clough's practice may be useful.

The quantitative prosody of Greek and Latin is based on the length of syllables, not on their accent or stress. A long vowel makes a long syllable, a short one a short, except when followed by certain combinations of consonants, which, by the rules, make the preceding syllable long, whatever its vowel. Two short syllables equal one long, as two semiquavers equal one quaver. A hexameter contains six feet and each foot, like a bar of music, has the same length: the first syllable is long, and may be followed by one long syllable (spondee) or two short (dactyl). The sixth foot must have only two syllables (the second of which may, in this case only, be long or short), and the fifth foot is almost invariably a dactyl. 'Happily married' is a typical ending for an English hexameter on classical principles.

Elizabethan poets thought that English verse might be written according to the same rules, but their attempts were not successful. They produced verses which, as Milford says, 'can neither be scanned for their false quantities nor read as verses for their false accents'. Later attempts have proved equally unconvincing, including those by Clough himself, in the short pieces 'Trunks the forest yielded', 'From thy far sources', and *Actaeon*. It will not do. The rhythm of English verse depends upon accent (among other things), not length of syllable, in the classical sense. Rébel, the noun, cannot have the same metrical value as rebél, the verb, though the length of the syllables is the same, and in a Latin hexameter the two words would be metrically interchangeable.

Clough's two long hexameter poems seem to show that he realized better than any of his contemporaries the difference between classical and English prosody. He let 'longs' and 'shorts' go by the board, and went by accent. Each of his hexameters has its six feet, and in each foot there should be one syllable—almost invariably the first—which has a naturally strong and predominant stress. There are thus six predominantly stressed syllables in each line, and each of these syllables is followed—or very occasionally preceded—by one or two unstressed, or less strongly stressed, syllables. Where there are three syllables in the foot, the two unstressed syllables are normally very light; where there are only two, the second syllable may, and quite often does, have almost as much weight as the first.

But some examples will perhaps make the matter clearer; and we will begin with straightforward examples which can hardly be read wrongly.

1. Ónly a / Líberal / mémber, a / wáy at the / énd of the / táble.
2. Dráwn by / móon and / sún from / Lábra / dór and / Gréenland.
3. Árchi / téctural / Beáuty in / Ápplic / átion to / Wómen.
4. Ráphael's / Jóys and / Gráces, and / thý clear / stárs, Gali / léo!

In 1 every foot but the last has three syllables, in 2 every foot is dissyllabic, while 3 and 4 are mixed. But whereas in 1, 2, and 3 no syllables except the first in each foot have any natural stress, in 4 there are two feet, the first and fourth, in which there is a secondary stress; indeed, the two syllables of the fourth foot should be read with almost equal weight.

But Clough was trying his hand out—'Experimental yet the prosody is of the English', as he wrote in one of his notebooks—and he wrote many lines over which the reader may well stumble at first sight, and some which it is frankly impossible to scan with confidence. The following passage from Section IX of the *Bothie* will be found to exhibit almost every conceivable irregularity:

All the great empty streets are flooded with broadening clearness,
Which, withal, by inscrutable simultaneous access
Permeates far and pierces to the very cellars lying in
Narrow high back-lane, and court, and alley of alleys:—
He that goes forth to his walks, while speeding to the suburb,
Sees sights only peaceful and pure; as labourers settling
Slowly to work, in their limbs the lingering sweetness of slumber;
Humble market-carts, coming-in, bringing-in, not only
Flower, fruit, farm-store, but sounds and sights of the country
Dwelling yet on the sense of the dreamy drivers; soon after
Half-awake servant-maids unfastening drowsy shutters
Up at the windows, or down, letting-in the air by the doorway;
School-boys, school-girls soon, with slate, portfolio, satchel,
Hampered as they haste, those running, these others maidenly tripping;
Early clerk anon turning out to stroll, or it may be
Meet his sweetheart—waiting behind the garden gate there;
Merchant on his grass-plat haply, bare-headed; and now by this time
Little child bringing breakfast to 'father' that sits on the timber
There by the scaffolding; see, she waits for the can beside him;
Meantime above purer air untarnished of new-lit fires:
So that the whole great wicked artificial civilized fabric—
All its unfinished houses, lots for sale, and railway outworks—
Seems reaccepted, resumed to Primal Nature and Beauty:—
—Such—in me, and to me, and on me the love of Elspie!

In l. 1 the last four feet are clear, but should the first two be 'Áll the great / émpty' or 'Áll the / gréat empty'? or even 'All the gréat / émpty', inverting the stress in the first foot? The answer is not quite any of these. The proper way to read it is 'Áll the greàt / émpty', with a secondary stress on the third syllable of the first foot—unusual in a trisyllabic foot.

In l. 2 the only difficulty is in the fourth foot, 'símul-', in which a stress heavier than is natural must be placed on the first syllable.

In l. 3 there are two departures from the normal. The third foot has four syllables, 'piérces to the', instead of three, and the last foot, 'lýing in', has three syllables, though the first two can be almost compressed into one.

In l. 5 the difficulty lies in the fourth and fifth feet, for which we have four syllables, 'speeding to the', with only one natural stress among them. The only way to mitigate the deficiency is to put a secondary stress on the second syllable of 'speeding', but it is a bad line.

In l. 9 'Flower' is a whole foot, and is to be read as a dissyllable.

Line 14 is no doubt intentionally unsteady at the outset. The first foot has four syllables, and the second and third feet both contain two natural stresses: 'Hámpered as they / háste, thòse / rúnning, thèse / óthers / máidenly / trípping'. The movement of the line is not ill-suited to the morning rush to school.

Here is the whole passage with the suggested scansion marked (the *grave* accents indicate secondary stress):

Áll the greàt / émpty / stréets are / floóded with / broádening / cleárness,
Whích, with / ál, by in / scrútable / símul / táneous / áccess
Pérmeàtes / fár and / piérces to the / véry / céllars / lýing in
Nárrow / hígh bàck / láne, and / coúrt, and / álley of / álleys:—
Hé that goes / fórth to his / wálks, whìle / spéedìng / to the / súburb,
Seés sìghts / ónly / peáceful and / púre; as / lábourers / séttling
Slówly to / wórk, in their / límbs the / língering / sweétness of / slúmber;
Húmble / márket / cárts, còming / ín, brìnging / ín, not / ónly
Flówer, / fruít, fàrm / stóre, but / soúnds and / síghts of the / coúntry
Dwélling / yét on the / sénse of the / dréamy / drívers; soòn / áfter
Hálf-awàke / sérvant / maíds un / fástening / drówsy / shútters
Úp at the / wíndows, or / dówn, lètting / ín the / aír by the / doórway;

Schoól-bòys, / schoól-gìrls / soón, with / sláte, pòrt / fólio, / sátchel,
Hámpered as they / háste, thòse / rúnning, thèse / óthers / máidenly /
  trípping;
Eárly / clérk a / nón tùrning / oút to / stróll, or it / máy be
Méet his / swéetheàrt / —waíting be / hínd the / gárden / gáte thère;
Mérchant on his / gráss-plat / háply, bàre / heáded; and / nów by / thís
  tìme
Líttle / chíld brìnging / breákfast to / 'fáther' that / síts on the / tímber
Thére by the / scáffolding; / seé, she / waíts for the / cán be / síde him;
Meántìme a / bóve pùrer / aír un / tárnished of / néw-lìt / fíres:
Só that the / whóle greàt / wícked / ártifìcial / cívilized / fábric—
Áll its un / fínished / hoúses, / lóts for sàle, and / raílway / oútworks—
Séems reac / cépted, re / súmed to / Prímal / Náture and / Beaúty:—
—Súch / —ín me, and / tó me, and / ón me the / lóve of / Élspie!

V

Walter Bagehot, reviewing the first posthumous collection of
Clough's poems in 1862, wrote of him as a man 'who seemed about
to do something, but who died before he did it'. Lowell described
him as 'dying before he had subdued his sensitive temperament to
the sterner requirements of his art'. This view of Clough as a poet
of unfulfilled promise has often been repeated. It is true, of course,
that he left much work, and some of his best, unfinished. But that is
not to say that if he had lived longer he would have written better.
The evidence points the other way.

He wrote almost all his poetry between 1839 and 1852. To the
period before he resigned his fellowship at Oriel in 1848 belong the
Ambarvalia poems and many other short pieces. In 1848, in a mood
of release, he wrote the *Bothie*, and continued to fill notebook after
notebook with verse during the next two or three years, to which
belong *Amours de Voyage*, *Dipsychus*, 'Say not the struggle nought
availeth', *Easter Day*, and much else. But the sequel to *Dipsychus*
which he wrote in 1852[1] is very inferior; for the next eight years he
wrote nothing; and when he began verse-making again, a few months

---

[1] Lady Chorley has proved beyond reasonable doubt that *Dipsychus Continued* was
written during his visit to America (op. cit. pp. 264 ff.).

xiii

before his death, the result was justly described by Professor Houghton as 'the most dated and least successful of Clough's longer poems', the unfinished *Mari Magno*. It is hard to avoid the suspicion that Clough would have become, had he lived longer, a poet less worth reading.

Secondly, anybody reading his poetry as a whole may well find it hard to recognize the familiar portrait drawn by Matthew Arnold in *Thyrsis*: the gentle shepherd-poet whose 'rustic flute kept not for long its happy, country tone', the 'too quick despairer' whose 'piping took a troubled sound'. Arnold seems to be saying that Clough showed his true bent as a poet in the *Bothie* and then, overcome by the contentions of the world and faltering in his quest for unattainable truth, began to sing out of tune. Nothing, certainly, could be blither than the 'happy country tone' of the *Bothie*, with its glowing pictures of Highland scenery 'where the great peaks look abroad over Skye to the westernmost islands', and its hilarious reading-party talk:

'Every woman is, or ought to be, a Cathedral.'
'Philip shall write us a book, a Treatise on *The Laws of Architectural Beauty in Application to Women*. . . .
Where shall in specimen seen be the sculliony stumpy-columnar,
(which to a reverent taste is perhaps the most moving of any,)
Rising to grace of true woman in English the Early and Later. . . .
Lost, ere we end, in the Lady-Debased and the Lady-Flamboyant.'

But it was not a feebler note that Clough struck in the poetry that he wrote after the *Bothie*, nor always a more melancholy note. What could be more airily and amusingly conversational than *Amours de Voyage*?

Rome, believe me, my friend, is like its own Monte Testaceo,
Merely a marvellous mass of broken and castaway wine-pots. . . .
No one can cavil, I grant, at the size of the great Coliseum.
Doubtless the notion of grand and capacious and massive amusement,
This the old Romans had; but tell me, is this an idea?

What, again, could be more vigorous than the satire of, for example,

The Latest Decalogue, or the Spirit's mockery of the *parvenu* in
Dipsychus:

> As I sat at the café, I said to myself,
> They may talk as they please about what they call pelf,
> They may sneer as they like about eating and drinking,
> But help it I cannot, I cannot help thinking
> How pleasant it is to have money, heigh ho!
> How pleasant it is to have money.

Poetry like this may lack the 'high seriousness' that Arnold thought
appropriate, but it was not the 'too quick despairer' of *Thyrsis* who
seemed to be talking to us in such a very contemporary voice when
the B.B.C. broadcast readings of *Amours de Voyage* in 1958,[1] a hundred years after it was first published.

Lastly, Clough has been pronounced a prosaic poet. It has been
maintained that it would have been better if he had said what he
wanted to say in prose, not verse. His lyrics (to call them such) are
too plain in language, too stiff and intricate in movement, his longer
poems too unbuttoned. He would not don the poet's singing robes.
'Consider whether you attain the *beautiful*', Arnold wrote to him,
'and whether your product gives PLEASURE.' Certainly he is an
unusual mid-nineteenth-century poet, sometimes a difficult poet,
but a poet he had to be.

[1] and again in 1967.

CONTENTS

SHORTER POEMS

CONTENTS

xix

II

Ah love, high love, she said and sighed,
    She said, the Poet's love!
A star upon a turbid tide,
    Reflected from above.
A marvel here, a glory there,
    But clouds will intervene,
And garish earthly noon outglare
    The purity serene.   20

I GIVE thee joy! O worthy word!
Congratulate—A courtier fine,
Transacts, politely shuffling by,
The civil ceremonial lie,
Which, quickly spoken, barely heard,
Can never hope, nor e'en design
                To give thee joy!

I give thee joy! O faithful word!
When heart with heart, and mind with mind
Shake hands; and eyes in outward sign   10
Of inward vision, rest in thine;
And feelings simply, truly stirred,
Emphatic utterance seek to find,
                And give thee joy!

I give thee joy! O word of power!
Believe, though slight the tie in sooth,
When heart to heart its fountain opes
The plant to water that with hopes
Is budding for fruition's flower—
The word, potential made, in truth   20
                Shall give thee joy!

3

Shall give thee joy! Oh, not in vain,
For erring child the mother's prayer;
The sigh, wherein a martyr's breath
Exhales from ignominious death
For some lost cause! In humbler strain
Shall this poor word a virtue bear,
    And give thee joy!

WHEN panting sighs the bosom fill,
And hands by chance united thrill
At once with one delicious pain
The pulses and the nerves of twain;
When eyes that erst could meet with ease,
Do seek, yet, seeking, shyly shun
Extatic conscious unison,—
The sure beginnings, say, be these,
Prelusive to the strain of love
Which angels sing in heaven above?   10

 Or is it but the vulgar tune,
Which all that breathe beneath the moon
So accurately learn—so soon?
With variations duly blent;
Yet that same song to all intent,
Set for the finer instrument;
It is; and it would sound the same
In beasts, were not the bestial frame,
Less subtly organised, to blame;
And but that soul and spirit add   20
To pleasures, even base and bad,
A zest the soulless never had.

 It may be—well indeed I deem;
But what if sympathy, it seem,
And admiration and esteem,

Commingling therewithal, do make
The passion prized for Reason's sake?
Yet, when my heart would fain rejoice,
A small expostulating voice
Falls in: Of this thou wilt not take   30
Thy one irrevocable choice?
In accent tremulous and thin
I hear high Prudence deep within,
Pleading the bitter, bitter sting,
Should slow-maturing seasons bring,
Too late, the veritable thing.
For if (the Poet's tale of bliss)
A love, wherewith commeasured this
Is weak, and beggarly, and none,
Exist a treasure to be won,   40
And if the vision, though it stay,
Be yet for an appointed day,—
This choice, if made, this deed, if done,
The memory of this present past,
With vague foreboding might o'ercast
The heart, or madden it at last.

  Let Reason first her office ply;
Esteem, and admiration high,
And mental, moral sympathy,
Exist they first, nor be they brought   50
By self-deceiving afterthought,—
What if an halo interfuse
With these again its opal hues,
That all o'erspreading and o'erlying,
Transmuting, mingling, glorifying,
About the beauteous various whole,
With beaming smile do dance and quiver;
Yet, is that halo of the soul?—
Or is it, as may sure be said,
Phosphoric exhalation bred   60

5

Of vapour, steaming from the bed
Of Fancy's brook, or Passion's river?
So when, as will be by-and-bye,
The stream is waterless and dry,
This halo and its hues will die;
And though the soul contented rest
With those substantial blessings blest,
Will not a longing, half-confest,
Betray that this is not the love,
The gift for which all gifts above   70
Him praise we, Who is Love, the giver?

    I cannot say—the things are good:
Bread is it, if not angels' food;
But Love? Alas! I cannot say;
A glory on the vision lay;
A light of more than mortal day
About it played, upon it rested;
It did not, faltering and weak,
Beg Reason on its side to speak:
Itself was Reason, or, if not,   80
Such substitute as is, I wot,
Of seraph-kind the loftier lot;—
Itself was of itself attested;—
To processes that, hard and dry,
Elaborate truth from fallacy,
With modes intuitive succeeding,
Including those and superseding;
Reason sublimed and Love most high
It was, a life that cannot die,
A dream of glory most exceeding.   90

SIC ITUR

As, at a railway junction, men
Who came together, taking then
One the train up, one down, again

Meet never! Ah, much more as they
Who take one street's two sides, and say
Hard parting words, but walk one way:

Though moving other mates between,
While carts and coaches intervene,
Each to the other goes unseen,

Yet seldom, surely, shall there lack   10
Knowledge they walk not back to back,
But with an unity of track,

Where common dangers each attend,
And common hopes their guidance lend
To light them to the self-same end.

Whether he then shall cross to thee,
Or thou go thither, or it be
Some midway point, ye yet shall see

Each other, yet again shall meet.
Ah, joy! when with the closing street,   20
Forgivingly at last ye greet!

COMMEMORATION SONNETS

OXFORD, 1844

I

AMIDST the fleeting many unforgot,
O Leonina! whether thou wert seen
Singling, upon the Isis' margent green,
From meaner flowers the frail forget-me-not,
Or, as the picture of a saintly queen,

7

Sitting, uplifting, betwixt fingers small,
A sceptre of the water-iris tall,
With pendent lily crowned of golden sheen;
So, or in gay and gorgeous gallery,
Where, amid splendours, like to those that far   10
Flame backward from the sun's invisible car,
Thou lookedst forth, as there the evening star;
Oh, Leonina! fair wert thou to see,
And unforgotten shall thine image be.

II

Thou whom thy danglers have ere this forgot,
O Leonina! whether thou wert seen
Waiting, upon the Isis' margent green,
The boats that should have passed there and did not;
Or at the ball, admiring crowds between,
To partner academical and slow   20
Teaching, upon the light Slavonic toe,
Polkas that were not, only should have been;
Or, in the crowded gallery crushed, didst hear
For bonnets white, blue, pink, the ladies' cheer
Multiplied while divided, and endure
(Thyself being seen) to see, not hear, rehearse
The long, long Proses, and the Latin Verse—
O Leonina! thou wert tired, I'm sure.

III

Not in thy robes of royal rich array,
As when thy state at Dresden thou art keeping;   30
Nor with the golden epaulettes outpeeping
From under pink and scarlet trappings gay
(Raiment of doctors) through the area led;
While galleries peal applause, and Phillimore
For the supreme superlative cons-o'er
The common-place-book of his classic head;

8

Uncrowned thou com'st, alone, or with a tribe
Of volant varlets scattering jest and jibe
Almost beside thee. Yet to thee, when rent
Was the Teutonic Caesar's robe, there went   40
One portion: and with Julius, thou to-day
Canst boast, I came, I saw, I went away!

COME back again, my olden heart!—
  Ah, fickle spirit and untrue,
I bade the only guide depart
  Whose faithfulness I surely knew:
I said, my heart is all too soft;
He who would climb and soar aloft
Must needs keep ever at his side
The tonic of a wholesome pride.

Come back again, my olden heart!—
  Alas, I called not then for thee;   10
I called for Courage, and apart
  From Pride if Courage could not be,
Then welcome, Pride! and I shall find
In thee a power to lift the mind
This low and grovelling joy above—
'Tis but the proud can truly love.

Come back again, my olden heart!—
  With incrustations of the years
Uncased as yet,—as then thou wert,
  Full-filled with shame and coward fears: 20
Wherewith, amidst a jostling throng
Of deeds, that each and all were wrong,
The doubting soul, from day to day,
Uneasy paralytic lay.

Come back again, my olden heart!
　I said, Perceptions contradict,
Convictions come, anon depart,
　And but themselves as false convict.
Assumptions hasty, crude and vain,
Full oft to use will Science deign;　　　　30
The corks the novice plies to-day
The swimmer soon shall cast away.

Come back again, my olden heart!
　I said, Behold, I perish quite,
Unless to give me strength to start,
　I make myself my rule of right:
It must be, if I act at all,
To save my shame I have at call
The plea of all men understood,
Because I willed it, it is good.　　　　40

Come back again, my olden heart!
　I know not if in very deed
This means alone could aid impart
　To serve my sickly spirit's need;
But clear alike of wild self-will,
And fear that faltered, paltered still,
Remorseful thoughts of after days
A way espy betwixt the ways.

Come back again, old heart! Ah me!
　Methinks in those thy coward fears　　　　50
There might, perchance, a courage be,
　That fails in these the manlier years;
Courage to let the courage sink,
Itself a coward base to think,
Rather than not for heavenly light
Wait on to show the truly right.

WHEN soft September brings again
   To yonder gorse its golden glow,
And Snowdon sends its autumn rain
   To bid thy current livelier flow;
Amid that ashen foliage light
When scarlet beads are glistering bright,
While alder boughs unchanged are seen
In summer livery of green;
When clouds before the cooler breeze
Are flying, white and large; with these   10
Returning, so may I return,
And find thee changeless, Pont-y-wern.

OH, ask not what is love, she said,
   Or ask it not of me;
Or of the heart, or of the head,
   Or if at all it be.

Oh, ask it not, she said, she said,
   Thou winn'st not word from me!
—Oh, silent as the long long dead,
   I, Lady, learn of thee.

I ask,—thou speakest not,—and still
   I ask, and look to thee;   10
And lo, without or with a will,
   The answer is in me.

Without thy will it came to me?
   Ah, with it let it stay;
Ah, with it, yes, abide in me,
   Nor only for to-day!

Thou claim'st it? nay, the deed is done;
   Ah, leave it with thy leave;
And thou a thousand loves for one
   Shalt day on day receive!   20

LIGHT words they were, and lightly, falsely said;
She heard them, and she started,—and she rose,
As in the act to speak; the sudden thought
And unconsidered impulse led her on.
In act to speak she rose, but with the sense
Of all the eyes of that mixed company
Now suddenly turned upon her, some with age
Hardened and dulled, some cold and critical;
Some in whom vapours of their own conceit,
As moist malarious mists the heavenly stars,   10
Still blotted out their good, the best at best
By frivolous laugh and prate conventional
All too untuned for all she thought to say—
With such a thought the mantling blood to her cheek
Flushèd-up, and o'er-flushed itself, blank night her soul
Made dark, and in her all her purpose swooned.
She stood as if for sinking. Yet anon
With recollections clear, august, sublime,
Of God's great truth, and right immutable,
Which, as obedient vassals, to her mind   20
Came summoned of her will, in self-negation
Quelling her troublous earthy consciousness,
She queened it o'er her weakness. At the spell
Back rolled the ruddy tide, and leaves her cheek
Paler than erst, and yet not ebbs so far
But that one pulse of one indignant thought
Might hurry it hither in flood. So as she stood
She spoke. God in her spoke, and made her heard.

QUI LABORAT, ORAT

O ONLY Source of all our light and life,
    Whom as our truth, our strength, we see and feel,
But whom the hours of mortal moral strife
    Alone aright reveal!

Mine inmost soul, before Thee inly brought,
  Thy presence owns ineffable, divine;
Chastised each rebel self-encentered thought,
  My will adoreth Thine.

With eye down-dropt, if then this earthly mind
  Speechless remain, or speechless e'en depart;   10
Nor seek to see—for what of earthly kind
  Can see Thee as Thou art?—

If well-assured 'tis but profanely bold
  In thought's abstractest forms to seem to see,
It dare not dare the dread communion hold
  In ways unworthy Thee,

O not unowned, Thou shalt unnamed forgive,
  In worldly walks the prayerless heart prepare;
And if in work its life it seem to live,
  Shalt make that work be prayer.   20

Nor times shall lack, when while the work it plies,
  Unsummoned powers the blinding film shall part,
And scarce by happy tears made dim, the eyes
  In recognition start.

But, as thou willest, give or e'en forbear
  The beatific supersensual sight,
So, with Thy blessing blest, that humbler prayer
  Approach Thee morn and night.

WITH graceful seat and skilful hand,
  Upon the fiery steed,
Prompt at a moment to command,
  As fittest, or concede,

O Lady! happy he whose will
  Shall manliest homage pay
To that which yielding ever, still
  Shall in its yielding sway:

Yea, happy he, whose willing soul
   In perfect love combined
With thine shall form one perfect whole,
   One happy heart and mind!   10

Fair, fair on fleeting steed to see,
   Boon Nature's child, nor less,
In gorgeous rooms, serene and free,
   'Midst etiquette and dress!

Thrice happy who, amidst the form
   And folly that must be,
Existence fresh, and true, and warm,
   Shall, Lady, own in thee!   20

Such dreams, in gay saloon, of days
   That shall be, 'midst the dance
And music, while I hear and gaze,
   My silent soul entrance.

As here the harp thy fingers wake
   To sounds melodious, he
To thy soul's touch shall music make,
   And his enstrengthen thee.

The notes, diverse in time and tone,
   The hearts shall image true,   30
That still, in some sweet ways unknown,
   Their harmonies renew.

The mazy dance, an emblem meet,
   Shall changeful life pourtray,
Whose changes all love's music sweet
   Expressively obey.

Then shall to waltz, though unexiled,
   And polka sometimes heard,
To songs capricious, wayward, wild,
   Be other strains preferred.   40

The heart that 'midst the petty strife,
    Whose ferment, day by day,
To strange realities of life
    Converts its trifling play,—

The heart, that here pursued the right,
    Shall then, in freer air,
Expand its wings, and drink the light
    Of life and reason there:

And quickening truth and living law,
    And large affections clear   50
Shall it to heights on heights updraw,
    To holiest hope and fear.

—Ah, moralizing premature!
    And yet words half-supprest
May find some secret thoughts ensure
    Acceptance half-confest.

Full oft concealed high meanings work;
    And, scorning observation,
In gay unthinking guise will lurk
    A saintly aspiration;   60

No sickly thing to sit and sun
    Its puny worth, to pause
And list, ere half the deed be done,
    Its echo—self-applause:

No idler, who its kindly cares
    To every gossip mentions,
And at its breast a posy wears
    Of laudable intentions.

As of itself, of others so
    Unrecognised to seek   70
Its aim content, and in the flow
    Of life and spirits meek.

WHEN ISRAEL CAME OUT OF EGYPT

Lo, here is God, and there is God!
  Believe it not, O Man;
In such vain sort to this and that
  The ancient heathen ran:
Though old Religion shake her head,
  And say in bitter grief,
The day behold, at first foretold,
  Of atheist unbelief:
Take better part, with manly heart,
  Thine adult spirit can;   10
Receive it not, believe it not,
  Believe it not, O Man!

As men at dead of night awaked
  With cries, 'The king is here,'
Rush forth and greet whome'er they meet,
  Whoe'er shall first appear;
And still repeat, to all the street,
  ' 'Tis he,—the king is here;'
The long procession moveth on,
  Each nobler form they see   20
With changeful suit they still salute,
  And cry, ' 'Tis he, 'tis he!'

So, even so, when men were young,
  And earth and heaven was new,
And His immediate presence He
  From human hearts withdrew,
The soul perplexed and daily vexed
  With sensuous False and True,
Amazed, bereaved, no less believed,
  And fain would see Him too: 30
He is! the prophet-tongues proclaimed;
  In joy and hasty fear,
He is! aloud replied the crowd,
  Is here, and here, and here.

He is! They are! in distance seen
  On yon Olympus high,
In those Avernian woods abide,
  And walk this azure sky:
They are, They are! to every show
  Its eyes the baby turned,   40
And blazes sacrificial, tall,
  On thousand altars burned:
They are, they are!—On Sinai's top
  Far seen the lightnings shone,
The thunder broke, a trumpet spoke,
  And God said, I am One.

God spake it out, I, God, am One;
  The unheeding ages ran,
And baby-thoughts again, again,
  Have dogged the growing man: 50
And as of old from Sinai's top
  God said that God is One,
By Science strict so speaks He now
  To tell us, There is None!
Earth goes by chemic forces; Heaven's
  A Mécanique Céleste!
And heart and mind of human kind
  A watch-work as the rest!

Is this a Voice, as was the Voice
  Whose speaking told abroad,   60
When thunder pealed, and mountain reeled,
  The ancient Truth of God?
Ah, not the Voice; 'tis but the cloud,
  Of outer darkness dense,
Where image none, nor e'er was seen
  Similitude of sense.
'Tis but the cloudy darkness dense

That wrapt the Mount around;
While in amaze the people stays,
To hear the Coming Sound.   70

Is there no chosen prophet-soul
    To dare, sublimely meek,
Within the shroud of blackest cloud
    The Deity to seek?
'Midst atheistic systems dark,
    And darker hearts' despair,
His very word it may have heard,
    And on the dusky air
His skirts, as passed He by, to see
    Have strained on their behalf,   80
Who on the plain, with dance amain,
    Adore the Golden Calf.

'Tis but the cloudy darkness dense;
    Though blank the tale it tells,
No God, no Truth! yet He, in sooth,
    Is there—within it dwells;
Within the sceptic darkness deep
    He dwells that none may see,
Till idol forms and idol thoughts
    Have passed and ceased to be: 90
No God, no Truth! ah though, in sooth
    So stand the doctrine's half;
On Egypt's track return not back,
    Nor own the Golden Calf.

Take better part, with manlier heart,
    Thine adult spirit can;
No God, no Truth, receive it ne'er—
    Believe it ne'er—O Man!
But turn not then to seek again
    What first the ill began;   100

No God, it saith; ah, wait in faith
    God's self-completing plan;
Receive it not, but leave it not,
    And wait it out, O Man!

'The Man that went the cloud within
    Is gone and vanished quite;
He cometh not,' the people cries,
    'Nor bringeth God to sight:'
'Lo these thy gods, that safety give,
    Adore and keep the feast!'   110
Deluding and deluded cries
    The Prophet's brother-Priest:
And Israel all bows down to fall
    Before the gilded beast.

Devout, indeed! that priestly creed,
    O Man, reject as sin;
The clouded hill attend thou still,
    And him that went within.
He yet shall bring some worthy thing
    For waiting souls to see: 120
Some sacred word that he hath heard
    Their light and life shall be;
Some lofty part, than which the heart
    Adopt no nobler can,
Thou shalt receive, thou shalt believe,
    And thou shalt do, O Man!

THE Silver Wedding! on some pensive ear
    From towers remote as sound the silvery bells,
To-day from one far unforgotten year
    A silvery faint memorial music swells.

And silver-pale the dim memorial light
    Of musing age on youthful joys is shed,

The golden joys of fancy's dawning bright,
   The golden bliss of, Woo'd, and won, and wed.

Ah, golden then, but silver now! In sooth,
   The years that pale the cheek, that dim the eyes,   10
And silver o'er the golden hairs of youth,
   Less prized can make its only priceless prize.

Not so; the voice this silver name that gave
   To this, the ripe and unenfeebled date,
For steps together tottering to the grave,
   Hath bid the perfect golden title wait.

Rather, if silver this, if that be gold,
   From good to better changed on age's track,
Must it as baser metal be enrolled,
   That day of days, a quarter-century back.   20

Yet ah, its hopes, its joys were golden too,
   But golden of the fairy gold of dreams:
To feel is but to dream; until we do,
   There's nought that is, and all we see but seems.

What was or seemed it needed cares and tears,
   And deeds together done, and trials past,
And all the subtlest alchemy of years,
   To change to genuine substance here at last.

Your fairy gold is silver sure to-day;
   Your ore by crosses many, many a loss,   30
As in refiners' fires, hath purged away
   What erst it had of earthy human dross.

Come years as many yet, and as they go,
   In human life's great crucible shall they
Transmute, so potent are the spells they know,
   Into pure gold the silver of to-day.

Strange metallurge is human life! 'Tis true;
   And Use and Wont in many a gorgeous case

Full specious fair for casual outward view
Electrotype the sordid and the base.　　　　40

Nor lack who praise, avowed, the spurious ware,
　　Who bid young hearts the one true love forego,
Conceit to feed, or fancy light as air,
　　Or greed of pelf and precedence and show.

True, false, as one to casual eyes appear,
　　To read men truly men may hardly learn;
Yet doubt it not that wariest glance would here
　　Faith, Hope and Love, the true Tower-stamp discern.

Come years again! as many yet! and purge
　　Less precious earthier elements away,　　　　50
And gently changed at life's extremest verge,
　　Bring bright in gold your perfect fiftieth day!

That sight may children see and parents show!
　　If not—yet earthly chains of metal true,
By love and duty wrought and fixed below,
　　Elsewhere will shine, transformed, celestial-new;

Will shine of gold, whose essence, heavenly bright,
　　No doubt-damps tarnish, worldly passions fray;
Gold into gold there mirrored, light in light,
　　Shall gleam in glories of a deathless day.　　　　60

I

WHY should I say I see the things I see not,
　　Why be and be not?
Show love for that I love not, and fear for what I fear not?
And dance about to music that I hear not?
　　Who standeth still i' the street
　　Shall be hustled and justled about;
And he that stops i' the dance shall be spurned by the dancers' feet,—
Shall be shoved and be twisted by all he shall meet,

21

And shall raise up an outcry and rout;
　And the partner, too,— 　　　　　　　　10
　What's the partner to do?
While all the while 'tis but, perchance, an humming in mine ear,
　That yet anon shall hear,
　And I anon, the music in my soul,
　In a moment read the whole;
　The music in my heart,
　Joyously take my part,
And hand in hand, and heart with heart, with these retreat, advance;
　And borne on wings of wavy sound,
　Whirl with these around, around, 　　　　20
　Who here are living in the living dance!
　Why forfeit that fair chance?
　Till that arrive, till thou awake,
　Of these, my soul, thy music make,
　And keep amid the throng,
And turn as they shall turn, and bound as they are bounding,—
Alas! alas! alas! and what if all along
　The music is not sounding?

II

Are there not, then, two musics unto men?—
　One loud and bold and coarse, 　　　　30
　And overpowering still perforce
　All tone and tune beside;
　Yet in despite its pride
Only of fumes of foolish fancy bred,
And sounding solely in the sounding head:
　The other, soft and low,
　Stealing whence we not know,
Painfully heard, and easily forgot,
With pauses oft and many a silence strange,
(And silent oft it seems, when silent it is not) 　　40
Revivals too of unexpected change:

Haply thou think'st 'twill never be begun,
Or that 't has come, and been, and passed away;
    Yet turn to other none,—
    Turn not, oh, turn not thou!
But listen, listen, listen,—if haply be heard it may;
Listen, listen, listen,—is it not sounding now?

III

Yea, and as thought of some beloved friend
By death or distance parted will descend,
Severing, in crowded rooms ablaze with light,   50
As by a magic screen, the seër from the sight
(Palsying the nerves that intervene
The eye and central sense between);
    So may the ear,
    Hearing, not hear,
Though drums do roll, and pipes and cymbals ring;
So the bare conscience of the better thing
Unfelt, unseen, unimaged, all unknown,
May fix the entrancèd soul 'mid multitudes alone.

    SWEET streamlet bason! at thy side
    Weary and faint within me cried
    My longing heart,—In such pure deep
    How sweet it were to sit and sleep;
    To feel each passage from without
    Close up,—above me and about,
    Those circling waters crystal clear,
    That calm impervious atmosphere!
    There on thy pearly pavement pure
    To lean, and feel myself secure,   10
    Or through the dim-lit inter-space,
    Afar at whiles upgazing trace
    The dimpling bubbles dance around

Upon thy smooth exterior face;
Or idly list the dreamy sound
Of ripples lightly flung, above
That home, of peace, if not of love.

AWAY, haunt not thou me,
Thou vain Philosophy!
Little hast thou bestead,
Save to perplex the head,
And leave the spirit dead.
Unto thy broken cisterns wherefore go,
While from the secret treasure-depths below,
Fed by the skiey shower,
And clouds that sink and rest on hill-tops high,
Wisdom at once, and Power,   10
Are welling, bubbling forth, unseen, incessantly?
Why labour at the dull mechanic oar,
When the fresh breeze is blowing,
And the strong current flowing,
Right onward to the Eternal Shore?

MY wind is turned to bitter north,
    That was so soft a south before;
My sky, that shone so sunny bright,
    With foggy gloom is clouded o'er:
My gay green leaves are yellow-black,
    Upon the dank autumnal floor;
For love, departed once, comes back
    No more again, no more.

A roofless ruin lies my home,
    For winds to blow and rains to pour;   10
One frosty night befell, and lo,
    I find my summer days are o'er:

The heart bereaved, of why and how
Unknowing, knows that yet before
It had what e'en to Memory now
Returns no more, no more.

LOOK you, my simple friend, 'tis one of those
(Alack, a common weed of our ill time),
Who, do whate'er they may, go where they will,
Must needs still carry about the looking-glass
Of vain philosophy. And if so be
That some small natural gesture shall escape them,
(Nature will out) straightway about they turn,
And con it duly there, and note it down,
With inward glee and much complacent chuckling,
Part in conceit of their superior science,   10
Part in forevision of the attentive look
And laughing glance that may one time reward them,
When the fresh ore, this day dug up, at last
Shall, thrice refined and purified, from the mint
Of conversation intellectual
Into the golden currency of wit
Issue—satirical or pointed sentence,
Impromptu, epigram, or it may be sonnet,
Heir undisputed to the pinkiest page
In the album of a literary lady.   20

And can it be, you ask me, that a man,
With the strong arm, the cunning faculties,
And keenest forethought gifted, and, within,
Longings unspeakable, the lingering echoes
Responsive to the still-still-calling voice
Of God Most High,—should disregard all these,
And half-employ all those for such an aim
As the light sympathy of successful wit,
Vain titillation of a moment's praise?

Why, so is good no longer good, but crime   30
Our truest, best advantage, since it lifts us
Out of the stifling gas of men's opinion
Into the vital atmosphere of Truth,
Where He again is visible, tho' in anger.

THOUGHT may well be ever ranging,
And opinion ever changing,
Task-work be, though ill begun,
Dealt with by experience better;
By the law and by the letter
Duty done is duty done:
Do it, Time is on the wing!

Hearts, 'tis quite another thing,
Must or once for all be given,
Or must not at all be given;   10
Hearts, 'tis quite another thing!

To bestow the soul away
In an idle duty-play!—
Why, to trust a life-long bliss
To caprices of a day,
Scarce were more depraved than this!

Men and maidens, see you mind it;
Show of love, where'er you find it,
Look if duty lurk behind it!
Duty-fancies, urging on   20
Whither love had never gone!

Loving—if the answering breast
Seem not to be thus possessed,
Still in hoping have a care;
If it do, beware, beware!
But if in yourself you find it,
Above all things—mind it, mind it!

26

Duty—that's to say complying
  With whate'er's expected here;
On your unknown cousin's dying,
  Straight be ready with the tear;
Upon etiquette relying,
Unto usage nought denying,
Lend your waist to be embraced,
  Blush not even, never fear;
Claims of kith and kin connection,
  Claims of manners honour still,   10
Ready money of affection
  Pay, whoever drew the bill.
With the form conforming duly,
Senseless what it meaneth truly,
Go to church—the world require you,
  To balls—the world require you too,
And marry—papa and mamma desire you,
  And your sisters and schoolfellows do.
Duty—'tis to take on trust
What things are good, and right, and just;   20
  And whether indeed they be or be not,
  Try not, test not, feel not, see not:
'Tis walk and dance, sit down and rise
  By leading, opening ne'er your eyes;
Stunt sturdy limbs that Nature gave,
And be drawn in a Bath chair along to the grave.

'Tis the stern and prompt suppressing,
  As an obvious deadly sin,
All the questing and the guessing
  Of the soul's own soul within: 30
    'Tis the coward acquiescence
      In a destiny's behest,
    To a shade by terror made,
    Sacrificing, aye, the essence
      Of all that's truest, noblest, best:

27

'Tis the blind non-recognition
    Either of goodness, truth, or beauty,
Except by precept and submission;
    Moral blank, and moral void,
    Life at very birth destroyed,   40
Atrophy, exinanition!
Duty! ——
Yea, by duty's prime condition
    Pure nonentity of duty!

'Blank Misgivings of a Creature moving about in Worlds not realised.'

I

HERE am I yet, another twelvemonth spent,
One-third departed of the mortal span,
Carrying on the child into the man,
Nothing into reality. Sails rent,
And rudder broken,—reason impotent,—
Affections all unfixed; so forth I fare
On the mid seas unheedingly, so dare
To do and to be done by, well content.
So was it from the first, so is it yet;
Yea, the first kiss that by these lips was set   10
On any human lips, methinks was sin—
Sin, cowardice, and falsehood; for the will
Into a deed e'en then advanced, wherein
God, unidentified, was thought-of still.

II

Though to the vilest things beneath the moon
For poor Ease' sake I give away my heart,
And for the moment's sympathy let part
My sight and sense of truth, Thy precious boon,
My painful earnings, lost, all lost, as soon,
Almost, as gained; and though aside I start,
Belie Thee daily, hourly,—still Thou art,

Art surely as in heaven the sun at noon:
How much so e'er I sin, whate'er I do
Of evil, still the sky above is blue,   10
The stars look down in beauty as before:
Is it enough to walk as best we may,
To walk, and, sighing, dream of that blest day
When ill we cannot quell shall be no more?

III

Well, well,—Heaven bless you all from day to day!
Forgiveness too, or e'er we part, from each,
As I do give it, so must I beseech:
I owe all much, much more than I can pay;
Therefore it is I go; how could I stay
Where every look commits me to fresh debt,
And to pay little I must borrow yet?
Enough of this already, now away!
With silent woods and hills untenanted
Let me go commune; under thy sweet gloom,   10
O kind maternal Darkness, hide my head:
The day may come I yet may re-assume
My place, and, these tired limbs recruited, seek
The task for which I now am all too weak.

IV

Yes, I have lied, and so must walk my way,
Bearing the liar's curse upon my head;
Letting my weak and sickly heart be fed
On food which does the present craving stay,
But may be clean-denied me e'en to-day,
And tho' 'twere certain, yet were ought but bread;
Letting—for so they say, it seems, I said,
And I am all too weak to disobey!
Therefore for me sweet Nature's scenes reveal not
Their charm; sweet Music greets me and I feel not;   10

29   D

Sweet eyes pass off me uninspired; yea, more,
The golden tide of opportunity
Flows wafting-in friendships and better,—I
Unseeing, listless, pace along the shore.

V

How often sit I, poring o'er
   My strange distorted youth,
Seeking in vain, in all my store,
   One feeling based on truth;
Amid the maze of petty life
   A clue whereby to move,
A spot whereon in toil and strife
   To dare to rest and love.
So constant as my heart would be,
   So fickle as it must,   10
'Twere well for others as for me
   'Twere dry as summer dust.
Excitements come, and act and speech
   Flow freely forth;—but no,
Nor they, nor ought beside can reach
   The buried world below.

VI

            ——Like a child
In some strange garden left awhile alone,
I pace about the pathways of the world,
Plucking light hopes and joys from every stem,
With qualms of vague misgiving in my heart
That payment at the last will be required,
Payment I cannot make, or guilt incurred,
And shame to be endured.

VII

          ——Roused by importunate knocks
I rose, I turned the key, and let them in,

First one, anon another, and at length
In troops they came; for how could I, who once
Had let in one, nor looked him in the face,
Show scruples e'er again? So in they came,
A noisy band of revellers,—vain hopes,
Wild fancies, fitful joys; and there they sit
In my heart's holy place, and through the night
Carouse, to leave it when the cold grey dawn   10
Gleams from the East, to tell me that the time
For watching and for thought bestowed is gone.

VIII

O kind protecting Darkness! as a child
Flies back to bury in his mother's lap
His shame and his confusion, so to thee,
O Mother Night, come I! within the folds
Of thy dark robe hide thou me close; for I
So long, so heedless, with external things
Have played the liar, that whate'er I see,
E'en these white glimmering curtains, yon bright stars,
Which to the rest rain comfort down, for me
Smiling those smiles, which I may not return,   10
Or frowning frowns of fierce triumphant malice,
As angry claimants or expectants sure
Of that I promised and may not perform,
Look me in the face! O hide me, Mother Night!

IX

Once more the wonted road I tread,
Once more dark heavens above me spread,
Upon the windy down I stand,
My station, whence the circling land
Lies mapped and pictured wide below;—
Such as it was, such e'en again,
Long dreary bank, and breadth of plain
By hedge or tree unbroken;—lo,

31

A few grey woods can only show
How vain their aid, and in the sense   10
Of one unaltering impotence,
Relieving not, meseems enhance
The sovereign dulness of the expanse.
Yet marks where human hand hath been,
Bare house, unsheltered village, space
Of ploughed and fenceless tilth between
(Such aspect as methinks may be
In some half-settled colony),
From Nature vindicate the scene;
A wide, and yet disheartening view,   20
A melancholy world.

                     'Tis true,
Most true; and yet, like those strange smiles
By fervent hope or tender thought
From distant happy regions brought,
Which upon some sick bed are seen
To glorify a pale worn face
With sudden beauty,—so at whiles
Lights have descended, hues have been,
To clothe with half-celestial grace
The bareness of the desert place.   30

Since so it is, so be it still!
Could only thou, my heart, be taught
To treasure, and in act fulfil
The lesson which the sight has brought;
In thine own dull and dreary state
To work and patiently to wait:
Little thou think'st in thy despair
How soon the o'ershaded sun may shine,
And e'en the dulling clouds combine
To bless with lights and hues divine   40
That region desolate and bare,
Those sad and sinful thoughts of thine!

Still doth the coward heart complain;
The hour may come, and come in vain;
The branch that withered lies and dead
No suns can force to lift its head.
True!—yet how little thou canst tell
How much in thee is ill or well;
Nor for thy neighbour, nor for thee,
Be sure, was life designed to be   50
A draught of dull complacency.
One Power too is it, who doth give
The food without us, and within
The strength that makes it nutritive;
He bids the dry bones rise and live,
And e'en in hearts depraved to sin
Some sudden, gracious influence,
May give the long-lost good again,
And wake within the dormant sense
And love of good;—for mortal men,   60
So but thou strive, thou soon shalt see
Defeat itself is victory.

So be it: yet, O Good and Great,
In whom in this bedarkened state
I fain am struggling to believe,
Let me not ever cease to grieve,
Nor lose the consciousness of ill
Within me;—and refusing still
To recognise in things around
What cannot truly there be found,   70
Let me not feel, nor be it true,
That while each daily task I do
I still am giving day by day
My precious things within away,
(Those thou didst give to keep as thine)
And casting, do whate'er I may,
My heavenly pearls to earthly swine.

33

X

I HAVE seen higher holier things than these,
    And therefore must to these refuse my heart,
Yet am I panting for a little ease;
    I'll take, and so depart.

Ah hold! the heart is prone to fall away,
    Her high and cherished visions to forget,
And if thou takest, how wilt thou repay
    So vast, so dread a debt?

How will the heart, which now thou trustest, then
    Corrupt, yet in corruption mindful yet,   10
Turn with sharp stings upon itself! Again,
    Bethink thee of the debt!

—Hast thou seen higher holier things than these,
    And therefore must to these thy heart refuse?
With the true best, alack, how ill agrees
    That best that thou wouldst choose!

The Summum Pulchrum rests in heaven above;
    Do thou, as best thou may'st, thy duty do:
Amid the things allowed thee live and love;
    Some day thou shalt it view.   20

QUA CURSUM VENTUS

As ships, becalmed at eve, that lay
    With canvas drooping, side by side,
Two towers of sail at dawn of day
    Are scarce long leagues apart descried;

When fell the night, upsprung the breeze,
    And all the darkling hours they plied,
Nor dreamt but each the self-same seas
    By each was cleaving, side by side:

E'en so—but why the tale reveal
  Of those, whom, year by year unchanged,   10
Brief absence joined anew, to feel
  Astounded, soul from soul estranged?

At dead of night their sails were filled,
  And onward each rejoicing steered—
Ah, neither blame, for neither willed,
  Or wist, what first with dawn appeared!

To veer, how vain! On, onward strain,
  Brave barks! In light, in darkness too,
Through winds and tides one compass guides—
  To that, and your own selves, be true.   20

But O blithe breeze! and O great seas,
  Though ne'er, that earliest parting past,
On your wide plain they join again,
  Together lead them home at last.

One port, methought, alike they sought,
  One purpose hold where'er they fare,—
O bounding breeze, O rushing seas!
  At last, at last, unite them there!

ALCAICS

So spake the Voice; and, as with a single life
Instinct, the whole mass, fierce, irretainable,
  Down on that unsuspecting host swept
  Down, with the fury of winds that all night
Up-brimming, sapping slowly the dyke, at dawn
Full through the breach, o'er homestead, and harvest, and
  Herd roll a deluge; while the milkmaid
  Trips i' the dew, and remissly guiding
Morn's first uneven furrow, the farmer's boy
Dreams out his dream: so over the multitude   10
  Safe-tented, uncontrolled and uncon-
  trollably sped the Avenger's fury.

NATURA NATURANS

BESIDE me,—in the car,—she sat,
  She spake not, no, nor looked to me:
From her to me, from me to her,
  What passed so subtly stealthily?
As rose to rose that by it blows
  Its interchanged aroma flings;
Or wake to sound of one sweet note
  The virtues of disparted strings.

Beside me, nought but this!—but this,
  That influent as within me dwelt   10
Her life, mine too within her breast,
  Her brain, her every limb she felt:
We sat; while o'er and in us, more
  And more, a power unknown prevailed,
Inhaling, and inhaled,—and still
  'Twas one, inhaling or inhaled.

Beside me, nought but this;—and passed;
  I passed; and know not to this day
If gold or jet her girlish hair,
  If black, or brown, or lucid-grey   20
Her eye's young glance: the fickle chance
  That joined us, yet may join again;
But I no face again could greet
  As hers, whose life was in me then.

As unsuspecting mere a maid
  As, fresh in maidhood's bloomiest bloom,
In casual second-class did e'er
  By casual youth her seat assume;
Or vestal, say, of saintliest clay,
  For once by balmiest airs betrayed   30
Unto emotions too too sweet
  To be unlingeringly gainsaid:

Unowning then, confusing soon
   With dreamier dreams that o'er the glass
Of shyly ripening woman-sense
   Reflected, scarce reflected, pass,
A wife may-be, a mother she
   In Hymen's shrine recalls not now,
She first in hour, ah, not profane,
   With me to Hymen learnt to bow.   40

Ah no!—Yet owned we, fused in one,
   The Power which e'en in stones and earths
By blind elections felt, in forms
   Organic breeds to myriad births;
By lichen small on granite wall
   Approved, its faintest feeblest stir
Slow-spreading, strengthening long, at last
   Vibrated full in me and her.

In me and her—sensation strange!
   The lily grew to pendent head,   50
To vernal airs the mossy bank
   Its sheeny primrose spangles spread,
In roof o'er roof of shade sun-proof
   Did cedar strong itself outclimb,
And altitude of aloe proud
   Aspire in floreal crown sublime;

Flashed flickering forth fantastic flies,
   Big bees their burly bodies swung,
Rooks roused with civic din the elms,
   And lark its wild reveillez rung;   60
In Libyan dell the light gazelle,
   The leopard lithe in Indian glade,
And dolphin, brightening tropic seas,
   In us were living, leapt and played:

37

Their shells did slow crustacea build,
   Their gilded skins did snakes renew,
While mightier spines for loftier kind
   Their types in amplest limbs outgrew;
Yea, close comprest in human breast,
   What moss, and tree, and livelier thing,   70
What Earth, Sun, Star of force possest,
   Lay budding, burgeoning forth for Spring.

Such sweet preluding sense of old
   Led on in Eden's sinless place
The hour when bodies human first
   Combined the primal prime embrace,
Such genial heat the blissful seat
   In man and woman owned unblamed,
When, naked both, its garden paths
   They walked unconscious, unashamed: 80

Ere, clouded yet in mistiest dawn,
   Above the horizon dusk and dun,
One mountain crest with light had tipped
   That Orb that is the Spirit's Sun;
Ere dreamed young flowers in vernal showers
   Of fruit to rise the flower above,
Or ever yet to young Desire
   Was told the mystic name of Love.

$$\delta \; \theta \epsilon \grave{o}s \; \mu \epsilon \tau \grave{\alpha} \; \sigma o \hat{u} \, ^{1}$$

*   *   *   *

FAREWELL, my Highland lassie! when the year returns around,
Be it Greece, or be it Norway, where my vagrant feet are found,
I shall call to mind the place, I shall call to mind the day,
The day that's gone for ever, and the glen that's far away;
I shall mind me, be it Rhine or Rhone, Italian land or France,
Of the laughings and the whispers, of the pipings and the dance;

        ¹ God be with you!

38

I shall see thy soft brown eyes dilate to wakening woman thought,
And whiter still the white cheek grow to which the blush was brought;
And oh, with mine commixing I thy breath of life shall feel,
And clasp the shyly passive hands in joyous Highland reel;　　　10
I shall hear, and see, and feel, and in sequence sadly true,
Shall repeat the bitter-sweet of the lingering last adieu;
I shall seem as now to leave thee, with the kiss upon the brow,
And the fervent benediction of—ὁ θεὸς μετὰ σοῦ!

Ah me, my Highland lassie! though in winter drear and long
Deep arose the heavy snows, and the stormy winds were strong,
Though the rain, in summer's brightest, it were raining every day,
With worldly comforts few and far, how glad were I to stay!
I fall to sleep with dreams of life in some black bothie spent,
Coarse poortith's ware thou changing there to gold of pure con-
　　　tent,　　　20
With barefoot lads and lassies round, and thee the cheery wife,
In the braes of old Lochaber a laborious homely life;
But I wake—to leave thee, smiling, with the kiss upon the brow,
And the peaceful benediction of—ὁ θεὸς μετὰ σοῦ!

*　　*　　*　　*　　*　　*

ἐπὶ Λάτμῳ[1]

ON the mountain, in the woodland,
In the shaded secret dell,
　　I have seen thee, I have met thee!
In the soft ambrosial hours of night,
In darkness silent sweet
　　I beheld thee, I was with thee,
　　I was thine, and thou wert mine!

When I gazed in palace-chambers,
When I trod the rustic dance,
Earthly maids were fair to look on,　　　10

[1] On Latmos.

39

Earthly maidens' hearts were kind:
Fair to look on, fair to love:
But the life, the life to me,
'Twas the death, the death to them,
In the spying, prying, prating
Of a curious cruel world.
At a touch, a breath they fade,
They languish, droop, and die;
Yea, the juices change to sourness,
And the tints to clammy brown;   20
And the softness unto foulness,
And the odour unto stench.
Let alone and leave to bloom;
Pass aside, nor make to die,
—In the woodland, on the mountain,
Thou art mine, and I am thine.

So I passed.—Amid the uplands,
In the forests, on whose skirts
Pace unstartled, feed unfearing
Do the roe-deer and the red,   30
While I hungered, while I thirsted,
While the night was deepest dark,
Who was I, that thou shouldst meet me?
Who was I, thou didst not pass?
Who was I, that I should say to thee,
Thou art mine, and I am thine?

To the air from whence thou camest
Thou returnest, thou art gone;
Self-created, dis-created,
Re-created, ever fresh,   40
Ever young!——
As a lake its mirrored mountains
At a moment, unregretting,
Unresisting, unreclaiming,
Without preface, without question,

On the silent shifting levels
Lets depart,
Shows, effaces and replaces!
For what is, anon is not;
What has been, again's to be;   50
Ever new and ever young
Thou art mine, and I am thine.

Art thou she that walks the skies,
That rides the starry night?
I know not———
For my meanness dares not claim the truth
Thy loveliness declares.
But the face thou show'st the world is not
The face thou show'st to me.
And the look that I have looked in   60
Is of none but me beheld.
I know not; but I know
I am thine, and thou art mine.

And I watch: the orb behind
As it fleeteth, faint and fair
In the depth of azure night,
In the violet blank, I trace
By an outline faint and fair
Her whom none but I beheld.
By her orb she moveth slow,   70
Graceful-slow, serenely firm,
Maiden-Goddess! while her robe
The adoring planets kiss.
And I too cower and ask,
Wert thou mine, and was I thine?

Hath a cloud o'ercast the sky?
Is it cloud upon the mountain-sides
Or haze of dewy river-banks
Below?—

41

Or around me,   80
To enfold me, to conceal,
Doth a mystic magic veil,
A celestial separation,
As of curtains hymeneal,
Undiscerned yet all excluding,
Interpose?
For the pine-tree boles are dimmer,
And the stars bedimmed above;
In perspective brief, uncertain,
Are the forest-alleys closed,   90
And to whispers indistinctest
The resounding torrents lulled.
Can it be, and can it be?
Upon Earth and here below,
In the woodland at my side
Thou art with me, thou art here.

'Twas the vapour of the perfume
Of the presence that should be,
That enwrapt me!
That enwraps us,   100
O my Goddess, O my Queen!
And I turn
At thy feet to fall before thee;
And thou wilt not:
At thy feet to kneel and reach and kiss thy finger-tips;
And thou wilt not:
And I feel thine arms that stay me,
And I feel————
O mine own, mine own, mine own,
I am thine, and thou art mine!   110

Χρυσέα κλὴς ἐπὶ γλώσσᾳ[1]

IF, when in cheerless wanderings, dull and cold,
A sense of human kindliness hath found us,
  We seem to have around us
  An atmosphere all gold,
'Mid darkest shades a halo rich of shine,
An element, that while the bleak wind bloweth,
  On the rich heart bestoweth
  Imbreathed draughts of wine;
Heaven guide, the cup be not, as chance may be,
To some vain mate given up as soon as tasted!   10
  No, nor on thee be wasted,
  Thou trifler, Poesy!
Heaven grant the manlier heart, that timely, ere
Youth fly, with life's real tempest would be coping;
  The fruit of dreamy hoping
  Is, waking, blank despair.

Is it true, ye gods, who treat us
As the gambling fool is treated,
O ye, who ever cheat us,
And let us feel we're cheated!
Is it true that poetical power,
The gift of heaven, the dower
Of Apollo and the Nine,
The inborn sense, 'the vision and the faculty divine,'
All we glorify and bless
In our rapturous exaltation,   10
All invention, and creation,
Exuberance of fancy, and sublime imagination,
All a poet's fame is built on,
The fame of Shakespeare, Milton,
Of Wordsworth, Byron, Shelley,

---

[1] 'A golden key on the tongue.'

Is in reason's grave precision,
Nothing more, nothing less,
Than a peculiar conformation,
Constitution, and condition
Of the brain and of the belly?   20
Is it true, ye gods who cheat us?
And that's the way ye treat us?

Oh say it, all who think it,
Look straight, and never blink it!
If it is so, let it be so,
And we will all agree so;
But the plot has counterplot,
It may be, and yet be not.

SHORTER POEMS

1

TRUTH is a golden thread, seen here and there
In small bright specks upon the visible side
Of our strange being's party-coloured web.
How rich the converse! 'Tis a vein of ore
Emerging now and then on Earth's rude breast,
But flowing full below. Like islands set
At distant intervals on Ocean's face,
We see it on our course; but in the depths
The mystic colonnade unbroken keeps
Its faithful way, invisible but sure.   10
Oh, if it be so, wherefore do we men
Pass by so many marks, so little heeding?

2

WHENCE com'st thou, shady lane, and why and how,
Wherein with idle heart ten years ago
I wandered, and with childhood's paces slow,
So long unthought of, and remembered now?
Again in vision clear thy pathwayed side
I tread, and view thine orchard plots again
With yellow fruitage hung, and glimmering grain
Standing or shocked through the thick hedge espied.
This hot still noon of August brings the sight,
This quelling silence as of eve or night,   10
Wherein Earth (feeling as a mother will
After her travail's latest bitterest throes)
Looks up, so seemeth it, one half repose,
One half in effort, straining, suffering still.

3

So I, as boyish years went by, went wrong
Plainly and grievously. For fond conceit
Led me astray, and my weak heart that long

In the wild wood of daily deeds had sought
A passage worthy her immortal part,
And found there none, or where mayhap she found
Had dared not duly follow, weary of pause
Went greedily at last as chance her led
E'en by the worst and meanest:

                    or say rather
Powerless to stand alone, and without faith   10
To lay her hand upon the outstretched arm
Of heavenly guidance, which in happy moments
Her eye was strong to see, she in the end
Out of sheer weakness was full fain to lean
On every common passer.

                  So I went wrong,
Grievously wrong; but folly crushed itself,
And vanity o'ertoppling fell, and time,
And healthy discipline, and some neglect
In those half friendships half-resolves had made,
Labour, and solitary thoughts revived   20
Somewhat at least of that original life.
Oh well do I remember then the days
When on some grassy slope, what time the sun
Was sinking and the solemn eve came down
With its blue vapour upon field and wood
And elm-embosomed spire, once more again
I fed on sweet emotions, and my soul
With love o'erflowed or hushed itself in fear
Unearthly, yea celestial, once again
My heart was hot within me, and meseemed   30
I too had in my body breath to sound
The magic horn of song, I too possessed
Upwelling in my being's depths a fount
Of the true poet-nectar, whence to fill
The golden urns of verse. ——

4

WHEN the dews are earliest falling,
When the evening glen is grey,
Ere thou lookest, ere thou speakest,
My beloved,
I depart, and I return to thee,—
Return, return, return.

Dost thou watch while I traverse
Haunts of men, beneath the sun—
Dost thou list while I bespeak them
With a voice whose cheer is thine?   10
O my brothers! men, my brothers,
You are mine, and I am yours;
I am yours to cheer and succour,
I am yours for hope and aid:
Lo, my hand to raise and stay you,
Lo, my arm to guard and keep,
My voice to rouse and warn you,
And my heart to warm and calm:
My heart to lend the life it owes
To her that is not here,   20
In the power of her that dwelleth
Where you know not—no, nor guess not—
Whom you see not; unto whom,—
Ere the evening star hath sunken,
Ere the glow-worm lights its lamp,
Ere the weariest workman slumbers,—
I return, return, return.

5

ENOUGH, small Room,—tho' all too true
Much ill in thee I daily do,—
Enough to make thy memory blest,
And thoughts of thee a place of rest,
If midst the ills that crowd me here,

Unvarying clouds that still appear
To dull Life's social atmosphere,
(Oh shame that things so base have power
To bind me down a single hour)
Vainglorious words of fond conceit,   10
Self-pleasures of successful wit,
And heartless jests and coward lies
And hollow sleek complacencies,—
Enough,—if, ever and anon
In thee secluded and alone,
On the dry dust of this weak breast
With conscious faultiness opprest,
And social levities distrest,
Hath fallen from sunny skies above
An April shower of genuine love: 20
If homeward thoughts and thoughts of one
Sincerely sought nor all unwon,
Of words once said and things once done
Mid simpler hearts and fresher faces
In happier times and holier places,
With penitential thoughts combine,
And hopes that ere life's day decline
Such lot may yet once more be mine,
And though with toil recalled and pain
My purer soul return again,   30
And I be wiser to retain.

6

TO THE GREAT METROPOLIS

TRAFFIC, to speak from knowledge but begun,
I saw, and travelling much, and fashion—Yea,
And if that Competition and Display
Make a great Capital, then thou art one,
One, it may be, unrivalled neath the sun.
But sovereign symbol of the Great and Good,
True Royalty, and genuine Statesmanhood,

Nobleness, Learning, Piety was none.
If such realities indeed there are
Working within unsignified, 'tis well;   10
The stranger's fancy of the thing thou art
Is rather truly of a huge Bazaar,
A railway terminus, a gay Hotel,
Anything but a mighty Nation's heart.

7

WOULD that I were,—O hear thy suppliant, thou,
   Whom fond belief still ventures here to see,—
Would that I were not that which I am now
   Nor yet became the thing I wish to be!
What wouldst thou? Poor suggestion of today
   Depart, vain fancy and fallacious thought!
Would I could wish my wishes all away,
   And learn to wish the wishes that I ought.

8

EPI-STRAUSS-IUM

MATTHEW and Mark and Luke and holy John
Evanished all and gone!
Yea, he that erst, his dusky curtains quitting,
Through Eastern pictured panes his level beams transmitting,
With gorgeous portraits blent,
On them his glories intercepted spent,
Southwestering now, through windows plainly glassed,
On the inside face his radiance keen hath cast,
And in the lustre lost, invisible and gone,
Are, say you, Matthew, Mark and Luke and holy John?   10
Lost, is it? lost, to be recovered never?
However,
The place of worship the meantime with light
Is, if less richly, more sincerely bright,
And in blue skies the Orb is manifest to sight.

9

THE SONG OF LAMECH

HEARKEN to me, ye mothers of my tent;
Ye wives of Lamech, listen to my speech;
Adah, let Jabal hither lead his goats,
And Tubal Cain, O Zillah, hush the forge;
Naamah her wheel shall ply beside, and thou
My Jubal, touch, before I speak, the string.

Yea, Jubal, touch, before I speak, the string.
Hear ye my voice, beloved of my tent,
Dear ones of Lamech listen to my speech.

For Eve made answer, Cain, my son, my own,   10
O first mysterious increase of my womb,
O, if I cursed thee, O my child, I sinned,
And He that heard me, heard and said me nay;
My first, my only one, thou shalt not go.

And Adam answered also, Cain, my son,
He that is gone forgiveth, we forgive:
Rob not thy mother of two sons at once,
My child, abide with us and comfort us.

Hear ye my voice, Adah and Zillah, hear;
Ye wives of Lamech, listen to my speech.   20

For Cain replied not. But, an hour more, sat
Where the night through he sat, his knit brows seen,
Scarce seen, amidst the foldings of his limbs.
But when the sun was bright upon the field
To Adam still and Eve still waiting by
And weeping, lift he up his voice and spake.

Cain said, The sun is risen upon the Earth;
The day demands my going; and I go.
As you from Paradise, so I from you;
As you to exile, into exile I: 30
My Father and my Mother, I depart.

As betwixt you and Paradise of old,
So betwixt me, my Parents, now and you
Cherubims I discern and in their hand
A flaming sword that turneth every way,
To keep the way of my one tree of life,
The way my spirit yearns to, of your love.

Yet not, O Adam, and O Eve, fear not.
For He that asked me, Where is Abel, He
Who called me cursed from the Earth, and said,   40
A fugitive and vagabond thou art,
He also said, when fear had slain my soul,
There shall not touch thee man nor beast; fear not.
Lo, I have spoke with God, and He hath said,
Fear not; and let me go as He hath said.

Cain also said (O Jubal, touch thy string),—
Moreover, in the darkness of my mind,
When the night's night of misery was most black,
A little star came twinkling up within,
And in myself I had a guide that led,   50
And in myself had knowledge of a soul.
Fear not, O Adam and O Eve: I go.

Children of Lamech, listen to my speech.

For when the years were multiplied, and Cain
Eastward of Eden, in this land of Nod,
Had sons and sons of sons, and sons of them,
Enoch and Irad and Mehujael
My father, and my children's grandsire he,
It came to pass, that Cain who dwelt alone
Met Adam at the nightfall in the field;   60
Who fell upon his neck, and wept, and said,
My son, hath God not spoken to thee, Cain?

And Cain replied, when weeping loosed his voice:
My dreams are double, O my father; good
And evil. Terror to my soul by night

And agony by day, when Abel stands
A dead black shade and speaks not neither looks,
Nor makes me any answer when I cry
Curse me, but let me know thou art alive.
But comfort also like a whisper comes,   70
In visions of a deeper sleep, when he,
Abel, as whom we knew, yours once and mine,
Comes with a free forgiveness in his face,
Seeming to speak, solicitous for words,
And wearing ere he go the old first look
Of unsuspecting, unforeboding love.
Three nights are gone, I saw him thus, my Sire.

Dear ones of Lamech, listen to my speech.

For Adam said, Three nights ago to me
Came Abel in my sleep as thou hast said,   80
And spake, and bade, Arise my father, go
Where in the land of exile dwells thy son.
Say to my brother, Abel bids thee come,
Abel would have thee; and lay thou thy hand,
My father, on his head that he may come;
Am I not weary, Father, for this hour?

Hear ye my voice, Adah and Zillah, hear:
Children of Lamech, listen to my speech:
And, son of Zillah, sound thy solemn string.

For Adam laid upon the head of Cain   90
His hand, and Cain bowed down, and slept and died.
And a deep sleep on Adam also fell,
And in his slumber's deepest he beheld,
Standing before the gate of Paradise
With Abel, hand in hand, our father Cain.

Hear ye my voice, Adah and Zillah, hear;
Ye wives of Lamech, listen to my speech.

Though to his wounding did he slay a man,
Yea, and a young man to his hurt he slew,
Fear not ye wives nor sons of Lamech fear: 100
If unto Cain was safety given and rest,
Shall Lamech surely and his people die?

10
BETHESDA
A SEQUEL

I SAW again the spirits on a day,
Where on the earth in mournful case they lay;
Five porches were there, and a pool, and round,
Huddling in blankets, strewn upon the ground,
Tied-up and bandaged, weary, sore and spent,
The maimed and halt, diseased and impotent.

For a great angel came, 'twas said, and stirred
The pool at certain seasons, and the word
Was, with this people of the sick, that they
Who in the waters here their limbs should lay   10
Before the motion on the surface ceased
Should of their torment straightway be released.

So with shrunk bodies and with heads down-dropt,
Stretched on the steps, and at the pillars propt,
Watching by day and listening through the night,
They filled the place, a miserable sight.

And I beheld that on the stony floor
He too, that spoke of duty once before,
No otherwise than others here to-day
Foredone and sick and sadly muttering lay.   20
'I know not, I will do—what is it I would say?
'What was that word which once sufficed alone for all,
'Which now I seek in vain, and never can recall?'
'I know not, I will do the work the world requires
'Asking no reason why, but serving its desires;

'Will do for daily bread, for wealth, respect, good name,
'The business of the day—alas, is that the same?'
And then, as weary of in vain renewing
His question, thus his mournful thought pursuing,
'I know not, I must do as other men are doing.'   30

But what the waters of that pool might be,
Of Lethe were they, or Philosophy;
And whether he, long waiting, did attain
Deliverance from the burden of his pain
There with the rest; or whether, yet before,
Some more diviner stranger passed the door
With his small company into that sad place,
And breathing hope into the sick man's face,
Bade him take up his bed, and rise and go,
What the end were, and whether it were so,   40
Further than this I saw not, neither know.

II

EASTER DAY

NAPLES, 1849

THROUGH the great sinful streets of Naples as I past,
With fiercer heat than flamed above my head
My heart was hot within me; till at last
My brain was lightened, when my tongue had said

      Christ is not risen!

    Christ is not risen, no,
    He lies and moulders low;
      Christ is not risen.

What though the stone were rolled away, and though
      The grave found empty there!—   10
      If not there, then elsewhere;
If not where Joseph laid Him first, why then
      Where other men

Translaid Him after; in some humbler clay
    Long ere to-day
Corruption that sad perfect work hath done,
Which here she scarcely, lightly had begun.
    The foul engendered worm
Feeds on the flesh of the life-giving form
Of our most Holy and Anointed One.   20

      He is not risen, no,
      He lies and moulders low;
        Christ is not risen.

      Ashes to ashes, dust to dust;
As of the unjust, also of the just—
        Christ is not risen.

What if the women, ere the dawn was grey,
Saw one or more great angels, as they say,
Angels, or Him himself? Yet neither there, nor then,
Nor afterward, nor elsewhere, nor at all,   30
Hath He appeared to Peter or the Ten,
Nor, save in thunderous terror, to blind Saul;
Save in an after-Gospel and late Creed
      He is not risen indeed,
        Christ is not risen.

Or what if e'en, as runs the tale, the Ten
Saw, heard, and touched, again and yet again?
What if at Emmaüs' inn and by Capernaum's lake
      Came One the bread that brake,
Came One that spake as never mortal spake,   40
And with them ate and drank and stood and walked about?
      Ah! 'some' did well to 'doubt'!
Ah! the true Christ, while these things came to pass,
Nor heard, nor spake, nor walked, nor dreamt, alas!
      He was not risen, no,
      He lay and mouldered low,
        Christ was not risen.

55

As circulates in some great city crowd
A rumour changeful, vague, importunate, and loud,
From no determined centre, or of fact,   50
    Or authorship exact,
    Which no man can deny
    Nor verify;
    So spread the wondrous fame;
      He all the same
    Lay senseless, mouldering, low.
He was not risen, no,
    Christ was not risen!

Ashes to ashes, dust to dust;
As of the unjust, also of the just—   60
    Yea, of that Just One too.
This is the one sad Gospel that is true,
    Christ is not risen.

————

Is He not risen, and shall we not rise?
    Oh, we unwise!
What did we dream, what wake we to discover?
Ye hills, fall on us, and ye mountains, cover!
    In darkness and great gloom
Come ere we thought it is *our* day of doom,
From the cursed world which is one tomb,   70
    Christ is not risen!

Eat, drink, and die, for we are men deceived,
Of all the creatures under heaven's wide cope
We are most hopeless who had once most hope
We are most wretched that had most believed.
    Christ is not risen.

Eat, drink, and play, and think that this is bliss!
    There is no Heaven but this!
    There is no Hell;—

Save Earth, which serves the purpose doubly well,   80
    Seeing it visits still
With equallest apportionments of ill
Both good and bad alike, and brings to one same dust
    The unjust and the just
    With Christ, who is not risen.

Eat, drink, and die, for we are souls bereaved,
Of all the creatures under this broad sky
We are most hopeless, that had hoped most high,
And most beliefless, that had most believed.
    Ashes to ashes, dust to dust;   90
    As of the unjust, also of the just—
      Yea, of that Just One too.
    It is the one sad Gospel that is true,
      Christ is not risen.

———

    Weep not beside the Tomb,
    Ye women, unto whom
He was great solace while ye tended Him;
    Ye who with napkin o'er His head
And folds of linen round each wounded limb
    Laid out the Sacred Dead;   100
And thou that bar'st Him in thy Wondering Womb.
Yea, Daughters of Jerusalem, depart,
Bind up as best ye may your own sad bleeding heart;
Go to your homes, your living children tend,
    Your earthly spouses love;
    Set your affections *not* on things above,
Which moth and rust corrupt, which quickliest come to end:
Or pray, if pray ye must, and pray, if pray ye can,
For death; since dead is He whom ye deemed more than man,
    Who is not risen, no,   110
    But lies and moulders low,
      Who is not risen.

Ye men of Galilee!
Why stand ye looking up to heaven, where Him ye ne'er may see,
Neither ascending hence, nor hither returning again?
   Ye ignorant and idle fishermen!
Hence to your huts and boats and inland native shore,
  And catch not men, but fish;
  Whate'er things ye might wish,
Him neither here nor there ye e'er shall meet with more. 120
   Ye poor deluded youths, go home,
   Mend the old nets ye left to roam,
   Tie the split oar, patch the torn sail;
   It was indeed 'an idle tale',
    He was not risen.

And oh, good men of ages yet to be,
Who shall believe *because* ye did not see,
   Oh, be ye warned! be wise!
   No more with pleading eyes,
   And sobs of strong desire, 130
 Unto the empty vacant void aspire,
Seeking another and impossible birth
That is not of your own and only Mother Earth.
But if there is no other life for you,
Sit down and be content, since this must even do:
   He is not risen.

   One look, and then depart,
   Ye humble and ye holy men of heart!
And ye! ye ministers and stewards of a word
Which ye would preach, because another heard,— 140
   Ye worshippers of that ye do not know,
   Take these things hence and go;
   He is not risen.

   Here on our Easter Day
We rise, we come, and lo! we find Him not;
Gardener nor other on the sacred spot,

Where they have laid Him is there none to say!
No sound, nor in, nor out; no word
Of where to seek the dead or meet the living Lord;
There is no glistering of an angel's wings,   150
There is no voice of heavenly clear behest:
Let us go hence, and think upon these things
In silence, which is best.
      Is He not risen? No—
      But lies and moulders low—
        Christ is not risen.

12

EASTER DAY

II

*   *   *   *

So in the sinful streets, abstracted and alone,
I with my secret self held communing of mine own.
So in the southern city spake the tongue
  Of one that somewhat overwildly sung;
  But in a later hour I sat and heard
  Another voice that spake, another graver word.
  Weep not, it bade, whatever hath been said,
  Though He be dead, He is not dead.
    In the true Creed
    He is yet risen indeed,   10
      Christ is yet risen.

    Weep not beside His tomb,
    Ye women unto whom
  He was great comfort and yet greater grief;
Nor ye faithful few that went with Him to roam,
Seek sadly what for Him ye left, go hopeless to your home;
Nor ye despair, ye sharers yet to be of their belief;
  Though He be dead, He is not dead,
    Not gone, though fled,
    Not lost, though vanished;   20

Though He return not, though
He lies and moulders low;
   In the true Creed
He is yet risen indeed,
   Christ is yet risen.

Sit if ye will, sit down upon the ground,
  Yet not to weep and wail, but calmly look around.
     Whate'er befell,
     Earth is not hell;
  Now, too, as when it first began,   30
  Life yet is Life and Man is Man.
For all that breathe beneath the heaven's high cope,
  Joy with grief mixes, with despondence hope.
  Hope conquers cowardice, joy grief:
  Or at the least, faith unbelief.
     Though dead, not dead;
     Not gone, though fled;
     Not lost, not vanished.
     In the great Gospel and true Creed,
     He is yet risen indeed;   40
       Christ is yet risen.

13

THE LATEST DECALOGUE

THOU shalt have one God only; who
Would be at the expense of two?
No graven images may be
Worshipped, except the currency:
Swear not at all; for for thy curse
Thine enemy is none the worse:
At church on Sunday to attend
Will serve to keep the world thy friend:
Honour thy parents; that is, all
From whom advancement may befall: 10

Thou shalt not kill; but needst not strive
Officiously to keep alive:
Do not adultery commit;
Advantage rarely comes of it:
Thou shalt not steal; an empty feat,
When it's so lucrative to cheat:
Bear not false witness; let the lie
Have time on its own wings to fly:
Thou shalt not covet; but tradition
Approves all forms of competition.   20

The sum of all is, thou shalt love,
If any body, God above:
At any rate shall never labour
More than thyself to love thy neighbour.

14

WHAT we, when face to face we see
The Father of our souls, shall be,
John tells us, doth not yet appear;
Ah! did he tell what we are here!

A mind for thoughts to pass into,
A heart for loves to travel through,
Five senses to detect things near,
Is this the whole that we are here?

Rules baffle instincts—instincts rules,
Wise men are bad—and good are fools,   10
Facts evil—wishes vain appear,
We cannot go, why are we here?

O may we for assurance' sake,
Some arbitrary judgement take,
And wilfully pronounce it clear,
For this or that 'tis we are here?

Or is it right, and will it do,
To pace the sad confusion through,
And say:—It doth not yet appear,
What we shall be, what we are here?   20

Ah yet, when all is thought and said,
The heart still overrules the head;
Still what we hope we must believe,
And what is given us receive;

Must still believe, for still we hope
That in a world of larger scope,
What here is faithfully begun
Will be completed, not undone.

My child, we still must think, when we
That ampler life together see,   30
Some true result will yet appear
Of what we are, together, here.

15

HOPE evermore and believe, O man, for e'en as thy thought
  So are the things that thou see'st; e'en as thy hope and belief.
Cowardly art thou and timid? they rise to provoke thee against them;
  Hast thou courage? enough, see them exulting to yield.
Yea, the rough rock, the dull earth, the wild sea's furying waters
  (Violent say'st thou and hard, mighty thou think'st to destroy),
All with ineffable longing are waiting their Invader,
  All, with one varying voice, call to him, Come and subdue;
Still for their Conqueror call, and, but for the joy of being conquered
  (Rapture they will not forego), dare to resist and rebel;   10
Still, when resisting and raging, in soft undervoice say unto him,
  Fear not, retire not, O man; hope evermore and believe.

Go from the east to the west, as the sun and the stars direct thee,
  Go with the girdle of man, go and encompass the earth.

Not for the gain of the gold, for the getting, the hoarding, the having,
   But for the joy of the deed; but for the Duty to do.
Go with the spiritual life, the higher volition and action,
   With the great girdle of God, go and encompass the earth.

Go; say not in thy heart, And what then were it accomplished,
   Were the wild impulse allayed, what were the use or the good!   20
Go, when the instinct is stilled, and when the deed is accomplished,
   What thou hast done and shalt do, shall be declared to thee then.
Go with the sun and the stars, and yet evermore in thy spirit
   Say to thyself: It is good: yet is there better than it.
This that I see is not all, and this that I do is but little;
   Nevertheless it is good, though there is better than it.

16

SAY not the struggle nought availeth,
   The labour and the wounds are vain,
The enemy faints not, nor faileth,
   And as things have been, things remain.

If hopes were dupes, fears may be liars;
   It may be, in yon smoke concealed,
Your comrades chase e'en now the fliers,
   And, but for you, possess the field.

For while the tired waves, vainly breaking,
   Seem here no painful inch to gain,   10
Far back through creeks and inlets making
   Came, silent, flooding in, the main,

And not by eastern windows only,
   When daylight comes, comes in the light,
In front the sun climbs slow, how slowly,
   But westward, look, the land is bright.

17

O LAND of Empire, art and love!
  What is it that you show me?
A sky for Gods to tread above,
  A soil for pigs below me!
O in all place and shape and kind
  Beyond all thought and thinking,
The graceful with the gross combined,
  The stately with the stinking!
Whilst words of mighty love to trace,
  Which thy great walls I see on,   10
Thy porch I pace or take my place
  Within thee, great Pantheon,
What sights untold of contrast bold
  My ranging eyes must be on!
What though uprolled by young and old
  In slumbrous convolution
Neath pillared shade must lie displayed
  Bare limbs that scorn ablution,
Should husks that swine would never pick
  Bestrew that patterned paving,   20
And sores to make a surgeon sick
  For charity come craving?
Though oft the meditative cur
  Account it small intrusion
Through that great gate to quit the stir
  Of market-place confusion,
True brother of the bipeds there,
  If Nature's need requireth,
Lifts up his leg with tranquil air
  And tranquilly retireth: 30
Though priest think fit to stop and spit
  Beside the altar solemn,
Yet, boy, that nuisance why commit
  On this Corinthian column?—

O richly soiled and richly sunned,
Exuberant, fervid, and fecund!
  Are these the fixed condition
On which may Northern pilgrim come
To imbibe thine ether-air, and sum
    Thy store of old tradition?   40
Must we be chill, if clean, and stand
Foot-deep in dirt in classic land?

So is it: in all ages so,
And in all places man can know,
From homely roots unseen below
In forest-shade in woodland bower
The stem that bears the ethereal flower
Derives that emanative power;
From mixtures fetid foul and sour
Draws juices that those petals fill.   50

Ah Nature, if indeed thy will
Thou own'st it, it shall not be ill!
And truly here, in this quick clime
Where, scarcely bound by space or time,
The elements in half a day
Toss off with exquisitest play
What our cold seasons toil and grieve,
And never quite at last achieve;
Where processes, with pain and fear
Disgust and horror wrought, appear   60
The quick mutations of a dance,
Wherein retiring but to advance,
Life, in brief interpause of death,
One moment sitting, taking breath,
Forth comes again as glad as e'er
In some new figure full as fair,
Where what has scarcely ceased to be,
Instinct with newer birth we see—

65

What dies already, look you, lives;
In such a clime, who thinks, forgives;   70
Who sees, will understand; who knows,
In calm of knowledge find repose,
And thoughtful as of glory gone,
So too of more to come anon,
Of permanent existence sure,
Brief intermediate breaks endure.

   O Nature, if indeed thy will,
Thou ownest it, it is not ill!
And e'en as oft on heathy hill,
On moorland black, and ferny fells,   80
Beside thy brooks and in thy dells,
Was welcomed erst the kindly stain
Of thy true earth, e'en so again
With resignation fair and meet
The dirt and refuse of thy street
My philosophic foot shall greet,
So leave but perfect to my eye
Thy columns set against thy sky!

18

URANUS

WHEN on the primal peaceful blank profound,
Which in its still unknowing silence holds
All knowledge, ever by withholding holds—
When on that void (like footfalls in far rooms),
In faint pulsations from the whitening East
Articulate voices first were felt to stir,
And the great child, in dreaming grown to man,
Losing his dream to piece it up began;
Then Plato in me said,
"'Tis but the figured ceiling overhead,   10
With cunning diagrams bestarred, that shine
In all the three dimensions, are endowed
With motion too by skill mechanical,

66

That thou in height, and depth, and breadth, and power,
Schooled unto pure Mathesis, might proceed
To higher entities, whereof in us
Copies are seen, existent they themselves
In the sole Kingdom of the Mind and God.
Mind not the stars, mind thou thy Mind and God.'
By that supremer Word   20
O'ermastered, deafly heard
Were hauntings dim of old astrologies;
Chaldean mumblings vast, with gossip light
From modern ologistic fancyings mixed,
Of suns and stars, by hypothetic men
Of other frame than ours inhabited,
Of lunar seas and lunar craters huge.
And was there atmosphere, or was there not?
And without oxygen could life subsist?
And was the world originally mist?—   30
Talk they as talk they list,
I, in that ampler voice,
Unheeding, did rejoice.

19
LES VACHES

THE skies have sunk and hid the upper snow,
Home, Rose, and home, Provence and La Palie,
The rainy clouds are filing fast below,
And wet will be the path, and wet shall we.
Home, Rose, and home, Provence and La Palie.

Ah dear, and where is he, a year agone
Who stepped beside and cheered us on and on?
My sweetheart wanders far away from me,
In foreign land or o'er a foreign sea.
Home, Rose, and home, Provence and La Palie.   10

The lightning zigzags shot across the sky,
(Home, Rose, and home, Provence and La Palie,)

And through the vale the rains go sweeping by,
Ah me, and when in shelter shall we be?
Home, Rose, and home, Provence and La Palie.

Cold, dreary cold, the stormy winds feel they
O'er foreign lands and foreign seas that stray.
(Home, Rose, and home, Provence and La Palie.)
And doth he e'er, I wonder, bring to mind
The pleasant huts and herds he left behind?   20
And doth he sometimes in his slumbering see
The feeding kine, and doth he think of me,
My sweetheart wandering wheresoe'er it be?
Home, Rose, and home, Provence and La Palie.

The thunder bellows far from snow to snow,
(Home, Rose, and home, Provence and La Palie)
And loud and louder roars the flood below.
Heigh ho! but soon in shelter shall we be.
Home, Rose, and home, Provence and La Palie.

Or shall he find before his term be sped,   30
Some comelier maid that he shall wish to wed?
(Home, Rose, and home, Provence and La Palie,)
For weary is work, and weary day by day
To have your comfort miles on miles away.
Home, Rose, and home, Provence and La Palie.
Or may it be 'tis I shall find my mate,
And he returning see himself too late?
For work we must, and what we see, we see,
And God he knows, and what must be, must be,
When sweethearts wander far away from me.   40
Home, Rose, and home, Provence and La Palie.

The sky behind is brightening up anew,
(Home, Rose, and home, Provence and La Palie),
The rain is ending, and our journey too;
Heigh ho! aha! for here at home are we:—
In, Rose, and in, Provence and La Palie.

20. *SA MAJESTÉ TRÈS CHRÉTIENNE*

'TIS true, Monseigneur, I am much to blame;
But we must all forgive; especially
Subjects their King; would I were one to do so
What could I do? and how was I to help it?
'Tis true it should not be so; true indeed,
I know I am not what I would I were.
I would I were, as God intended me,
A little quiet harmless acolyte,
Clothed in long serge and linen shoulder-piece,
Day after day   10
To pace serenely through the sacred fane,
Bearing the sacred things before the priest,
Curtsey before that altar as we pass,
And place our burden reverently on this.
There—by his side to stand and minister,
To swing the censer and to sound the bell,
Uphold the book, the patin change and cup—
Ah me—
And why does childhood ever change to man?
Oh, underneath the black and sacred serge   20
Would yet uneasy uncontented blood
Swell to revolt? Beneath the tippet's white
Would harassed nerves by sacred music soothed,
By solemn sights and peaceful tasks composed,
Demand more potent medicine than these,
Or ask from pleasure more than duty gives?

                    Ah, holy father, yes.
Without the appointed,
Without the sweet confessional relief,
Without the welcome all-absolving words,   30
The mystic rite, the solemn soothing forms,
Our human life were miserable indeed.
And yet methinks our holy Mother Church
Deals hardly, very, with her eldest born,

Her chosen, sacred, and most Christian Kings.
To younger pets, the blind, the halt, the sick,
The outcast child, the sinners of the street,
Her doors are open and her precinct free:
The beggar finds a nest, the slave a home,
Even thy altars, O my Mother Church—   40
O templa quam dilecta. We, the while,
Poor Kings, must forth to action, as you say;
Action, that slaves us, drives us, fretted, worn,
To pleasure, which anon enslaves us too;
Action, and what is Action, O my God?
Alas, and can it be
In this perplexing labyrinth I see,
This waste and wild infinity of ways
Where all are like, and each each other meets,
Quits, meets, and quits a many hundred times,   50
That this path more than that conducts to Thee?
Alas, and is it true
Ought I can purpose, say, or will, or do,
My fancy choose, my changeful silly heart
Resolve, my puny petty hand enact,
To that great glory can in ought conduce
Which from the old eternities is Thine?
Ah never, no!
If ought there be for sinful souls below
To do, 'tis rather to forbear to do;   60
If ought there be of action that contains
The sense of sweet identity with God,
It is, methinks, it is inaction only.
To walk with God I know not; let me kneel.
Ah yes, the livelong day
To watch before the altar where they pray:
To muse and wait,
On sacred stones lie down and meditate.
No, through the long and dark and dismal night
We will not turn and seek the city streets,   70

We will not stir, we should but lose our way;
But faithful stay
And watch the tomb where He, our Saviour, lies
Till his great day of Resurrection rise.

Yes, the commandments you remind me, yes,
The Sacred Word has pointed out the way,
The Priest is here for our unfailing guide;
Do this, not that, to right hand and to left,
A voice is with us ever at our ear.
Yes, holy Father, I am thankful for it;   80
Most thankful I am not, as other men,
A lonely Lutheran English Heretic;
If I had so by God's despite been born,
Alas, methinks I had but passed my life
In sitting motionless beside the fire,
Not daring to remove the once-placed chair,
Nor stir my foot for fear it should be sin.
Thank God indeed,
Thank God for his infallible certain creed.
Yes, the commandments, precepts of good life,   90
And counsels of perfection and the like,—
'Thou knowest the commandments'—Yes indeed,
Yes, I suppose. But it is weary work;
For Kings I think they are not plain to read;
Ministers somehow have small faith in them.
Ah, holy father, would I were as you.
But you, no less, have trials as you say;
Inaction vexes you, and action tempts,
And the bad prickings of the animal heats,
As in the palace, to the cell will come.   100
Ah, well a day!
Would I were out in quiet Paraguay,
Mending the Jesuits' shoes!—

You drive us into action as our duty.
Then action persecutes and tortures us.

To pleasures and to loving soft delights
We fly for solace and for peace; and gain
Vexation, Persecution also here.
We hurry from the tyranny of man
Into the tyranny yet worse of woman.   110
No satisfaction find I any more
In the old pleasant evil ways; but less,
Less, I believe, of those uneasy stirs
Of discontented and rebellious will
That once with self-contempt tormented me.
Depraved, that is, degraded am I—Sins,
Which yet I see not how I should have shunned,
Have, in despite of all the means of grace,
Submission perfect to the appointed creed,
And absolution-plenary and prayers,   120
Possessed me, held, and changed—yet after all
Somehow I think my heart within is pure.

21

PESCHIERA

WHAT voice did on my spirit fall,
Peschiera, when thy bridge I crost?
' 'Tis better to have fought and lost,
Than never to have fought at all.'

The tricolor a trampled rag
Lies, dirt and dust; the lines I track
By sentry boxes yellow-black
Lead up to no Italian flag.

I see the Croat soldier stand
Upon the grass of your redoubts;   10
The Eagle with his black wing flouts
The breadth and beauty of your land.

Yet not in vain, although in vain,
O men of Brescia, on the day

Of loss past hope, I heard you say
Your welcome to the noble pain.

You said, 'Since so it is, good-bye
Sweet life, high hope; but whatsoe'er
May be, or must, no tongue shall dare
To tell, "The Lombard feared to die."'   20

You said (there shall be answer fit)
'And if our children must obey,
They must; but thinking on this day
'Twill less debase them to submit.'

You said (Oh not in vain you said),
'Haste, brothers, haste while yet we may:
The hours ebb fast of this one day
When blood may yet be nobly shed.'

Ah! not for idle hatred, not
For honour, fame, nor self-applause,   30
But for the glory of the cause,
You did, what will not be forgot.

And though the Stranger stand, 'tis true,
By force and fortune's right he stands;
By fortune which is in God's hands,
And strength which yet shall spring in you.

This voice did on my spirit fall,
Peschiera, when thy bridge I crost,
' 'Tis better to have fought and lost,
Than never to have fought at all.'   40

22

ALTERAM PARTEM

OR shall I say, Vain word, false thought,
Since Prudence hath her martyrs too,
And Wisdom dictates not to do,
Till doing shall be not for nought?

Not ours to give or lose is life;
Will Nature when her brave ones fall,
Remake her work? or songs recall
Death's victim slain in useless strife?

That rivers flow into the sea
Is loss and waste, the foolish say,   10
Nor know that back they find their way,
Unseen, to where they wont to be.

Showers fall upon the hills, springs flow,
The river runneth still at hand,
Brave men are born into the land,
And whence the foolish do not know.

No! no vain voice did on me fall,
Peschiera, when thy bridge I crost,
''*Tis* better to have fought and lost,
Than never to have fought at all.'   20

23

THESE vulgar ways that round me be,
These faces shabby, sordid, mean,
Shall they be daily, hourly seen
And not affect the eyes that see?

Long months to play the censor's part,
Lie down at night and rise at morn
In mere defiance and stern scorn
Is scarcely well for human heart.

Accept, O soul, not in disdain,
But patience, faith and simple sooth;   10
Poise all things in the scales of truth,
And one day they shall pay thy pain.

24

IT fortifies my soul to know
That, though I perish, Truth is so:
That, howsoe'er I stray and range,
Whate'er I do, Thou dost not change.
I steadier step when I recall
That, if I slip, Thou dost not fall.

25

JULY'S FAREWELL

YET once again, ye banks and bowery nooks,
And once again, ye dells and flowing brooks,
I come to list the plashing of your fountains
And lie within the foldings of your mountains.
Yet once again, ye mossy flowery plots,
And once again, ye leaf-enguarded grots,
And breathing fields and soft enclosing shades,
And once again, ye fair and loving maids,
I come to twist my fingers in your tresses,
And watch your eyes and laugh in your caresses,   10
And beg or steal or seize your pouting kisses,
And live and die in your oblivious blisses;
Yet once again, ye banks and bowers, I hie to you,
And once again, ye loves and graces, fly to you.

I come, I come, upon the heart's wings fly to you,
Ye dreary lengths of brick and flag, good-bye to you,
Ambitious hopes and money's mean anxieties,
And worldly-wise decorum's false proprieties,
And politics and news and fates of nations too,
And philanthropic sick investigations too,   20
And company, and jests, and feeble witticisms,
And talk of talk, and criticism of criticisms;
I come, I come, ye banks and bowers, to hide in you,
And once again, ye loves and joys, confide in you.

75

Yet once again, and why not once again?
The leaves they tumbled, but the boughs remain;
Cold winds they blew, and biting frosts they dried them,
But didn't wholly kill the old life inside them;
What winter numbed, sweet spring anon revisiteth,
And vernal airs to vernal stir soliciteth,   30
No scruples fond, no shy fastidious tarrying here,
Sweet air and earth forthwith are intermarrying here;
To intermixtures subtle, strange, mysterious
A voice, an impulse soft, sublime, imperious,
Calls all around us; shall we deaf remain?
Yet once again, and why not once again,
Yet once again, ye leafy bowers, I hide in you
And once again, ye tender loves, confide in you.

I come, I come, upon the soul's wings hie to you,
Ye weary lines of printer's ink, good-bye to you,   40
With all the tomes of all the hundred pages there,
The mighty books of all the World's great sages there,
Grammarians old, and modern fine Philologists,
And Poets gone, and going Ideologists,
From old solemnities, new trivialities,
Philosophies, economies, moralities,
I come, I come, ye banks and bowers, I hie to you,
And once again, ye loves and graces, fly to you.

Yet once again—how often once again?
The days die fast, old age comes on amain: 50
Age, loss, decay. Ah come, if come they will,
The leaf shall fall, the tree subsisteth still:
Age, weakness, death. Ah come, if come they must,
Age, weakness, death; and over our cold dust
The joyous spring shall lead, as erst, her flowers
To deck, as erst, our fresh reviving bowers,
And with the spring and flowers the youth and maid
Shall laugh and kiss and play as we have played,

Shall part and meet and kiss old kisses o'er
And sing old verses we had sung before,   60
'Yet once again, ye banks and bowers, we hie to you,
And once again, ye loves and graces, fly to you'.

26

CHORUS

Now the birds have ceased their singing
    And the sun has sunk below
And the bedtime bell is ringing,
        Let us go!
    Let us go!

Business ceases, joy decreases,
    We have had enough we know;
Where our slumber soft and peace is
    We will go, We will go!

If to wake us up to-morrow   10
    Rays of day shall prick our eyes,
For that morrow's joy or sorrow
    We will rise, We will rise.

When the carts begin to clatter,
    Then it will be time we know,
Surely now it cannot matter,
    Let us go, Let us go.

When the birds have ceased their singing
    And all's over for to-day
And the bedtime bell's done ringing,   20
        Wherefore stay,
    Wherefore stay?
        No! No!
        Let us go!
    Let us go!

27

Go, foolish thoughts, and join the throng
  Of myriads gone before;
To flutter and flap and flit along
  The airy limbo shore.

Go, words of sport and words of wit,
  Sarcastic points and fine,
And words of wisdom wholly fit
  With folly's to combine.

Go, words of wisdom, words of sense,
  Which, while the heart belied,   10
The tongue still uttered for pretence,
  The inner blank to hide.

Go, words of wit, so gay, so light,
  That still were meant express
To soothe the smart of fancied slight
  By fancies of success.

Go, broodings vain o'er fancied wrong;
  Go, love-dreams vainer still;
And scorn that's not, but would be, strong;
  And Pride without a Will.   20

Go, foolish thoughts, and find your way
  Where myriads went before,
To linger, languish and decay
  Upon the limbo shore.

28

GENESIS XXIV

WHO is this Man
        that walketh in the field,
O Eleazar,
        steward to my lord?

And Eleazar
   answered her and said,
Daughter of Bethuel,
   it is other none
But my lord Isaac,
   son unto my lord;
Who, as his wont is,
   walketh in the field
In the hour of evening
   meditating there.

Therefore Rebekah
   hasted where she sat,
And from her camel
   lighting to the earth
Sought for a veil,
   and put it on her face.   10

But Isaac also,
   walking in the field,
Saw from afar
   a company that came,
Camels, and a seat
   as where a woman sat;
Wherefore he came,
   and met them on the way.

Whom, when Rebekah
   saw, she came before,
Saying, Behold
   the handmaid of my lord,
Who for my lord's sake
   travel from my land.

But he said, O
   thou blessed of our God,
Come, for the tent
   is eager for thy face.

79

Shall not thy husband
     be unto thee more than   **20**
Hundreds of kinsmen
     living in thy land?

And Eleazar answered,
     Thus and thus,
Even according
     as thy father bade,
Did we; and thus and
     thus it came to pass;
Lo! is not this
     Rebekah, Bethuel's child?

And as he ended
     Isaac spoke and said,
Surely my heart
     went with you on the way,
When with the beasts
     ye came unto the place.

Truly, O child
     of Nahor, I was there,
When to thy mother
     and thy mother's son   **30**
Thou madest answer,
     saying, I will go.
And Isaac brought her
     to his mother's tent.

29
JACOB'S WIVES

THESE are the words of Jacob's wives; the words
Which Leah spake and Rachel to his ears,
When in the shade at eventide he sat
By the tent-door, a palm tree overhead,
A spring beside him, and the sheep around.

And Rachel spake and said, The nightfall comes;
Night, which all day I wait for, and for thee.

And Leah also spake, The day is done;
My lord with toil is weary, and would rest.

And Rachel said, Come, O my Jacob, come;   10
And we will think we sit beside the well,
As in that day the long long years agone
When first I met thee with my father's flock.

And Leah said, Come, Israel, unto me;
And thou shalt reap an harvest of fair sons,
E'en as before I bare thee goodly babes;
For when was Leah fruitless to my lord?

And Rachel said, Ah come, as then thou cam'st;
Come once again to set thy seal of love,
As then, down bending, when the sheep had drunk,   20
Then settedst it, my shepherd—O sweet seal!—
Upon the unwitting half-foretasting lips,
Which shy and trembling thirsted yet for thine
As cattle thirsted never for the spring.

And Leah answered, Are not these their names,
As Reuben, Simeon, Levi, Judah, four?
Like four young saplings by the water's brim,
Where straining rivers through the great plain wind,
Four saplings soon to rise to goodly trees,
Four trees whose growth shall cast an huger shade   30
Than ever yet on river-side was seen.

And Rachel said, And shall it be again
As when dissevered far, unheard, alone,
Consumed in bitter anger all night long,
I moaned and wept, while, silent and discreet,
One reaped the fruit of love that Rachel's was
Upon the breast of him that knew her not?

And Leah said, And was it then a wrong
That, in submission to a father's word,
Trembling yet hopeful to that bond I crept,   40
Which God hath greatly prospered, and my lord
Content in after-wisdom not disowned,
Joyful in after-thankfulness approved?

And Rachel said, But we will not complain,
Though all life long an alien unsought third
She trouble our companionship of love.

And Leah answered, No; complain we not,
Though year on year she loiter in the tent,
A fretful, vain, unprofitable wife.

And Rachel answered, Ah! she little knows   50
What in old days to Jacob Rachel was.

And Leah said, And wilt thou dare to say,
Because my lord was gracious to thee then,
No deeper thought his riper cares hath claimed,
No stronger purpose passed into his life?
That, youth and maid once fondly, softly touched,
Time's years must still the casual dream repeat,
And all the river far, from source to sea,
One flitting moment's chance reflection bear?

Also she added, Who is she to judge   60
Of thoughts maternal, and a father's heart?

And Rachel said, But what to supersede
The rights which choice bestowed hath Leah done?
What which my handmaid or which hers hath not?
Is Simeon more than Naphthali? is Dan
Less than his brother Levi in the house?
That part that Billah and that Zilpah have,
That, and no more, hath Leah in her lord,
And let her with the same be satisfied.

Leah asked then, And shall these things compare   70
(Fond wishes, and the pastime and the play)
With serious aims and forward-working hopes—
Aims as far-reaching as to Earth's last age,
And hopes far-travelling as from East to West?

Rachel replied, That love which in his youth,
Through trial proved, consoles his perfect age,
Shall this with project and with plan compare?
Or is forever shorter than all time,
And love more straitened than from East to West?

Leah spake further, Hath my lord not told   80
How in the visions of the night his God,
The God of Abraham and of Isaac, spake
And said, Increase, and multiply, and fill
With sons to serve Me this thy land and mine,
And I will surely do thee good, and make
Thy seed as is the sand beside the sea,
Which is not numbered for its multitude?
Shall [Rachel] bear this progeny to God?

But Rachel wept and answered, And if God
Hath closed the womb of Rachel until now,   90
Shall He not at His pleasure open it?
Hath Leah read the counsels of the Lord?
Was it not told her in the ancient days
How Sarah, mother of great Israel's sire,
Lived to long years insulted of her slave
Or e'er to light the Child of Promise came,
Whom Rachel too to Jacob yet may bear?

Moreover Rachel said, Shall Leah mock,
Who stole the prime embraces of my love,
My first long-destined, long-withheld caress?   100

But not, she said, methought, but not for this,
In the old days did Jacob seek his bride;

83

Where art thou now, O thou that sought'st me then?
Where is thy loving tenderness of old?
And where that fervency of faith to which
Seven weary years were even as a few days?

And Rachel wept and ended, Ah, my life!
Though Leah bear thee sons on sons, methought
The Child of love, late-born, were worth them all.

And Leah groaned and answered, It is well: 110
She that hath kept from me my husband's heart
Will set their father's soul against my sons.

Yet, also, not, she said, I thought, for this,
Not for the feverish nor the doting love
Doth Israel, father of a Nation, seek;
Nor to light dalliance as of boy and girl
Incline the thoughts of matron and of man,
Or lapse the wisdoms of maturer mind.

And Leah ended, Father of my sons,
Come, thou shalt dream of Rachel if thou wilt,   120
So Leah fold thee in a wife's embrace.

These are the words of Jacob's wives, who sat
In the tent door, and listened to their speech,
The spring beside him, and above the palm,
While all the sheep were gathered for the night.

30

JACOB

My sons, and ye the children of my sons,
Jacob your father goes upon his way,
His pilgrimage is being accomplished.
Come near, and hear him ere his words are o'er.
Not as my father's or his father's days,
As Isaac's days or Abraham's, have been mine;

Not as the days of those that in the field
Walked at the eventide to meditate,
And haply to the tent returning found
Angels at nightfall waiting at their door.   10
They communed, Israel wrestled with the Lord.
No, not as Abraham's or as Isaac's days,
My sons, have been Jacob your father's days,
Evil and few, attaining not to theirs
In number, and in worth inferior much.
As a man with his friend, walked they with God,
In his abiding presence they abode,
And all their acts were open to his face.
But I have had to force mine eyes away,
To lose, almost to shun, the thoughts I loved,   20
To bend down to the work, to bare the breast,
And struggle, feet and hands, with enemies;
To buffet and to battle with hard men,
With men of selfishness and violence;
To watch by day and calculate by night,
To plot and think of plots, and through a land
Ambushed with guile, and with strong foes beset,
To win with art safe wisdom's peaceful way.
Alas! I know, and from the outset knew,
The first-born faith, the singleness of soul,   30
The antique pure simplicity with which
God and good angels communed undispleased,
Is not; it shall not any more be said
That of a blameless and a holy kind
The chosen race, the seed of promise, comes.
The royal high prerogatives, the dower
Of innocence and perfectness of life,
Pass not unto my children from their sire
As unto me they came of mine; they fit
Neither to Jacob nor to Jacob's race.   40
Think ye, my sons, in this extreme old age
And in this failing breath, that I forget

How on the day when from my father's door,
In bitterness and ruefulness of heart,
I from my parents set my face and felt
I never more again should look on theirs,—
How on that day I seemed unto myself
Another Adam from his home cast out,
And driven abroad into a barren land,
Cursed for his sake, and mocking still with thorns   50
And briars that labour and that sweat of brow
He still must spend to live? Sick of my days,
I wished not life, but cried out, Let me die;
But at Luz God came to me; in my heart
He put a better mind, and showed me how,
While we discern it not and least believe,
On stairs invisible betwixt his heaven
And our unholy, sinful, toilsome earth
Celestial messengers of loftiest good
Upward and downward pass continually.   60
Many, since Jacob on the field of Luz
Set up the stone he slept on, unto God,
Many have been the troubles of my life;
Sins in the field and sorrows in the tent,
In mine own household anguish and despair,
And gall and wormwood mingled with my love.
The time would fail me should I seek to tell
Of a child wronged and cruelly revenged
(Accursed was that anger, it was fierce,
That wrath, for it was cruel), or of strife   70
And jealousy and cowardice, with lies
Mocking a father's misery; deeds of blood,
Pollutions, sicknesses, and sudden deaths,
These many things against me many times.
The ploughers have ploughed deep upon my back,
And made deep furrows; blessed be his name
Who hath delivered Jacob out of all,
And left within his spirit hope of good.

Come near to me, my sons: your father goes,
The hour of his departure draweth nigh.   80
Ah me! this eager rivalry of life,
This cruel conflict for pre-eminence,
This keen supplanting of the dearest kin,
Quick seizure and fast unrelaxing hold
Of vantage-place; the stony-hard resolve,
The chase, the competition, and the craft
Which seems to be the poison of our life
And yet is the condition of our life!
To have done things on which the eye with shame
Looks back, the closed hand clutching still the prize!   90
Alas! what of all these things shall I say?
Take me away unto thy sleep, O God!
I thank thee it is over, yet I think
It was a work appointed me of thee.
How is it? I have striven all my days
To do my duty to my house and hearth,
And to the purpose of my father's race,
Yet is my heart therewith not satisfied.

31

ὕμνος ἄυμνος[1]

O THOU whose image in the shrine
Of human spirits dwells divine;
Which from that precinct once conveyed,
To be to outer day displayed,
Doth vanish, part, and leave behind
Mere blank and void of empty mind,
Which wilful fancy seeks in vain
With casual shapes to fill again—

O thou that in our bosoms' shrine
Dost dwell, because unknown, divine!   10

[1] A hymn, yet not a hymn.

I thought to speak, I thought to say,
'The light is here,' 'behold the way,'
'The voice was thus,' and 'thus the word,'
And 'thus I saw,' and 'that I heard,'—
But from the lips but half essayed
The imperfect utterance fell unmade.

O thou, in that mysterious shrine
Enthroned, as we must say, divine!
I will not frame one thought of what
Thou mayest either be or not.   20
I will not prate of 'thus' and 'so',
And be profane with 'yes' and 'no.'
Enough that in our soul and heart
Thou, whatsoe'er thou may'st be, art.

Unseen, secure in that high shrine
Acknowledged present and divine,
I will not ask some upper air,
Some future day, to place thee there;
Nor say, nor yet deny, Such men
Or women saw thee thus and then: 30
Thy name was such, and there or here
To him or her thou didst appear.

Do only thou in that dim shrine,
Unknown or known, remain, divine;
There, or if not, at least in eyes
That scan the fact that round them lies.
The hand to sway, the judgment guide,
In sight and sense thyself divide:
Be thou but there,—in soul and heart,
I will not ask to feel thou art.   40

32

'OLD things need not be therefore true,'
O brother men, nor yet the new;
Ah! still awhile the old thought retain,
And yet consider it again!

The souls of now two thousand years
Have laid up here their toils and tears,
And all the earnings of their pain,—
Ah, yet consider that again!

We! what do *we* see? each a space
Of some few yards before his face;   10
Does that the whole wide plan explain?
Ah, yet consider it again!

Alas! the great World goes its way,
And takes its truth from each new day;
They do not quit, nor can retain,
Far less consider it again!

33

ACROSS the sea, along the shore,
In numbers more and ever more,
From lonely hut and busy town,
The valley through, the mountain down,
What was it ye went out to see,
Ye silly folk of Galilee?
The reed that in the wind doth shake?
The weed that washes in the lake?
The reeds that waver, the weeds that float?—
A young man preaching in a boat.   10

What was it ye went out to hear
By sea and land from far and near?
A teacher? Rather seek the feet
Of those who sit in Moses' seat.
Go humbly seek, and bow to them,
Far off in great Jerusalem.

From them that in her courts ye saw,
Her perfect doctors of the law,
What is it came ye here to note?—
A young man preaching in a boat.   20

A prophet! Boys and women weak!
    Declare, or cease to rave;
Whence is it he hath learned to speak?
    Say, who his doctrine gave?
A prophet? Prophet wherefore he
    Of all in Israel tribes?—
He teacheth with authority,
    And not as do the Scribes.

34

To spend uncounted years of pain,
Again, again, and yet again,
In working out in heart and brain
    The problem of our being here;
To gather facts from far and near,
Upon the mind to hold them clear,
And, knowing more may yet appear,
Unto one's latest breath to fear
The premature result to draw—
Is this the object, end and law,   10
    And purpose of our being here?

35

It is not sweet content, be sure,
    That moves the nobler Muse to song,
Yet when could truth come whole and pure
    From hearts that inly writhe with wrong?

It is not calm and peaceful breasts
    That see or read the problem true;
They only know on whom 't has prest
    Too hard to hope to solve it too.

Our ills are worse than at their ease
   Mere blameless happy souls suspect;   **10**
They only study the disease,
   Alas, who live not to detect.

36
IN THE GREAT METROPOLIS

EACH for himself is still the rule,
We learn it when we go to school—
   The devil take the hindmost, o!

And when the schoolboys grow to men,
In life they learn it o'er again—
   The devil take the hindmost, o!

For in the church, and at the bar,
On 'Change, at court, where'er they are,
   The devil takes the hindmost, o!

Husband for husband, wife for wife,   **10**
Are careful that in married life
   The devil take the hindmost, o!

From youth to age, whate'er the game,
The unvarying practice is the same—
   The devil take the hindmost, o!

And after death, we do not know,
But scarce can doubt, where'er we go,
   The devil takes the hindmost, o!

Tol rol de rol, tol rol de ro,
The devil take the hindmost, o!   **20**

37

BLESSED are those who have not seen,
   And who have yet believed
The witness, here that has not been,
   From heaven they have received.

Blessed are those who have not known
   The things that stand before them,
And for a vision of their own
   Can piously ignore them.

So let me think whate'er befall,
   That in the city duly   10
Some men there are who love at all,
   Some women who love truly;

And that upon two million odd
   Transgressors in sad plenty,
Mercy will of a gracious God
   Be shown—because of twenty.

38

PUT forth thy leaf, thou lofty plane,
   East wind and frost are safely gone;
With zephyr mild and balmy rain
   The summer comes serenely on;
Earth, air, and sun and skies combine
   To promise all that's kind and fair:—
But thou, O human heart of mine,
   Be still, contain thyself, and bear.

December days were brief and chill,
   The winds of March were wild and drear,   10
And, nearing and receding still,
   Spring never would, we thought, be here.
The leaves that burst, the suns that shine,
   Had, not the less, their certain date:—
And thou, O human heart of mine,
   Be still, refrain thyself, and wait.

39. LAST WORDS. NAPOLEON AND WELLINGTON

NAPOLEON

Is it this, then, O world-warrior,
  That, exulting, through the folds
Of the dark and cloudy barrier
  Thine enfranchised eye beholds?
Is, when blessed hands relieve thee
  From the gross and mortal clay,
This the heaven that should receive thee?
        'Tête d'armée.'

Now the final link is breaking,
  Of the fierce, corroding chain,   10
And the ships, their watch forsaking,
  Bid the seas no more detain.
Whither is it, freed and risen,
  The pure spirit seeks away,
Quits for what the weary prison?
        'Tête d'armée.'

Doubtless—angels, hovering o'er thee
  In thine exile's sad abode,
Marshalled even now before thee,
  Move upon that chosen road!   20
Thither they, ere friends have laid thee
  Where sad willows o'er thee play,
Shall already have conveyed thee!
        'Tête d'armée.'

Shall great captains, foiled and broken,
  Hear from thee on each great day,
At the crisis, a word spoken—
  Word that battles still obey—
'Cuirassiers here, here those cannon;
  Quick, those squadrons, up—away!   30
To the charge, on—as one man, on!'
        'Tête d'armée.'

(Yes, too true, alas! while sated
    Of the wars so slow to cease,
Nations, once that scorned and hated,
    Would to Wisdom turn, and Peace;
Thy dire impulse still obeying,
    Fevered youths, as in the old day,
In their hearts still find thee saying,
            'Tête d'armée.')   40

Oh, poor soul!—Or do I view thee,
    From earth's battle-fields withheld,
In a dream, assembling to thee
    Troops that quell not, nor are quelled,
Breaking airy lines, defeating
    Limbo-kings, and, as to-day,
Idly to all time repeating
            'Tête d'armée'?

WELLINGTON

And what the words that with his failing breath
    Did England hear her aged soldier say?
I know not. Yielding tranquilly to death,
    With no proud speech, no boast, he passed away.

Not stirring words, nor gallant deeds alone,
    Plain patient work fulfilled that length of life;
Duty, not glory—Service, not a throne,
    Inspired his effort, set for him the strife.

Therefore just Fortune, with one hasty blow,
    Spurning her minion, Glory's, Victory's lord,   10
Gave all to him that was content to know
    In service done its own supreme reward.

The words he said, if haply words there were,
    When full of years and works he passed away,
Most naturally might, methinks, refer
    To some poor humble business of to-day.

'That humble simple duty of the day
  Perform,' he bids; 'ask not if small or great:
Serve in thy post; be faithful, and obey;
  Who serves her truly, sometimes saves the State.'   20

40

FAREWELL, farewell! Her vans the vessel tries,
His iron might the potent engine plies;
Haste, wingèd words, and ere 'tis useless, tell,
Farewell, farewell, yet once again, farewell.

The docks, the streets, the houses past us fly,
Without a strain the great ship marches by;
Ye fleeting banks take up the words we tell,
And say for us yet once again, farewell.

The waters widen—but with calm disdain
The proud ship cleaves the liquid yielding plain;   10
She knows the seas, she hears the true waves swell,
She seems to say farewell, again farewell.

The billows whiten and the deep seas heave;
Fly once again, sweet words, to her I leave,
With winds that blow return, and seas that swell,
Farewell, farewell, say once again, farewell.

Fresh in my face and rippling to my feet
The winds and waves an answer soft repeat,
In sweet, sweet words far brought they seem to tell,
Farewell, farewell, yet once again, farewell.   20

Night gathers fast; adieu, thou fading shore!
The land we look for next must lie before;
Hence, foolish tears! weak thoughts, no more rebel,
Farewell, farewell, a last, a last farewell.

Yet not, indeed, ah not till more than sea
And more than space divide my love and me,
Till more than waves and winds between us swell,
Farewell, a last, indeed, a last farewell.

41

YE flags of Piccadilly,
  Where I posted up and down,
And wished myself so often
  Well away from you and Town,—

Are the people walking quietly
  And steady on their feet,
Cabs and omnibuses plying
  Just as usual in the street?

Do the houses look as upright
  As of old they used to be,   10
And does nothing seem affected
  By the pitching of the sea?

Through the Green Park iron railings
  Do the quick pedestrians pass?
Are the little children playing
  Round the plane-tree in the grass?

This squally wild north-wester
  With which our vessel fights,
Does it merely serve with you to
  Carry up some paper kites?   20

Ye flags of Piccadilly,
  Which I hated so, I vow
I could wish with all my heart
  You were underneath me now!

42

COME home, come home! and where an home hath he
Whose ship is driving o'er the driving sea?
To the frail bark here plunging on its way
To the wild waters shall I turn and say
          Ye are my home?

Fields once I walked in, faces once I knew,
Familiar things my heart had grown unto,

Far away hence behind me lie; before
The dark clouds mutter and the deep seas roar
      Not words of home.   10

Beyond the clouds, beyond the waves that roar
There may indeed, or may not be, a shore,
Where fields as green and friendly hearts as true
The old foregone appearance may renew
      As of an home.

But toil and care must add day on to day,
And weeks bear months and months bear years away,
Ere, if at all, the way-worn traveller hear
A voice he dare believe say in his ear
      Come to thy home.   20

Come home, come home! and where an home hath he
Whose ship is driving o'er the driving sea?
Through clouds that mutter and o'er seas that roar
Is there indeed, or is there not a shore
      That is our home?

43

    GREEN fields of England! wheresoe'er
    Across this watery waste we fare,
    Your image at our hearts we bear,
    Green fields of England, everywhere.

    Sweet eyes in England, I must flee
    Past where the waves' last confines be,
    Ere your loved smile I cease to see,
    Sweet eyes in England, dear to me.

    Dear home in England, safe and fast
    If but in thee my lot be cast,   10
    The past shall seem a nothing past
    To thee, dear home, if won at last;
    Dear home in England, won at last.

44

COME back, come back, behold with straining mast
And swelling sail, behold her steaming fast;
With one new sun to see her voyage o'er,
With morning light to touch her native shore.
    Come back, come back.

Come back, come back, while westward labouring by,
With sail-less yards, a bare black hulk we fly,
See how the gale we fight with, sweeps her back,
To our last home, on our forsaken track.
    Come back, come back.   10

Come back, come back, across the flying foam
We hear faint far-off voices call us home,
Come back, ye seem to say; ye seek in vain;
We went, we sought, and homeward turned again.
    Come back, come back.

Come back, come back; and whither back or why?
To fan quenched hopes, forsaken schemes to try;
Walk the old fields; pace the familiar street;
Dream with the idlers, with the base compete.
    Come back, come back.   20

Come back, come back; and whither and for what?
To finger idly some old Gordian knot,
Unskilled to sunder, and too weak to cleave,
And with much toil attain to half-believe.
    Come back, come back.

Come back, come back; yea back, indeed, do go
Sighs panting thick, and tears that want to flow;
Fond fluttering hopes upraise their useless wings,
And wishes idly struggle in the strings;
    Come back, come back.   30

Come back, come back, more eager than the breeze,
The flying fancies sweep across the seas,
And lighter far than ocean's flying foam
The heart's fond message hurries to its home.
       Come back, come back!

Come back, come back!
Back flies the foam; the hoisted flag streams back;
The long smoke wavers on the homeward track,
Back fly with winds things which the winds obey,
The strong ship follows its appointed way.   40

45

SOME future day when what is now is not,
When all old faults and follies are forgot,
And thoughts of difference passed like dreams away,
We'll meet again, upon some future day.

When all that hindered, all that vexed our love
As tall rank weeds will climb the blade above,
When all but it has yielded to decay,
We'll meet again upon some future day.

When we have proved, each on his course alone,
The wider world, and learnt what's now unknown,   10
Have made life clear, and worked out each a way,
We'll meet again,—we shall have much to say.

With happier mood, and feelings born anew,
Our boyhood's bygone fancies we'll review,
Talk o'er old talks, play as we used to play,
And meet again, on many a future day.

Some day, which oft our hearts shall yearn to see,
In some far year, though distant, yet to be,
Shall we indeed,—ye winds and waters, say!—
Meet yet again, upon some future day?   20

46

WERE I with you, or you with me,
My love, how happy should we be;
Day after day it is sad cheer
To have you there, while I am here.

My darling's face I cannot see,
My darling's voice is mute for me,
My fingers vainly seek the hair
Of her that is not here, but there.

In a strange land, to her unknown,
I sit and think of her alone;   10
And in that happy chamber where
We sat, she sits, nor has me there.

Yet still the happy thought recurs
That she is mine, as I am hers,
That she is there, as I am here,
And loves me, whether far or near.

The mere assurance that she lives
And loves me, full contentment gives;
I need not doubt, despond, or fear,
For, she is there, and I am here.   20

47

WERE you with me, or I with you,
There's nought, methinks, I might not do;
Could venture here, and venture there,
And never fear, nor ever care.

To things before, and things behind,
Could turn my thoughts, and turn my mind,
On this and that, day after day,
Could dare to throw myself away.

Secure, when all was o'er, to find
My proper thought, my perfect mind,   10
And unimpaired receive anew
My own and better self in you.

48

THAT out of sight is out of mind
Is true of most we leave behind;
It is not, sure, nor can be true,
My own and dearest love, of you.

They were my friends, 'twas sad to part;
Almost a tear began to start;
But yet as things run on they find
That out of sight is out of mind.

For men that will not idlers be
Must lend their hearts to things they see;   10
And friends who leave them far behind,
Being out of sight are out of mind.

I do not blame; I think that when
The cold and silent see again,
Kind hearts will yet as erst be kind,
'Twas out of sight was out of mind.

I knew it, when we parted, well,
I knew it, but was loth to tell;
I knew before, what now I find,
That out of sight was out of mind.   20

That friends, however friends they were,
Still deal with things as things occur,
And that, excepting for the blind,
What's out of sight is out of mind.

But love *is*, as they tell us, blind;
So out of sight and out of mind
Need not, nor will, I think, be true,
My own and dearest love, of you.

49

THE mighty ocean rolls and raves,
My child, to part us with its waves;
But arch on arch from shore to shore,
In a vast fabric reaching o'er,

With careful labours daily wrought
By steady hope and tender thought,
The wide and weltering waste above—
Our hearts have bridged it with their love.

There fond anticipations fly
To rear the growing structure high;   10
Dear memories upon either side
Combine to make it large and wide.

There happy fancies day by day
New courses sedulously lay;
There soft solicitudes, sweet fears,
And doubts accumulate, and tears.

While the pure purpose of the soul,
To form of many parts a whole,
To make them strong and hold them true
From end to end is carried through,   20

Then while the waters war between,
Upon the masonry unseen,
Secure and swift, from shore to shore,
With silent footfall travelling o'er,

Our sundered spirits come and go,
Hither and thither, to and fro,
Pass and repass, now linger near,
Now part, anew to reappear.

With motions of a glad surprise,
We meet each other's wondering eyes,   30
At work, at play, while people talk,
And when we sleep, and when we walk.

Each dawning day my eyelids see
You come, methinks, across to me,
And I, at every hour anew,
I start to fly to bliss and you.

50

AM I with you, or you with me?
   Or in some blessed place above,
Where neither lands divide nor sea,
   Are we united in our love?

Oft while in longing here I lie,
   That wasting ever still endures,
My soul out from me seems to fly,
   And half-way, somewhere, meet with yours.

Somewhere—but where I cannot guess—
   Beyond, may be, the bound of space,   10
The liberated spirits press
   And meet, bless heaven, and embrace.

It seems not either here nor there,
   Somewhere between us up above,
A region of a clearer air,
   The dwelling of a purer love.

51

O SHIP, ship, ship,
   That travellest over the sea,
What are the tidings, I pray thee,
   Thou bearest hither to me?

Are they tidings of comfort and joy,
   That shall make me seem to see
The sweet lips softly moving
   And whispering love to me?

Or are they of trouble and grief,
    Estrangement, [sorrow, and] doubt,   10
To turn into torture my hopes,
    And drive me from Paradise out?

O ship, ship, ship,
    That comest over the sea,
Whatever it be thou bringest,
    Come quickly with it to me.

52

WHERE lies the land to which the ship would go?
Far, far ahead, is all her seamen know.
And where the land she travels from? Away,
Far, far behind, is all that they can say.

On sunny noons upon the deck's smooth face,
Linked arm in arm, how pleasant here to pace;
Or, o'er the stern reclining, watch below
The foaming wake far widening as we go.

On stormy nights when wild north-westers rave,
How proud a thing to fight with wind and wave!   10
The dripping sailor on the reeling mast
Exults to bear, and scorns to wish it past.

Where lies the land to which the ship would go?
Far, far ahead, is all her seamen know.
And where the land she travels from? Away,
Far, far behind, is all that they can say.

53

How in all wonder Columbus got over,
    That is a marvel to me, I protest,
Cabot, and Raleigh too, that well-read rover,
    Frobisher, Dampier, Drake, and the rest.

Bad enough all the same,
For them that after came,
But, in great Heaven's name,
How *he* should ever think
That on the other brink
Of this huge waste terra firma should be,　　　　10
Is a pure wonder, I must say, to me.

(*bis*)

How a man ever should hope to get thither,
　E'en if he knew of there being another side;
But to suppose he should come any whither,
　Sailing right on into chaos untried,
　　　　Across the whole ocean,
　　　　In spite of the motion,
　　　　To stick to the notion
　　　　That in some nook or bend
　　　　Of a sea without end　　　　20
He should find North and South Amerikee,
Was a pure madness as it seems to me.

(*bis*)

What if wise men had, as far back as Ptolemy,
　Judged that the earth like an orange was round,
None of them ever said, 'Come along, follow me,
　Sail to the West, and the East will be found.'
　　　　Many a day before
　　　　Ever they'd touched the shore
　　　　Of the San Salvador,
　　　　Sadder and wiser men　　　　30
　　　　They'd have turned back again;
And that *he* did not, but did cross the sea,
Is a pure wonder, I must say, to me.
And that he crossed and that we cross the sea
Is a pure wonder, I must say, to me.

54

O QUI ME—

AMID these crowded pews must I sit and seem to pray,
All the blessed Sunday morning while I wish to be away,
While in the fields I long to be or on the hill-tops high,
The air of heaven about me, above, the sacred sky?

Why stay and form my features to a 'foolish face of' prayer,
Play postures with the body, while the Spirit is not there?
Not there, but wandering off to woods, or pining to adore
Where mountains rise or where the waves are breaking on the shore.

In a calm sabbatic chamber when I could sit alone,
And feed upon pure thoughts to work-day hours unknown,   10
Amidst a crowd of lookers-on why come, and sham to pray,
While the blessed Sunday morning wastes uselessly away?

Upon the sacred morning that comes but once a week,
Where'er the Voice is speaking, there let me hear it speak;
Await it in the chamber, abroad to seek it roam,
The Worship of the heavens attend, the Services of home.

Pent-up in crowded pews am I really bound to stay,
And to edify my neighbours make a sad pretence to pray,
And where the Truth indeed speaks, neglect to hear it speak,
On the blessed Sunday morning that comes but once a week?   20

55

LIPS, lips, open!
Up comes a little bird that lives inside,
Up comes a little bird, and peeps and out he flies.

All the day he sits inside, and sometimes he sings,
Up he comes and out he goes at night to spread his wings.

Little bird, little bird, whither will you go?
Round about the world, while nobody can know.

Little bird, little bird, whither do you flee?
Far away round the world while nobody can see.

Little bird, little bird, how long will you roam?　　10
All round the world and around again home.

Round the round world, and back through the air,
When the morning comes, the little bird is there.

Back comes the little bird, and looks, and in he flies,
Up wakes the little boy, and opens both his eyes.

Sleep, sleep, little boy, little bird's away,
Little bird will come again, by the peep of day;

Sleep, sleep, little boy, little bird must go
Round about the world, while nobody can know.

Sleep, sleep sound, little bird goes round,　　20
Round and round he goes—sleep, sleep sound.

56

Come, Poet, come!
A thousand labourers ply their task,
And what it tends to scarcely ask,
And trembling thinkers on the brink
Shiver, and know not how to think.
To tell the purport of their pain,
And what our silly joys contain;
In lasting lineaments pourtray
The substance of the shadowy day;
Our real and inner deeds rehearse,　　10
And make our meaning clear in verse:
Come, Poet, come! for but in vain
We do the work or feel the pain,
And gather up the seeming gain,
Unless before the end thou come
To take, ere they are lost, their sum.

Come, Poet, come!
To give an utterance to the dumb,
And make vain babblers silent, come;

A thousand dupes point here and there, 20
Bewildered by the show and glare;
And wise men half have learned to doubt
Whether we are not best without.
Come, Poet; both but wait to see
Their error proved to them in thee.

Come, Poet, come!
In vain I seem to call. And yet
Think not the living times forget.
Ages of heroes fought and fell
That Homer in the end might tell; 30
O'er grovelling generations past
Upstood the Doric fane at last;
And countless hearts on countless years
Had wasted thoughts, and hopes, and fears,
Rude laughter and unmeaning tears,
Ere England Shakespeare saw, or Rome
The pure perfection of her dome.
Others, I doubt not, if not we,
The issue of our toils shall see;
Young children gather as their own 40
The harvest that the dead had sown,
The dead forgotten and unknown.

57

Upon the water, in the boat,
I sit and sketch as down I float:
The stream is wide, the view is fair,
I sketch it looking backward there.

The stream is strong, and as I sit
And view the picture that we quit,
It flows and flows, and bears the boat,
And I sit sketching as we float.

Still as we go the things I see,
E'en as I see them, cease to be;   10
Their angles swerve, and with the boat
The whole perspective seems to float.

Each pointed height, each wavy line,
To wholly other forms combine;
Proportions vary, colours fade,
And all the landscape is remade.

Depicted neither far nor near
And larger there and smaller here,
And varying down from old to new,
E'en I can hardly think it true.   20

Yet still I look, and still I sit,
Adjusting, shaping, altering it;
And still the current bears the boat
And me, still sketching as I float.

58

O STREAM, descending to the sea,
  Thy mossy banks between,
The flowrets blow, the grasses grow,
  The leafy trees are green.

In garden plots the children play,
  The fields the labourers till,
And houses stand on either hand,—
  And thou descendest still.

O life, descending unto death,
  Our waking eyes behold   10
Parent and friend thy lapse attend,
  Companions young and old;

Strong purposes our minds possess,
    Our hearts affections fill,
We toil and earn, we seek and learn,—
    And thou descendest still.

O end, to which our currents tend,
    Inevitable sea,
To which we flow, what do we know,
    What shall we guess of thee?   20

A roar we hear upon thy shore
    As we our course fulfil;
Scarce we divine a sun will shine
    And be above us still.

59

CEASE, empty Faith, the Spectrum saith,
    I was, and lo, have been;
I, God, am nought: a shade of thought,
    Which, but by darkness seen,
Upon the unknown yourselves have thrown,
    Placed it and light between.

At morning's birth on darkened earth,
    And as the evening sinks,
Awfully vast abroad is cast
    The lengthened form that shrinks   10
In midday light, and shuns the sight,
    And underneath you slinks.

From barren strands of wintry lands
    Across the seas of time,
Borne onward fast ye touch at last
    An equatorial clime;

In equatorial noon sublime
  At zenith stands the sun,
And lo, around, far, near, are found
  Yourselves, and Shadow none.   20

A moment! yea, but when the day
  Indeed was perfect day!
A moment! so! and light we know
  With dark exchanges aye,

Nor morn nor eve shall shadow leave
  Your sunny paths secure,
And in your sight that orb of light
  Shall humbler orbs obscure.

And yet withal, 'tis shadow all
  Whate'er your fancies dream,   30
And I (misdeemed) that was, that seemed,
  Am not, whate'er I seem.

60

REPOSE IN EGYPT

O HAPPY mother, while the man wayworn
Sleeps by his ass and dreams of daily bread,
Wakeful and heedful for thy infant care,
O happy mother, while thy husband sleeps,
Art privileged, O blessed one, to see
Celestial strangers sharing in thy task,
And visible angels waiting on thy child.

Take, O young soul, O infant heaven-desired,
Take and fear not the cates, although of earth,
Which to thy hands celestial hands extend.   10
Take and fear not: such vulgar meats of life
Thy spirit lips no more must scorn to pass;
The seeming ill, contaminating joys,
Thy sense divine no more be loth to allow.

The pleasures as the pains of our strange life
Thou art engaged, self-compromised, to share.
Look up, upon thy mother's face there sits
No sad suspicion of a lurking ill,
No shamed confession of a needful sin.
Mistrust her not, albeit of earth she too.   20
Look up! the bright-eyed cherubs overhead
Strew from mid air fresh flowers to crown the feast.
Look! thy own father's servants these, and thine,
Who at his bidding and at thine are here.
In thine own word was it not said long since
Butter and honey shall he eat, and learn
The evil to refuse and choose the good?
Fear not, O babe divine, fear not, accept.
O happy mother, privileged to see,
While the man sleeps, the sacred mystery.   30

61

TRUNKS the forest yielded with gums ambrosial oozing,
    Boughs with apples laden beautiful, Hesperian,
Golden, odoriferous, perfume exhaling about them,
    Orbs in a dark umbrage luminous and radiant;
To the palate grateful, more luscious were not in Eden,
    Or in that fabled garden of Alcinoüs;
Out of a dark umbrage sounds also musical issued,
    Birds their sweet transports uttering in melody,
Thrushes clear-piping, wood-pigeons cooing, arousing
    Loudly the nightingale, loudly, the sylvan echoes;   10
Waters transpicuous flowed under, flowed to the list'ning
    Ear with a soft murmur, softly soporiferous;
Nor, with ebon locks too, there wanted, circling, attentive
    Unto the sweet fluting, girls, of a swarthy shepherd.
Over a sunny level their flocks are lazily feeding,
    They of Amor musing rest in a leafy cavern.

62

FROM thy far sources, 'mid mountains airily climbing,
    Pass to the rich lowland, thou busy sunny river;
Murmuring once, dimpling, pellucid, limpid, abundant,
    Deepening now, widening, swelling, a lordly river.
Through woodlands steering, with branches waving above thee,
    Through the meadows sinuous, wandering irriguous;
Farms, hamlets leaving, towns by thee, bridges across thee,
    Pass to palace garden, pass to cities populous.
Murmuring once, dimpling, 'mid woodlands wandering idly,
    Now with mighty vessels loaded, a mighty river.   10
Pass to the great waters, though tides may seem to resist thee,
    Tides to resist seeming, quickly will lend thee passage,
Pass to the dark waters that roaring wait to receive thee;
    Pass them thou wilt not, thou busy sunny river.

63

ACTÆON

OVER a mountain-slope with lentisk, and with abounding
Arbutus, and the red oak overtufted, 'mid a noontide
Now glowing fervidly, the Leto-born, the divine one,
Artemis, Arcadian wood-rover, alone, hunt-weary,
Unto a dell cent'ring many streamlets her foot unerring
Had guided. Platanus with fig-tree shaded a hollow,
Shaded a waterfall, where pellucid yet abundant
Streams from perpetual full-flowing sources a current:
Lower on either bank in sunshine flowered the' oleanders:
Plenteous under a rock green herbage here to the margin   10
Grew with white poplars o'ercrowning. She, thither arrived,
Unloosing joyfully the vest enfolded upon her,
Swift the divine shoulders discovering, swiftly revealing
Her maidenly bosom and all her beauty beneath it,
To the river waters overflowing to receive her
Yielded her ambrosial nakedness. But with an instant
Conscious, with the' instant the' immortal terrific anger
Flew to the guilty doer: that moment, where amid amply

Concealing plane leaves he the' opportunity, pursued
Long fruitlessly, possessed, unwise, Actæon, of hunters,   20
Hapless of Arcadian and most misguided of hunters,
Knew the divine mandate, knew fate directed upon him.
He, crouching, furtively, with audacious tremulous glance,
Espied approaching, saw descending, disarraying,
And the' unclad shoulders awestruck, awestruck let his eyes see
The maidenly bosom, but not—dim fear fell upon them—
Not more had witnessed. Not, therefore, less the forest through
Ranging, their master ceasing thenceforth to remember,
With the' instant together trooping came as to devour him
His dogs from the' ambush.—Transformed suddenly before them, 30
He fled, an antlered stag wild with terror to the mountain.
She, the liquid stream in, her limbs carelessly reclining,
The flowing waters collected grateful about her.

THE BOTHIE OF
TOBER-NA-VUOLICH

A LONG-VACATION PASTORAL

Nunc formosissimus annus
Ite meæ felix quondam pecus, ite camenæ

THE BOTHIE OF TOBER-NA-VUOLICH

I

IT was the afternoon; and the sports were now at the ending.
Long had the stone been put, tree cast, and thrown the hammer;
Up the perpendicular hill, Sir Hector so called it,
Eight stout gillies had run, with speed and agility wondrous;
Run too the course on the level had been; the leaping was over:
Last in the show of dress, a novelty recently added,
Noble ladies their prizes adjudged for costume that was perfect,
Turning the clansmen about, as they stood with upraised elbows,
Bowing their eye-glassed brows, and fingering kilt and sporran.
It was four of the clock, and the sports were come to the ending, 10
Therefore the Oxford party went off to adorn for the dinner.
  Be it recorded in song who was first, who last, in dressing.
Hope was first, black-tied, white-waistcoated, simple, His Honour;
For the postman made out he was heir to the Earldom of Ilay,
(Being the younger son of the younger brother, the Colonel,)
Treated him therefore with special respect; doffed bonnet, and ever
Called him his Honour: his Honour he therefore was at the cottage.
Always his Honour at least, sometimes the Viscount of Ilay.
  Hope was first, his Honour, and next to his Honour the Tutor.
Still more plain the Tutor, the grave man, nicknamed Adam, 20
White-tied, clerical, silent, with antique square-cut waistcoat
Formal, unchanged, of black cloth, but with sense and feeling be-
      neath it;
Skilful in Ethics and Logic, in Pindar and Poets unrivalled;
Shady in Latin, said Lindsay, but *topping* in Plays and Aldrich.
  Somewhat more splendid in dress, in a waistcoat work of a lady,
Lindsay succeeded; the lively, the cheery, cigar-loving Lindsay,
Lindsay the ready of speech, the Piper, the Dialectician,
This was his title from Adam because of the words he invented,
Who in three weeks had created a dialect new for the party;

This was his title from Adam, but mostly they called him the Piper. 30
Lindsay succeeded, the lively, the cheery, cigar-loving Lindsay.
  Hewson and Hobbes were down at the *matutine* bathing; of
    course too
Arthur, the bather of bathers *par excellence*, Audley by surname,
Arthur they called him for love and for euphony; they had been
    bathing,
Where in the morning was custom, where over a ledge of granite
Into a granite bason the amber torrent descended,
Only a step from the cottage, the road and larches between them.
Hewson and Hobbes followed quick upon Adam; on them followed
    Arthur.
  Airlie descended the last, effulgent as god of Olympus;
Blue, perceptibly blue, was the coat that had white silk facings, 40
Waistcoat blue, coral-buttoned, the white-tie finely adjusted,
Coral moreover the studs on a shirt as of crochet of women:
When the fourwheel for ten minutes already had stood at the
    gateway,
He, like a god, came leaving his ample Olympian chamber.
  And in the fourwheel they drove to the place of the clansmen's
    meeting.
  So in the fourwheel they came; and Donald the innkeeper showed
    them
Up to the barn where the dinner should be. Four tables were in it;
Two at the top and the bottom, a little upraised from the level,
These for Chairman and Croupier, and gentry fit to be with them,
Two lengthways in the midst for keeper and gillie and peasant. 50
Here were clansmen many in kilt and bonnet assembled;
Keepers a dozen at least; the Marquis's targeted gillies;
Pipers five or six, among them the young one, the drunkard;
Many with silver brooches, and some with those brilliant crystals
Found amid granite-dust on the frosty scalp of the Cairn-Gorm;
But with snuff-boxes all, and all of them using the boxes.
Here too were Catholic Priest, and Established Minister standing;
Catholic Priest; for many still clung to the Ancient Worship,
And Sir Hector's father himself had built them a chapel;

So stood Priest and Minister, near to each other, but silent,   60
One to say grace before, the other after the dinner.
Hither anon too came the shrewd, ever-ciphering Factor,
Hither anon the Attaché, the Guardsman mute and stately,
Hither from lodge and bothie in all the adjoining shootings
Members of Parliament many, forgetful of votes and blue-books,
Here, amid heathery hills, upon beast and bird of the forest
Venting the murderous spleen of the endless Railway Committee.
Hither the Marquis of Ayr, and Dalgarnish Earl and Croupier,
And at their side, amid murmurs of welcome, long-looked for,
  himself too
Eager, the grey, but boy-hearted Sir Hector, the Chief and the
  Chairman.   70
  Then was the dinner served, and the Minister prayed for a blessing,
And to the viands before them with knife and with fork they beset
  them;
Venison, the red and the roe, with mutton; and grouse succeeding;
Such was the feast, with whisky of course, and at top and bottom
Small decanters of Sherry, not overchoice, for the gentry.
So to the viands before them with laughter and chat they beset them.
And, when on flesh and on fowl had appetite duly been sated,
Up rose the Catholic Priest and returned God thanks for the dinner.
Then on all tables were set black bottles of well-mixed toddy,
And, with the bottles and glasses before them, they sat, digesting, 80
Talking, enjoying, but chiefly awaiting the toasts and speeches.

  Spare me, O great Recollection! for words to the task were unequal,
Spare me, O mistress of Song! nor bid me remember minutely
All that was said and done o'er the well-mixed tempting toddy;
How were healths proposed and drunk 'with all the honours,'
Glasses and bonnets waving, and three-times-three thrice over,
Queen, and Prince, and Army, and Landlords all, and Keepers;
Bid me not, grammar defying, repeat from grammar-defiers
Long constructions strange and plusquam-Thucydidean,
Tell how, as sudden torrent in time of speat[1] in the mountain   90

  [1] Flood.

Hurries six ways at once, and takes at last to the roughest,
Or as the practised rider at Astley's or Franconi's
Skilfully, boldly bestrides many steeds at once in the gallop,
Crossing from this to that, with one leg here, one yonder,
So, less skilful, but equally bold, and wild as the torrent,
All through sentences six at a time, unsuspecting of syntax,
Hurried the lively good-will and garrulous tale of Sir Hector.
Left to oblivion be it, the memory, faithful as ever,
How the Marquis of Ayr, with wonderful gesticulation,
Floundering on through game and mess-room recollections,   100
Gossip of neighbouring forest, praise of targeted gillies,
Anticipation of royal visit, skits at pedestrians,
Swore he would never abandon his country, nor give up deer-
    stalking;
How, too, more brief, and plainer in spite of the Gaelic accent,
Highland peasants gave courteous answer to flattering nobles.
    Two orations alone the memorial song will render;
For at the banquet's close spake thus the lively Sir Hector,
Somewhat husky with praises exuberant, often repeated,
Pleasant to him and to them, of the gallant Highland soldiers
Whom he erst led in the fight;—something husky, but ready,
    though weary,   110
Up to them rose and spoke the grey but gladsome chieftain:—
    Fill up your glasses, my friends, once more,—With all the honours!
There was a toast I forgot, which our gallant Highland homes have
Always welcomed the stranger, delighted, I may say, to see such
Fine young men at my table—My friends! are you ready? the
    Strangers.
Gentlemen, here are your healths,—and I wish you—With all the
    honours!
    So he said, and the cheers ensued, and all the honours,
All our Collegians were bowed to, the Attaché detecting his Honour,
Guardsman moving to Arthur, and Marquis sidling to Airlie,
And the small Piper below getting up and nodding to Lindsay. 120
    But, while the healths were being drunk, was much tribulation
    and trouble,

Nodding and beckoning across, observed of Attaché and Guardsman:
Adam wouldn't speak,—indeed it was certain he couldn't;
Hewson could, and would if they wished; Philip Hewson a poet,
Hewson a radical hot, hating lords and scorning ladies,
Silent mostly, but often reviling in fire and fury
Feudal tenures, mercantile lords, competition and bishops,
Liveries, armorial bearings, amongst other matters the Game-laws:
He could speak, and was asked-to by Adam, but Lindsay aloud cried
(Whisky was hot in his brain), Confound it, no, not Hewson,   130
A'nt he cock-sure to bring in his eternal political humbug?
However, so it must be, and after due pause of silence,
Waving his hand to Lindsay, and smiling oddly to Adam,
Up to them rose and spoke the poet and radical Hewson.
    I am, I think, perhaps the most perfect stranger present.
I have not, as have some of my friends, in my veins some tincture,
Some few ounces of Scottish blood; no, nothing like it.
I am therefore perhaps the fittest to answer and thank you.
So I thank you, sir, for myself and for my companions,
Heartily thank you all for this unexpected greeting,   140
All the more welcome, as showing you do not account us intruders,
Are not unwilling to see the north and the south forgather.
And, surely, seldom have Scotch and English more thoroughly
    mingled;
Scarcely with warmer hearts, and clearer feeling of manhood,
Even in tourney, and foray, and fray, and regular battle,
Where the life and the strength came out in the tug and tussle,
Scarcely, where man met man, and soul encountered with soul, as
Close as do the bodies and twining limbs of the wrestlers,
When for a final bout are a day's two champions mated,—
In the grand old times of bows, and bills, and claymores,   150
At the old Flodden-field—or Bannockburn—or Culloden.
—(And he paused a moment, for breath, and because of some
    cheering,)
We are the better friends, I fancy, for that old fighting,
Better friends, inasmuch as we know each other the better,
We can now shake hands without pretending or shuffling.

On this passage followed a great tornado of cheering,
Tables were rapped, feet stamped, a glass or two got broken:
He, ere the cheers died wholly away, and while still there was
     stamping,
Added, in altered voice, with a smile, his doubtful conclusion.
   I have, however, less claim than others perhaps to this honour, 160
For, let me say, I am neither game-keeper, nor game-preserver.
   So he said, and sat down, but his satire had not been taken.
Only the *men*, who were all on their legs as concerned in the thanking,
Were a trifle confused, but mostly sat down without laughing;
Lindsay alone, close-facing the chair, shook his fist at the speaker.
Only a Liberal member, away at the end of the table,
Started, remembering sadly the cry of a coming election,
Only the Attaché glanced at the Guardsman, who twirled his
     moustachio,
Only the Marquis faced round, but, not quite clear of the meaning,
Joined with the joyous Sir Hector, who lustily beat on the table. 170
   And soon after the chairman arose, and the feast was over:
Now should the barn be cleared and forthwith adorned for the
     dancing,
And, to make way for this purpose, the tutor and pupils retiring
Were by the chieftain addressed and invited to come to the castle.
But ere the door-way they quitted, a thin man clad as the Saxon,
Trouser and cap and jacket of homespun blue, hand-woven,
Singled out, and said with determined accent to Hewson,
Touching his arm: Young man, if ye pass through the Braes o'
     Lochaber,
See by the loch-side ye come to the Bothie of Tober-na-vuolich.

II

Et certamen erat, Corydon cum Thyrside, magnum

MORN, in yellow and white, came broadening out from the mountains,
Long ere music and reel were hushed in the barn of the dancers.
Duly in *matutine* bathed before eight some two of the party,
Where in the morning was custom, where over a ledge of granite
Into a granite bason the amber torrent descended.
There two plunges each took Philip and Arthur together,
Duly in *matutine* bathed, and read, and waited for breakfast:
Breakfast, commencing at nine, lingered lazily on to noon-day.
   Tea and coffee were there; a jug of water for Hewson;
Tea and coffee; and four cold grouse upon the sideboard;   10
Gaily they talked, as they sat, some late and lazy at breakfast,
Some professing a book, some smoking outside at the window.
By an aurora soft-pouring a still sheeny tide to the zenith,
Hewson and Arthur, with Adam, had walked and got home by
      eleven;
Hope and the others had staid till the round sun lighted them
      bedward.
They of the lovely aurora, but these of the lovelier women
Spoke—of noble ladies and rustic girls, their partners.
   Turned to them Hewson, the chartist, the poet, the eloquent
      speaker.
Sick of the very names of your Lady Augustas and Floras
Am I, as ever I was of the dreary botanical titles   20
Of the exotic plants, their antitypes, in the hot-house:
Roses, violets, lilies for me! the out-of-door beauties;
Meadow and woodland sweets, forget-me-nots and heartsease!
   Pausing awhile, he proceeded anon, for none made answer.
Oh, if our high-born girls knew only the grace, the attraction,
Labour, and labour alone, can add to the beauty of women,
Truly the milliner's trade would quickly, I think, be at discount,
All the waste and loss in silk and satin be saved us,
Saved for purposes truly and widely productive——

That's right,
Take off your coat to it, Philip, cried Lindsay, outside in the garden,
Take off your coat to it, Philip.   31
Well, then, said Hewson, resuming;
Laugh if you please at my novel economy; listen to this, though;
As for myself, and apart from economy wholly, believe me,
Never I properly felt the relation between men and women,
Though to the dancing-master I went, perforce, for a quarter,
Where, in dismal quadrille, were good-looking girls in abundance,
Though, too, school-girl cousins were mine—a bevy of beauties,—
Never, (of course you will laugh, but of course all the same I shall
    say it,)
Never, believe me, I knew of the feelings between men and women,
Till in some village fields in holidays now getting stupid,   40
One day sauntering 'long and listless,' as Tennyson has it,
Long and listless strolling, ungainly in hobbadiboyhood,
Chanced it my eye fell aside on a capless, bonnetless maiden,
Bending with three-pronged fork in a garden uprooting potatoes.
Was it the air? who can say? or herself, or the charm of the labour?
But a new thing was in me; and longing delicious possessed me,
Longing to take her and lift her, and put her away from her slaving.
Was it embracing or aiding was most in my mind? hard question!
But a new thing was in me, I, too, was a youth among maidens:
Was it the air? who can say? but in part 't was the charm of the
    labour.   50
Still, though a new thing was in me, the poets revealed themselves
    to me,
And in my dreams by Miranda, her Ferdinand, often I wandered,
Though all the fuss about girls, the giggling, and toying, and coying,
Were not so strange as before, so incomprehensible purely;
Still, as before (and as now), balls, dances, and evening parties,
Shooting with bows, going shopping together, and hearing them
    singing,
Dangling beside them, and turning the leaves on the dreary piano,
Offering unneeded arms, performing dull farces of escort,
Seemed like a sort of unnatural up-in-the-air balloon-work,

(Or what to me is as hateful, a riding about in a carriage,)   60
Utter removal from work, mother earth, and the objects of living.
Hungry and fainting for food, you ask me to join you in snapping—
What but a pink-paper comfit, with motto romantic inside it?
Wishing to stock me a garden, I'm sent to a table of nosegays;
Better a crust of black bread than a mountain of paper confections,
Better a daisy in earth than a dahlia cut and gathered,
Better a cowslip with root than a prize carnation without it.

    That I allow, said Adam.

                  But he, with the bit in his teeth, scarce
Breathed a brief moment, and hurried exultingly on with his rider,
Far over hillock, and runnel, and bramble, away in the champaign,
Snorting defiance and force, the white foam flecking his flanks, the
Rein hanging loose to his neck, and head projecting before him.

    Oh, if they knew and considered, unhappy ones! oh, could they
      see, could   73
But for a moment discern, how the blood of true gallantry kindles,
How the old knightly religion, the chivalry semi-quixotic
Stirs in the veins of a man at seeing some delicate woman
Serving him, toiling—for him, and the world; some tenderest
    girl, now
Over-weighted, expectant, of him, is it? who shall, if only
Duly her burden be lightened, not wholly removed from her,
    mind you,
Lightened if but by the love, the devotion man only can offer,   80
Grand on her pedestal rise as urn-bearing statue of Hellas;—
Oh, could they feel at such moments how man's heart, as into Eden
Carried anew, seems to see, like the gardener of earth uncorrupted,
Eve from the hand of her Maker advancing, an helpmeet for him,
Eve from his own flesh taken, a spirit restored to his spirit,
Spirit but not spirit only, himself whatever himself is,
Unto the mystery's end sole helpmate meet to be with him;—
Oh, if they saw it and knew it; we soon should see them abandon
Boudoir, toilette, carriage, drawing-room, and ball-room,
Satin for worsted exchange, gros-de-naples for plain linsey-woolsey,

Sandals of silk for clogs, for health lackadaisical fancies!   91
So, feel women, not dolls; so feel the sap of existence
Circulate up through their roots from the far-away centre of all
   things,
Circulate up from the depths to the bud on the twig that is topmost!
Yes, we should see them delighted, delighted ourselves in the seeing,
Bending with blue cotton gown skirted-up over striped linsey-
   woolsey,
Milking the kine in the field, like Rachel, watering cattle,
Rachel, when at the well the predestined beheld and kissed her,
Or, with pail upon head, like Dora beloved of Alexis,
Comely, with well-poised pail over neck arching soft to the shoulders,
Comely in gracefullest act, one arm uplifted to stay it,   101
Home from the river or pump moving stately and calm to the
   laundry;
Ay, doing household work, as many sweet girls I have looked at,
Needful household work, which some one, after all, must do,
Needful, graceful therefore, as washing, cooking, and scouring,
Or, if you please, with the fork in the garden uprooting potatoes.—
   Or,—high-kilted perhaps, cried Lindsay, at last successful,
Lindsay, this long time swelling with scorn and pent-up fury,
Or high-kilted perhaps, as once at Dundee I saw them,
Petticoats up to the knees, or even, it might be, above them,   110
Matching their lily-white legs with the clothes that they trod in the
   wash-tub!
   Laughter ensued at this; and seeing the Tutor embarrassed,
It was from them, I suppose, said Arthur, smiling sedately,
Lindsay learnt the tune we all have learnt from Lindsay,
For oh, he was a roguey, the Piper o' Dundee.
   Laughter ensued again; and the Tutor, recovering slowly,
Said, Are not these perhaps as doubtful as other attractions?
There is a truth in your view, but I think extremely distorted;
Still there is a truth, I own, I understand you entirely.   119
   While the Tutor was gathering his purposes, Arthur continued,
Is not all this the same that one hears at common-room breakfasts,
Or perhaps Trinity wines, about Gothic buildings and Beauty?

And with a start from the sofa came Hobbes; with a cry from the
    sofa,
Where he was laid, the great Hobbes, contemplative, corpulent,
    witty,
Author forgotten and silent of currentest phrases and fancies,
Mute and exuberant by turns, a fountain at intervals playing,
Mute and abstracted, or strong and abundant as rain in the tropics;
Studious; careless of dress; inobservant; by smooth persuasions
Lately decoyed into kilt on example of Hope and the Piper,
Hope an Antinoüs mere, Hyperion of calves the Piper.   130
    Beautiful! cried he upleaping, analogy perfect to madness!
O inexhaustible source of thought, shall I call it, or fancy!
Wonderful spring, at whose touch doors fly, what a vista disclosing!
Exquisite germ! Ah no, crude fingers shall not soil thee;
Rest, lovely pearl, in my brain, and slowly mature in the oyster.
    While at the exquisite pearl they were laughing and corpulent
        oyster,
Ah, could they only be taught, he resumed, by a Pugin of women,
How even churning and washing, the dairy, the scullery duties,
Wait but a touch to redeem and convert them to charms and
    attractions,
Scrubbing requires for true grace but frank and artistical handling,
And the removal of slops to be ornamentally treated.   141
    Philip who speaks like a book (retiring and pausing he added),
Philip here, who speaks—like a folio, say'st thou, Piper?
Philip shall write us a book, a Treatise upon *The Laws of
Architectural Beauty in Application to Women*;
Illustrations, of course, and a Parker's Glossary pendent,
Where shall in specimen seen be the sculliony stumpy-columnar,
(Which to a reverent taste is perhaps the most moving of any,)
Rising to grace of true woman in English the Early and Later,
Charming us still in fulfilling the Richer and Loftier stages,   150
Lost, ere we end, in the Lady-Debased and the Lady-Flamboyant:
Whence why in satire and spite too merciless onward pursue her
Hither to hideous close, Modern-Florid, modern-fine-lady?
No, I will leave it to you, my Philip, my Pugin of women.

Leave it to Arthur, said Adam, to think of, and not to play with.
You are young, you know, he said, resuming, to Philip,
You are young, he proceeded, with something of fervour to Hewson,
You are a boy; when you grow to a man you'll find things alter.
You will then seek only the good, will scorn the attractive,
Scorn all mere cosmetics, as now of rank and fashion,   160
Delicate hands, and wealth, so then of poverty also,
Poverty truly attractive, more truly, I bear you witness.
Good, wherever it's found, you will choose, be it humble or stately,
Happy if only you find, and finding do not lose it.
Yes, we must seek what is good, it always and it only;
Not indeed absolute good, good for us, as is said in the Ethics,
That which is good for ourselves, our proper selves, our best selves.
Ah, you have much to learn, we can't know all things at twenty.
Partly you rest on truth, old truth, the duty of Duty,
Partly on error, you long for equality.

                        Ay, cried the Piper,   170
That's what it is, that confounded *égalité*, French manufacture,
He is the same as the Chartist who spoke at a meeting in Ireland,
What, and is not one man, fellow-men, as good as another?
Faith, replied Pat, *and a deal better too!*

                        So rattled the Piper:
But undisturbed in his tenor, the Tutor.

                        Partly in error
Seeking equality, *is not one woman as good as another?*
I with the Irishman answer, *Yes, better too*; the poorer
Better full oft than richer, than loftier better the lower.
Irrespective of wealth and of poverty, pain and enjoyment,
Women all have their duties, the one as well as the other;   180
Are all duties alike? Do all alike fulfil them?
However noble the dream of equality, mark you, Philip,
Nowhere equality reigns in all the world of creation,
Star is not equal to star, nor blossom the same as blossom;
Herb is not equal to herb, any more than planet to planet.
There is a glory of daisies, a glory again of carnations;
Were the carnation wise, in gay parterre by greenhouse,

Should it decline to accept the nurture the gardener gives it,
Should it refuse to expand to sun and genial summer,
Simply because the field-daisy, that grows in the grass-plat beside it,
Cannot, for some cause or other, develope and be a carnation?   191
Would not the daisy itself petition its scrupulous neighbour?
Up, grow, bloom, and forget me; be beautiful even to proudness,
E'en for the sake of myself and other poor daisies like me.
Education and manners, accomplishments and refinements,
Waltz, peradventure, and polka, the knowledge of music and drawing,
All these things are Nature's, to Nature dear and precious.
We have all something to do, man, woman alike, I own it;
We have all something to do, and in my judgement should do it
In our station; not thinking about it, but not disregarding;   200
Holding it, not for enjoyment, but simply because we are in it.

Ah! replied Philip, Alas! the noted phrase of the prayer-book,
Doing our duty in that state of life to which God has called us,
Seems to me always to mean, when the little rich boys say it,
Standing in velvet frock by mama's brocaded flounces,
Eying her gold-fastened book and the watch and chain at her bosom,
Seems to me always to mean, Eat, drink, and never mind others.

Nay, replied Adam, smiling, so far your economy leads me,
Velvet and gold and brocade are nowise to my fancy.
Nay, he added, believe me, I like luxurious living   210
Even as little as you, and grieve in my soul not seldom,
More for the rich indeed than the poor, who are not so guilty.

So the discussion closed; and, said Arthur, Now it is my turn,
How will my argument please you? To-morrow we start on our
        travel.
And took up Hope the chorus.
                            To-morrow we start on our travel.
Lo, the weather is golden, the weather-glass, say they, rising;
Four weeks here have we read; four weeks will we read hereafter;
Three weeks hence will return and think of classes and classics.
Fare ye well, meantime, forgotten, unnamed, undreamt of,
History, Science, and Poets! lo, deep in dustiest cupboard,   220
Thookydid, Oloros' son, Halimoosian, here lieth buried!

Slumber in Liddell-and-Scott, O musical chaff of old Athens,
Dishes, and fishes, bird, beast, and sesquipedalian blackguard!
Sleep, weary ghosts, be at peace and abide in your lexicon-limbo!
Sleep, as in lava for ages your Herculanean kindred,
Sleep, and for aught that I care, 'the sleep that knows no waking,'
Æschylus, Sophocles, Homer, Herodotus, Pindar, and Plato.
Three weeks hence be it time to exhume our dreary classics.
   And in the chorus joined Lindsay, the Piper, the Dialectician.
Three weeks hence we return to the *shop* and the *wash-hand-stand-
      basin*,   230
(These are the Piper's names for the bathing-place and the cottage)
Three weeks hence unbury *Thicksides* and *hairy* Aldrich.
   But the Tutor enquired, the grave man, nick-named Adam,
Who are they that go, and when do they promise returning?
   And a silence ensued, and the Tutor himself continued,
Airlie remains, I presume, he continued, and Hobbes and Hewson.
   Answer was made him by Philip, the poet, the eloquent speaker:
Airlie remains, I presume, was the answer, and Hobbes, perad-
      venture;
Tarry let Airlie May-fairly, and Hobbes, brief-kilted hero,
Tarry let Hobbes in kilt, and Airlie 'abide in his breeches;'   240
Tarry let these, and read, four Pindars apiece an it like them!
Weary of reading am I, and weary of walks prescribed us;
Weary of Ethic and Logic, of Rhetoric yet more weary,
Eager to range over heather unfettered of gillie and marquis,
I will away with the rest, and bury my dismal classics.
   And to the Tutor rejoining, Be mindful; you go up at Easter,
This was the answer returned by Philip, the Pugin of Women.
Good are the Ethics, I wis; good absolute, not for me, though;
Good, too, Logic, of course; in itself, but not in fine weather.
Three weeks hence, with the rain, to Prudence, Temperance,
      Justice,   250
Virtues Moral and Mental, with Latin prose included,
Three weeks hence we return, to cares of classes and classics.
I will away with the rest, and bury my dismal classics.
   But the Tutor enquired, the grave man, nick-named Adam,

Where do you mean to go, and whom do you mean to visit?
And he was answered by Hope, the Viscount, His Honour, of Ilay.
Kitcat, a Trinity *coach*, has a party at Drumnadrochet,
Up on the side of Loch Ness, in the beautiful valley of Urquhart;
Mainwaring says they will lodge us, and feed us, and give us a
lift too:
Only they talk ere long to remove to Glenmorison. Then at   260
Castleton, high in Braemar, strange home, with his earliest party,
Harrison, fresh from the schools, has James and Jones and Lauder.
Thirdly, a Cambridge man I know, Smith, a senior wrangler,
With a mathematical score hangs-out at Inverary.
Finally, too, from the kilt and the sofa said Hobbes in conclusion,
Finally Philip must hunt for that home of the probable poacher,
Hid in the braes of Lochaber, the Bothie of *What-did-he-call-it.*
Hopeless of you and of us, of gillies and marquises hopeless,
Weary of Ethic and Logic, of Rhetoric yet more weary,
There shall he, smit by the charm of a lovely potato-uprooter,   270
Study the question of sex in the Bothie of *What-did-he-call-it.*

III

So in the golden morning they parted and went to the westward.
And in the cottage with Airlie and Hobbes remained the Tutor;
Reading nine hours a day with the Tutor Hobbes and Airlie;
One between bathing and breakfast, and six before it was dinner,
(Breakfast at eight, at four, after bathing again, the dinner)
Finally, two after walking and tea, from nine to eleven.
Airlie and Adam at evening their quiet stroll together
Took on the terrace-road, with the western hills before them;
Hobbes, only rarely a third, now and then in the cottage remaining,
E'en after dinner, eupeptic, would rush yet again to his reading; 10
Other times, stung by the œstrum of some swift-working conception,
Ranged, tearing-on in his fury, an Io-cow, through the mountains,
Heedless of scenery, heedless of bogs, and of perspiration,
On the high peaks, unwitting, the hares and ptarmigan starting.
   And the three weeks past, the three weeks, three days over,
Neither letter had come, nor casual tidings any,
And the pupils grumbled, the Tutor became uneasy,
And in the golden weather they wondered, and watched to the
   westward.
   There is a stream, I name not its name, lest inquisitive tourist
Hunt it, and make it a lion, and get it at last into guide-books, 20
Springing far off from a loch unexplored in the folds of great
   mountains,
Falling two miles through rowan and stunted alder, enveloped
Then for four more in a forest of pine, where broad and ample
Spreads, to convey it, the glen with heathery slopes on both sides:
Broad and fair the stream, with occasional falls and narrows;
But, where the glen of its course approaches the vale of the river,
Met and blocked by a huge interposing mass of granite,
Scarce by a channel deep-cut, raging up, and raging onward,
Forces its flood through a passage so narrow a lady would step it.
There, across the great rocky wharves, a wooden bridge goes,   30

131

Carrying a path to the forest; below, three hundred yards, say,
Lower in level some twenty-five feet, through flats of shingle,
Stepping-stones and a cart-track cross in the open valley.
   But in the interval here the boiling, pent-up water
Frees itself by a final descent, attaining a bason,
Ten feet wide and eighteen long, with whiteness and fury
Occupied partly, but mostly pellucid, pure, a mirror;
Beautiful there for the colour derived from green rocks under;
Beautiful, most of all, where beads of foam uprising
Mingle their clouds of white with the delicate hue of the stillness. 40
Cliff over cliff for its sides, with rowan and pendent birch boughs,
Here it lies, unthought of above at the bridge and pathway,
Still more enclosed from below by wood and rocky projection.
You are shut in, left alone with yourself and perfection of water,
Hid on all sides, left alone with yourself and the goddess of bathing.
   Here, the pride of the plunger, you stride the fall and clear it;
Here, the delight of the bather, you roll in beaded sparklings,
Here into pure green depth drop down from lofty ledges.
   Hither, a month agone, they had come, and discovered it; hither
(Long a design, but long unaccountably left unaccomplished,)   50
Leaving the well-known bridge and pathway above to the forest,
Turning below from the track of the carts over stone and shingle,
Piercing a wood, and skirting a narrow and natural causeway
Under the rocky wall that hedges the bed of the streamlet,
Rounded a craggy point, and saw on a sudden before them
Slabs of rock, and a tiny beach, and perfection of water,
Picture-like beauty, seclusion sublime, and the goddess of bathing.
There they bathed, of course, and Arthur, the Glory of headers,
Leapt from the ledges with Hope, he twenty feet, he thirty;
There, overbold, great Hobbes from a ten-foot height descended, 60
Prone, as a quadruped, prone with hands and feet protending;
There in the sparkling champagne, ecstatic, they shrieked and
    shouted.
   'Hobbes's gutter' the Piper entitles the spot, profanely,
Hope 'the Glory' would have, after Arthur, the Glory of headers:
But, for before they departed, in shy and fugitive reflex

Here in the eddies and there did the splendour of Jupiter glimmer,
Adam adjudged it the name of Hesperus, star of the evening.
    Hither, to Hesperus, now, the star of evening above them,
Come in their lonelier walk the pupils twain and Tutor;
Turned from the track of the carts, and passing the stone and
        shingle,   70
Piercing the wood, and skirting the stream by the natural causeway,
Rounded the craggy point, and now at their ease looked up; and
Lo, on the rocky ledge, regardant, the Glory of headers,
Lo, on the beach, expecting the plunge, not cigarless, the Piper.—
    And they looked, and wondered, incredulous, looking yet once
        more.
Yes, it was he, on the ledge, bare-limbed, an Apollo, down-gazing,
Eyeing one moment the beauty, the life, ere he flung himself in it,
Eyeing through eddying green waters the green-tinting floor under-
        neath them,
Eying the bead on the surface, the bead, like a cloud, rising to it,
Drinking-in, deep in his soul, the beautiful hue and the clearness, 80
Arthur, the shapely, the brave, the unboasting, the Glory of headers;
Yes, and with fragrant weed, by his knapsack, spectator and critic,
Seated on slab by the margin, the Piper, the Cloud-compeller.
    Yes, they were come; were restored to the party, its grace and its
        gladness,
Yes, were here, as of old; the light-giving orb of the household,
Arthur, the shapely, the tranquil, the strength-and-contentment-
        diffusing,
In the pure presence of whom none could quarrel long, nor be
        pettish,
And, the gay fountain of mirth, their dearly beloved of Pipers.
Yes, they were come, were here: but Hewson and Hope—where
        they then?
Are they behind, travel-sore, or ahead, going straight, by the
        pathway?   90
    And from his seat and cigar spoke the Piper, the Cloud-compeller.
Hope with the uncle abideth for shooting. Ah me, were I with him!
Ah, good boy that I am, to have stuck to my word and my reading!

133

Good, good boy to be here, far away, who might be at Balloch!
Only one day to have stayed who might have been welcome for seven,
Seven whole days in castle and forest—gay in the mazy
Moving, imbibing the rosy, and pointing a gun at the horny!
   And the Tutor impatient, expectant, interrupted,
Hope with the uncle, and Hewson—with him? or where have you
   left him?
   And from his seat and cigar spoke the Piper, the Cloud-com-
   peller.   100
Hope with the uncle, and Hewson—Why, Hewson we left in
   Rannoch,
By the lochside and the pines, in a farmer's house,—reflecting—
Helping to shear,[1] and dry clothes, and bring in peat from the
   peat-stack.
   And the Tutor's countenance fell, perplexed, dumb-foundered
Stood he,—slow and with pain disengaging jest from earnest.
   He is not far from home, said Arthur from the water,
He will be with us to-morrow, at latest, or the next day.
   And he was even more reassured by the Piper's rejoinder.
Can he have come by the mail, and have got to the cottage before us?
   So to the cottage they went, and Philip was not at the cottage; 110
But by the mail was a letter from Hope, who himself was to follow.
   Two whole days and nights succeeding brought not Philip,
Two whole days and nights exhausted not question and story.
   For it was told, the Piper narrating, corrected of Arthur,
Often by word corrected, more often by smile and motion,
How they had been to Iona, to Staffa, to Skye, to Culloden,
Seen Loch Awe, Loch Tay, Loch Fyne, Loch Ness, Loch Arkaig,
Been up Ben-nevis, Ben-more, Ben-cruachan, Ben-muick-dhui;
How they had walked, and eaten, and drunken, and slept in kitchens,
Slept upon floors of kitchens, and tasted the real Glen-livat,   120
Walked up perpendicular hills, and also down them,
Hither and thither had been, and this and that had witnessed,
Left not a thing to be done, and had not a copper remaining.
   For it was told withal, he telling, and he correcting,

---

[1] Reap.

How in the race they had run, and beaten the gillies of Rannoch,
How in forbidden glens, in Mar and midmost Athol,
Philip insisting hotly, and Arthur and Hope compliant,
They had defied the keepers; the Piper alone protesting,
Liking the fun, it was plain, in his heart, but tender of game-law;
Yea, too, in Meäly glen, the heart of Lochiel's fair forest,   130
Where Scotch firs are darkest and amplest, and intermingle
Grandly with rowan and ash—in Mar you have no ashes,
There the pine is alone, or relieved by the birch and the alder—
How in Meäly glen, while stags were starting before, they
Made the watcher believe they were guests from Achnacarry.

    And there was told moreover, he telling, the other correcting,
Often by word, more often by mute significant motion,
Much of the Cambridge *coach* and his pupils at Inverary,
Huge barbarian pupils, Expanded in Infinite Series,
Firing-off signal guns (great scandal) from window to window,   140
(For they were lodging perforce in distant and numerous houses,)
Signals, when, one retiring, another should go to the Tutor:—
Much too of Kitcat, of course, and the party at Drumnadrochet,
Mainwaring, Foley, and Fraser, their idleness horrid and dog-cart;
Drumnadrochet was *seedy*, Glenmorison *adequate*, but at
Castleton, high in Braemar, were the *clippingest* places for bathing,
One by the bridge in the village, indecent, *the Town-Hall* christened,
Where had Lauder howbeit been bathing, and Harrison also,
Harrison even, the Tutor; another like Hesperus here, and
Up the water of Eye half-a-dozen at least, all *stunners*.   150
    And it was told, the Piper narrating and Arthur correcting,
Colouring he, dilating, magniloquent, glorying in picture,
He to a matter-of-fact still softening, paring, abating,
He to the great might-have-been upsoaring, sublime and ideal,
He to the merest it-was restricting, diminishing, dwarfing,
River to streamlet reducing, and fall to slope subduing,
So was it told, the Piper narrating, corrected of Arthur,
How under Linn of Dee, where over rocks, between rocks,
Freed from prison the river comes, pouring, rolling, rushing,

Then at a sudden descent goes sliding, gliding, unbroken,   160
Falling, sliding, gliding, in narrow space collected,
Save for a ripple at last, a sheeted descent unbroken,—
How to the element offering their bodies, downshooting the fall, they
Mingled themselves with the flood and the force of imperious water.
  And it was told too, Arthur narrating, the Piper correcting,
How, as one comes to the level, the weight of the downward impulse
Carries the head under water, delightful, unspeakable; how the
Piper, here ducked and blinded, got stray, and borne-off by the
    current
Wounded his lily-white thighs, below, at the craggy corner.
  And it was told, the Piper resuming, corrected of Arthur,   170
More by word than motion, change ominous, noted of Adam,
How at the floating-bridge of Laggan, one morning at sunrise,
Came, in default of the ferryman, out of her bed a brave lassie;
And, as Philip and she together were turning the handles,
Winding the chain by which the boat works over the water,
Hands intermingled with hands, and at last, as they stept from the
    boatie,
Turning about, they saw lips also mingle with lips; but
That was flatly denied and loudly exclaimed at by Arthur:
How at the General's hut, the Inn by the Foyers Fall, where
Over the loch looks at you the summit of Méalfourvónie,   180
How here too he was hunted at morning, and found in the kitchen
Watching the porridge being made, pronouncing them smoked for
    certain,
Watching the porridge being made, and asking the lassie that made
    them,
What was the Gaelic for *girl*, and what was the Gaelic for *pretty*;
How in confusion he shouldered his knapsack, yet blushingly
    stammered,
Waving a hand to the lassie, that blushingly bent o'er the porridge,
Something outlandish—*Slan*-something, *Slan leat*, he believed,
    Caleg Looach,
That was the Gaelic it seemed for 'I bid you good-bye, bonnie
    lassie;'

Arthur admitted it true, not of Philip, but of the Piper.

And it was told by the Piper, while Arthur looked out at the
window,   190
How in thunder and rain—it is wetter far to the westward,—
Thunder and rain and wind, losing heart and road, they were
welcomed,
Welcomed, and three days detained at a farm by the lochside of
Rannoch;
How in the three days' detention was Philip observed to be smitten,
Smitten by golden-haired Katie, the youngest and comeliest
daughter;
Was he not seen, even Arthur observed it, from breakfast to bed-
time,
Following her motions with eyes ever brightening, softening ever?
Did he not fume, fret, and fidget to find her stand waiting at table?
Was he not one mere St. Vitus' dance, when he saw her at nightfall
Go through the rain to fetch peat, through beating rain to the
peat-stack?   200
How too a dance, as it happened, was given by Grant of Glenurchie,
And with the farmer they went as the farmer's guests to attend it;
Philip stayed dancing till daylight,—and evermore with Katie;
How the whole next afternoon he was with her away in the shearing,[1]
And the next morning ensuing was found in the ingle beside her
Kneeling, picking the peats from her apron,—blowing together,
Both, between laughing, with lips distended, to kindle the embers;
Lips were so near to lips, one living cheek to another,—
Though, it was true, he was shy, very shy,—yet it wasn't in nature,
Wasn't in nature, the Piper averred, there shouldn't be kissing; 210
So when at noon they had packed up the things, and proposed to be
starting,
Philip professed he was lame, would leave in the morning and follow;
Follow he did not; do burns, when you go up a glen, follow after?
Follow, he had not, nor left; do needles leave the loadstone?
Nay, they had turned after starting, and looked through the trees at
the corner,

---

[1] Reaping.

Lo, on the rocks by the lake there he was, the lassie beside him,
Lo, there he was, stooping by her, and helping with stones from the
      water
Safe in the wind to keep down the clothes she would spread for the
      drying.
There they had left him, and there, if Katie was there, was Philip,
There drying clothes, making fires, making love, getting on too by
      this time,   220
Though he was shy, so exceedingly shy.
                                    You may say so, said Arthur,
For the first time they had known with a peevish intonation,—
Did not the Piper himself flirt more in a single evening,
Namely, with Janet the elder, than Philip in all our sojourn?
Philip had stayed, it was true; the Piper was loth to depart too,
Harder his parting from Janet than e'en from the keeper at Balloch;
And it was certain that Philip was lame.
                                    Yes, in his excuses,
Answered the Piper, indeed!—
                              But tell me, said Hobbes, interposing,
Did you not say she was seen every day in her beauty and bedgown
Doing plain household work, as washing, cooking, scouring?   230
How could he help but love her? nor lacked there perhaps the
      attraction
That, in a blue cotton print tucked up over striped linsey-woolsey,
Barefoot, barelegged, he beheld her, with arms bare up to the elbows,
Bending with fork in her hand in a garden uprooting potatoes?
Is not Katie as Rachel, and is not Philip a Jacob?
Truly Jacob, supplanting an hairy Highland Esau?
Shall he not, love-entertained, feed sheep for the Laban of Rannoch?
Patriarch happier he, the long servitude ended of wooing,
If when he wake in the morning he find not a Leah beside him!
    But the Tutor enquired, who had bit his lip to bleeding,   240
How far off is the place? who will guide me thither to-morrow?

    But by the mail, ere the morrow, came Hope, and brought new
      tidings;

Round by Rannoch had come, and Philip was not at Rannoch;
He had left that noon, an hour ago.
                                    With the lassie?—
With her? the Piper exclaimed, Undoubtedly! By great Jingo!
And upon that he arose, slapping both his thighs like a hero,
Partly, for emphasis only, to mark his conviction, but also
Part, in delight at the fun, and the joy of eventful living.
   Hope couldn't tell him, of course, but thought it improbable
      wholly;
Janet, the Piper's friend, he had seen, and she didn't say so,   250
Though she asked a good deal about Philip, and where he was
      gone to:
One odd thing by the bye, he continued, befell me while with her;
Standing beside her, I saw a girl pass; I thought I had seen her,
Somewhat remarkable-looking, elsewhere; and asked what her name
      was;
Elspie Mackaye, was the answer, the daughter of David! she's
      stopping
Just above here, with her uncle. And David Mackaye, where lives he?
It's away west, she said, they call it Tober-na-vuolich.

IV

Ut vidi, ut perii, ut me malus abstulit error

So in the golden weather they waited. But Philip returned not.
Sunday six days thence a letter arrived in his writing.—
But, O Muse, that encompassest Earth like the ambient ether,
Swifter than steamer or railway or magical missive electric
Belting like Ariel the sphere with the star-like trail of thy travel,
Thou with thy Poet, to mortals mere post-office second-hand
    knowledge
Leaving, wilt seek in the moorland of Rannoch the wandering hero.
  There is it, there, or in lofty Lochaber, where, silent upheaving,
Heaving from ocean to sky, and under snow-winds of September,
Visibly whitening at morn to darken by noon in the shining,   10
Rise on their mighty foundations the brethren huge of Ben-nevis?
There, or westward away, where roads are unknown to Loch Nevish,
And the great peaks look abroad over Skye to the westernmost
    islands?
There is it? there? or there? we shall find our wandering hero?
  Here, in Badenoch, here, in Lochaber anon, in Lochiel, in
Knoydart, Moydart, Morrer, Ardgower, and Ardnamurchan,
Here I see him and here: I see him; anon I lose him!
Even as cloud passing subtly unseen from mountain to mountain,
Leaving the crest of Ben-more to be palpable next on Ben-vohrlich,
Or like to hawk of the hill which ranges and soars in its hunting, 20
Seen and unseen by turns, now here, now in ether eludent.
  Wherefore as cloud of Ben-more or hawk over-ranging the
    mountains,
Wherefore in Badenoch drear, in lofty Lochaber, Lochiel, and
Knoydart, Moydart, Morrer, Ardgower, and Ardnamurchan,
Wandereth he, who should either with Adam be studying logic,
Or by the lochside of Rannoch on Katie his rhetoric using;
He who, his three weeks past, past now long ago, to the cottage
Punctual promised return to cares of classes and classics,
He who, smit to the heart by that youngest comeliest daughter,

Bent, unregardful of spies, at her feet, spreading clothes from her
      wash-tub?
                                                                        30
Can it be with him through Badenoch, Morrer, and Ardnamurchan,
Can it be with him he beareth the golden-haired lassie of Rannoch?
This fierce, furious walking—o'er mountain-top and moorland,
Sleeping in shieling and bothie, with drover on hill-side sleeping,
Folded in plaid, where sheep are strewn thicker than rocks by Loch
      Awen,
This fierce, furious travel unwearying—cannot in truth be
Merely the wedding tour succeeding the week of wooing!
   No, wherever be Katie, with Philip she is not; I see him,
Lo, and he sitteth alone, and these are his words in the mountain.
   Spirits escaped from the body can enter and be with the living; 40
Entering unseen, and retiring unquestioned, they bring,—do they
      feel too?—
Joy, pure joy, as they mingle and mix inner essence with essence;
Would I were dead, I keep saying, that so I could go and uphold her!
Joy, pure joy, bringing with them, and when they retire leaving after
No cruel shame, no prostration, despondency; memories rather
Sweet, happy hopes bequeathing. Ah! wherefore not thus with the
      living?
Would I were dead, I keep saying, that so I could go and uphold her!
   Is it impossible, say you, these passionate, fervent impulsions,
These projections of spirit to spirit, these inward embraces,
Should in strange ways, in her dreams, should visit her, strengthen
      her, shield her?
                                                                        50
Is it possible, rather, that these great floods of feeling
Setting-in daily from me towards her should, impotent wholly,
Bring neither sound nor motion to that sweet shore they heave to?
Efflux here, and there no stir nor pulse of influx!
Would I were dead, I keep saying, that so I could go and uphold her!
   Surely, surely, when sleepless I lie in the mountain lamenting,
Surely, surely, she hears in her dreams a voice, 'I am with thee,'
Saying, 'although not with thee; behold, for we mated our spirits,
Then, when we stood in the chamber, and knew not the words we
      were saying;'

Yea, if she felt me within her, when not with one finger I touched
  her,   60
Surely she knows it, and feels it, while sorrowing here in the moor-
  land.
Would I were dead, I keep saying, that so I could go and uphold her!
  Spirits with spirits commingle and separate; lightly as winds do,
Spice-laden South with the ocean-born Zephyr; they mingle and
  sunder;
No sad remorses for them, no visions of horror and vileness;
Would I were dead, I keep saying, that so I could go and uphold
  her!
  Surely the force that here sweeps me along in its violent impulse,
Surely my strength shall be in her, my help and protection about her,
Surely in inner-sweet gladness and vigour of joy shall sustain her,
Till, the brief winter o'er-past, her own true sap in the springtide 70
Rise, and the tree I have bared be verdurous e'en as aforetime:
Surely it may be, it should be, it must be. Yet ever and ever,
Would I were dead, I keep saying, that so I could go and uphold her!
  No, wherever be Katie, with Philip she is not: behold, for
Here he is sitting alone, and these are his words in the mountain
  And, at the farm on the lochside of Rannoch in parlour and
  kitchen
Hark! there is music—the flowing of music, of milk, and of whiskey;
Lo, I see piping and dancing! and whom in the midst of the battle
Cantering loudly along there, or, look you, with arms uplifted
Whistling, and snapping his fingers, and seizing his gay-smiling
  Janet,   80
Whom?—whom else but the Piper? the wary precognizant Piper,
Who, for the love of gay Janet, and mindful of old invitation,
Putting it quite as a duty and urging grave claims to attention,
True to his night had crossed over: there goeth he, brimfull of music,
Like to cork tossed by the eddies that foam under furious lasher,
Like to skiff lifted, uplifted, in lock, by the swift-swelling sluices,
So with the music possessing him, swaying him, goeth he, look you,
Swinging and flinging, and stamping and tramping, and grasping
  and clasping

Whom but gay Janet?—Him rivalling Hobbes, briefest-kilted of
   heroes,
Enters, O stoutest, O rashest of creatures, mere fool of a Saxon, 90
Skill-less of philabeg, skill-less of reel too,—the whirl and the
   twirl o't:
Him see I frisking, and whisking, and ever at swifter gyration
Under brief curtain revealing broad acres—not of broad cloth.
Him see I there and the Piper—the Piper what vision beholds not?
Him and His Honour and Arthur, with Janet our Piper, and is it,
Is it, O marvel of marvels! he too in the maze of the mazy,
Skipping, and tripping, though stately, though languid, with head on
   one shoulder,
Airlie, with sight of the waistcoat the golden-haired Katie consoling?
Katie, who simple and comely, and smiling and blushing as ever,
What though she wear on that neck a blue kerchief remembered as
   Philip's,   100
Seems in her maidenly freedom to need small consolement of
   waistcoats!—
   Wherefore in Badenoch then, far-away, in Lochaber, Lochiel, in
Knoydart, Moydart, Morrer, Ardgower, or Ardnamurchan,
Wanders o'er mountain and moorland, in shieling or bothie is
   sleeping,
He, who,—and why should he not then? capricious? or is it rejected?
Might to the piping of Rannoch be pressing the thrilling fair fingers,
Might, as he clasped her, transmit to her bosom the throb of his
   own,—yea,—
Might in the joy of the reel be wooing and winning his Katie?
   What is it Adam reads far off by himself in the Cottage?
Reads yet again with emotion, again is preparing to answer?   110
What is it Adam is reading? What was it Philip had written?
   There was it writ, how Philip possessed undoubtedly had been,
Deeply, entirely possessed by the charm of the maiden of Rannoch;
Deeply as never before! how sweet and bewitching he felt her
Seen still before him at work, in the garden, the byre, the kitchen;
How it was beautiful to him to stoop at her side in the shearing,
Binding uncouthly the ears, that fell from her dexterous sickle,

Building uncouthly the stooks,[1] which she laid-by her sickle to
  straighten;
How at the dance he had broken through shyness; for four days after
Lived on her eyes, unspeaking what lacked not articulate speaking;
Felt too that she too was feeling what he did.—Howbeit they
  parted!   121
How by a kiss from her lips he had seemed made nobler and stronger,
Yea, for the first time in life a man complete and perfect,
So forth! much that before has been heard of.—Howbeit they
  parted.
  What had ended it all, he said, was singular, very.—
I was walking along some two miles off from the cottage
Full of my dreamings—a girl went by in a party with others;
She had a cloak on, was stepping on quickly, for rain was beginning;
But as she passed, from her hood I saw her eyes look at me.
So quick a glance, so regardless I, that although I had felt it,   130
You couldn't properly say our eyes met. She cast it, and left it:
It was three minutes perhaps ere I knew what it was. I had seen her
Somewhere before I am sure, but that wasn't it; not its import;
No, it had seemed to regard me with simple superior insight,
Quietly saying to itself—Yes, there he is still in his fancy,
Letting drop from him at random as things not worth his considering
All the benefits gathered and put in his hands by fortune,
Loosing a hold which others, contented and unambitious,
Trying down here to keep-up, know the value of better than he does.
Was it this? Was it perhaps?—Yes, there he is still in his fancy, 140
Doesn't yet see we have here just the things he is used-to elsewhere;
People here too are people, and not as fairy-land creatures;
He is in a trance, and possessed; I wonder how long to continue;
It is a shame and a pity—and no good likely to follow.—
Something like this, but indeed I cannot attempt to define it.
Only, three hours thence I was off and away in the moorland,
Hiding myself from myself if I could; the arrow within me.
Katie was not in the house, thank God: I saw her in passing,
Saw her, unseen myself, with the pang of a cruel desertion;

[1] Shocks.

What she thinks about it, God knows; poor child; may she only 150
Think me a fool and a madman, and no more worth her remembering.
Meantime all through the mountains I hurry and know not whither,
Tramp along here, and think, and know not what I should think.
  Tell me then, why, as I sleep amid hill-tops high in the moorland,
Still in my dreams I am pacing the streets of the dissolute city,
Where dressy girls slithering-by upon pavements give sign for
    accosting,
Paint on their beautiless cheeks, and hunger and shame in their
    bosoms;
Hunger by drink, and by that which they shudder yet burn for,
    appeasing,—
Hiding their shame—ah God!—in the glare of the public gas-lights?
Why, while I feel my ears catching through slumber the run of the
    streamlet,   160
Still am I pacing the pavement, and seeing the sign for accosting,
Still am I passing those figures, nor daring to look in their faces?
Why, when the chill, ere the light, of the daybreak uneasily wakes me,
Find I a cry in my heart crying up to the heaven of heavens,
No, Great Unjust Judge! she is purity; I am the lost one.
  You will not think that I soberly look for such things for sweet
    Katie;
No, but the vision is on me; I now first see how it happens,
Feel how tender and soft is the heart of a girl; how passive
Fain would it be, how helpless; and helplessness leads to destruction.
Maiden reserve torn from off it, grows never again to reclothe it, 170
Modesty broken-through once to immodesty flies for protection.
Oh, who saws through the trunk, though he leave the tree up in the
    forest,
When the next wind casts it down,—is *his* not the hand that smote it?

  This is the answer, the second, which, pondering long with
    emotion,
There by himself in the cottage the Tutor addressed to Philip.
  I have perhaps been severe, dear Philip, and hasty; forgive me;
For I was fain to reply ere I wholly had read through your letter;

And it was written in scraps with crossings and counter-crossings
Hard to connect with each other correctly, and hard to decipher;
Paper was scarce, I suppose: forgive me; I write to console you. 180
   Grace is given of God, but knowledge is bought in the market;
Knowledge needful for all, yet cannot be had for the asking.
There are exceptional beings, one finds them distant and rarely,
Who, endowed with the vision alike and the interpretation,
See, by their neighbours' eyes and their own still motions enlightened,
In the beginning the end, in the acorn the oak of the forest,
In the child of to-day its children to long generations,
In a thought or a wish a life, a drama, an epos.
There are inheritors, is it? by mystical generation,
Heiring the wisdom and ripeness of spirits gone-by; without labour
Owning what others by doing and suffering earn; what old men 191
After long years of mistake and erasure are proud to have come to,
Sick with mistake and erasure possess when possession is idle.
Yes, there is power upon earth, seen feebly in women and children,
Which can, laying one hand on the cover, read-off, unfaltering,
Leaf after leaf unlifted, the words of the closed book under,
Words which we are poring at, hammering at, stumbling at, spelling.
Rare is this; wisdom mostly is bought for a price in the market;—
Rare is this; and happy, who buy so much for so little,
As I conceive have you, and as I will hope has Katie.   200
Knowledge is needful for man,—needful no less for woman,
Even in Highland glens, were they vacant of shooter and tourist.
   Not that, of course, I mean to prefer your blindfold hurry
Unto a soul that abides most loving yet most withholding;
Least unfeeling though calm, self-contained yet most unselfish;
Renders help and accepts it, a man among men that are brothers,
Views, not plucks the beauty, adores, and demands no embracing,
So in its peaceful passage whatever is lovely and gracious
Still without seizing or spoiling, itself in itself reproducing.
No, I do not set Philip herein on the level of Arthur,   210
No, I do not compare still tarn with furious torrent,
Yet will the tarn overflow, assuaged in the lake be the torrent.
   Women are weak, as you say, and love of all things to be passive,

Passive, patient, receptive, yea, even of wrong and misdoing,
Even to force and misdoing with joy and victorious feeling
Passive, patient, receptive; for that is the strength of their being,
Like to the earth taking all things, and all to good converting.
Oh 'tis a snare indeed!—Moreover, remember it, Philip,
To the prestige of the richer the lowly are prone to be yielding,
Think that in dealing with them they are raised to a different region,
Where old laws and morals are modified, lost, exist not;   221
Ignorant they as they are, they have but to conform and be yielding.
   But I have spoken of this already, and need not repeat it.
You will not now run after what merely attracts and entices,
Every-day things highly coloured, and common-place carved and
      gilded.
You will henceforth seek only the good: and seek it, Philip,
Where it is—not more abundant perhaps, but—more easily met
      with;
Where you are surer to find it, less likely to run into error,
In your station, not thinking about it, but not disregarding.
   So was the letter completed: a postscript afterward added,   230
Telling the tale that was told by the dancers returning from Rannoch.
So was the letter completed: but query, whither to send it?
Not for the will of the wisp, the cloud, and the hawk of the moorland,
Ranging afar thro' Lochaber, Lochiel, and Knoydart, and Moydart,
Have even latest extensions adjusted a postal arrangement.
Query resolved very shortly, when Hope, from his chamber
      descending,
Came with a note in his hand from the Lady, his aunt, at the Castle;
Came and revealed the contents of a missive that brought strange
      tidings;
Came and announced to the friends in a voice that was husky with
      wonder,
Philip was staying at Balloch, was there in the room with the
      Countess,   240
Philip to Balloch had come and was dancing with Lady Maria.
   Philip at Balloch, he said, after all that stately refusal,
He there at last—O strange! O marvel, marvel of marvels!

Airlie, the Waistcoat, with Katie, we left him this morning at
    Rannoch;
Airlie with Katie, he said, and Philip with Lady Maria.
    And amid laughter Adam paced up and down, repeating
Over and over, unconscious, the phrase which Hope had lent him,
Dancing at Balloch, you say, in the Castle, with Lady Maria.

V

——*Putavi*
Stultus ego huic nostræ similem

So in the cottage with Adam the pupils five together
Duly remained, and read, and looked no more for Philip,
Philip at Balloch shooting and dancing with Lady Maria.
Breakfast at eight, and now, for brief September daylight,
Luncheon at two, and dinner at seven, or even later,
Five full hours between for the loch and the glen and the mountain,—
So in the joy of their life and glory of shooting-jackets,
So they read and roamed, the pupils five with Adam.
  What if autumnal shower came frequent and chill from the
    westward,
What if on browner sward with yellow leaves besprinkled   10
Gemming the crispy blade, the delicate gossamer gemming,
Frequent and thick lay at morning the chilly beads of hoar-frost,
Duly in *matutine* still, and daily, whatever the weather,
Bathed in the rain and the frost and the mist with the Glory of
    headers
Hope. Thither also at times, of cold and of possible gutters
Careless, unmindful, unconscious, would Hobbes, or e'er they
    departed,
Come, in heavy pea-coat his trouserless trunk enfolding,
Come, under coat over-brief those lusty legs displaying,
All from the shirt to the slipper the natural man revealing.
  Duly there they bathed and daily, the twain or the trio,   20
Where in the morning was custom, where over a ledge of granite
Into a granite bason the amber torrent descended;
Beautiful, very, to gaze-in ere plunging; beautiful also,
Perfect as picture, as vision entrancing that comes to the sightless,
Through the great granite jambs the stream, the glen, and the
    mountain,
Beautiful, seen by snatches in intervals of dressing,
Morn after morn, unsought for, recurring; themselves too seeming

Not as spectators, accepted into it, immingled, as truly
Part of it as are the kine in the field lying there by the birches.
  So they bathed, they read, they roamed in glen and forest;   30
Far amid blackest pines to the waterfalls they shadow,
Far up the long, long glen to the loch, and the loch beyond it,
Deep under huge red cliffs, a secret; and oft by the starlight,
Or the aurora perchance, racing home for the eight o'clock mutton.
So they bathed, and read, and roamed in heathery Highland;
There in the joy of their life and glory of shooting-jackets
Bathed and read and roamed, and looked no more for Philip.

List to a letter that came from Philip at Balloch to Adam.
  I am here, O my friend!—idle, but learning wisdom.
Doing penance, you think; content, if so, in my penance.   40
  Often I find myself saying, while watching in dance or on horseback
One that is here, in her freedom, and grace, and imperial sweetness,
Often I find myself saying, old faith and doctrine abjuring,
Into the crucible casting philosophies, facts, convictions,—
Were it not well that the stem should be naked of leaf and of tendril,
Poverty-stricken, the barest, the dismallest stick of the garden;
Flowerless, leafless, unlovely, for ninety-and-nine long summers,
So in the hundredth, at last, were bloom for one day at the summit,
So but that fleeting flower were lovely as Lady Maria.
  Often I find myself saying, and know not myself as I say it,   50
What of the poor and the weary? their labour and pain is needed.
Perish the poor and the weary! what can they better than perish,
Perish in labour for her, who is worth the destruction of empires?
What! for a mite, for a mote, an impalpable odour of honour,
Armies shall bleed; cities burn; and the soldier red from the
    storming
Carry hot rancour and lust into chambers of mothers and daughters:
What! would ourselves for the cause of an hour encounter the battle,
Slay and be slain; lie rotting in hospital, hulk, and prison;
Die as a dog dies; die mistaken perhaps, and dishonoured.
Yea,—and shall hodmen in beer-shops complain of a glory denied
    them,   60

Which could not ever be theirs more than now it is theirs as spec-
    tators?
Which could not be, in all earth, if it were not for labour of hodmen?
    And I find myself saying, and what I am saying, discern not,
Dig in thy deep dark prison, O miner! and finding be thankful;
Though unpolished by thee, unto thee unseen in perfection,
While thou art eating black bread in the poisonous air of thy cavern,
Far away glitters the gem on the peerless neck of a Princess,
Dig, and starve, and be thankful; it is so, and thou hast been aiding.
    Often I find myself saying, in irony is it, or earnest?
Yea, what is more, be rich, O ye rich! be sublime in great houses, 70
Purple and delicate linen endure; be of Burgundy patient;
Suffer that service be done you, permit of the page and the valet,
Vex not your souls with annoyance of charity schools or of districts,
Cast not to swine of the sty the pearls that should gleam in your
    foreheads.
Live, be lovely, forget them, be beautiful even to proudness,
Even for their poor sakes whose happiness is to behold you;
Live, be uncaring, be joyous, be sumptuous; only be lovely,—
Sumptuous not for display, and joyous, not for enjoyment;
Not for enjoyment truly; for Beauty and God's great glory!
    Yes, and I say, and it seems inspiration—of Good or of Evil! 80
Is it not He that hath done it, and who shall dare gainsay it?
Is it not even of Him, who hath made us?—Yea, *for the lions,*
Roaring after their prey, do seek their meat from God!—
Is it not even of Him, who one kind over another
All the works of His hand hath disposed in a wonderful order?
Who hath made man, as the beasts, to live the one on the other,
Who hath made man as Himself to know the law—and accept it!
    You will wonder at this, no doubt! I also wonder!
But we must live and learn; we can't know all things at twenty.

List to a letter of Hobbes to Philip his friend at Balloch.   90
    All Cathedrals are Christian, all Christians are Cathedrals,
Such is the Catholic doctrine; 'tis ours with a slight variation;
Every Woman is, or ought to be, a Cathedral,

Built on the ancient plan, a Cathedral pure and perfect,
Built by that only law, that Use be suggester of Beauty,
Nothing concealed that is done, but all things done to adornment,
Meanest utilities seized as occasions to grace and embellish.—
  So had I duly commenced in the spirit and style of my Philip,
So had I formally opened the Treatise upon *the Laws of*
Architectural Beauty in Application to Women,   100
So had I writ.—But my fancies are palsied by tidings they tell me,
Tidings—ah me, can it be then? that I, the blasphemer accounted,
Here am with reverent heed at the wondrous Analogy working,
Pondering thy words and thy gestures, whilst thou, a prophet
      apostate,
(How are the mighty fallen!) whilst thou, a shepherd travestie,
(How are the mighty fallen!) with gun,—with pipe no longer,
Teachest the woods to re-echo thy game-killing recantations,
Teachest thy verse to exalt Amaryllis, a Countess's daughter?
  What, thou forgettest, bewildered, my Master, that rightly considered
Beauty must ever be useful, what truly is useful is graceful?   110
She that is handy is handsome, good dairy-maids must be good-
      looking,
If but the butter be nice, the tournure of the elbow is shapely,
If the cream-cheeses be white, far whiter the hands that made them,
If—but alas, is it true? while the pupil alone in the cottage
Slowly elaborates here thy System of Feminine Graces,
Thou in the palace, its author, art dining, small-talking and dancing,
Dancing and pressing the fingers kid-gloved of a Lady Maria.

  These are the final words, that came to the Tutor from Balloch.
I am conquered, it seems! you will meet me, I hope, in Oxford,
Altered in manners and mind. I yield to the laws and arrangements,
Yield to the ancient existent decrees: who am I to resist them? 121
Yes, you will find me altered in mind, I think, as in manners,
Anxious too to atone for six weeks' loss of your Logic.

  So in the cottage with Adam, the Pupils five together,
Read, and bathed, and roamed, and thought not now of Philip,
All in the joy of their life, and glory of shooting-jackets.

VI

Ducite ab urbe domum, mea carmina, ducite Daphnin

BRIGHT October was come, the misty-bright October,
Bright October was come to burn and glen and cottage;
But the cottage was empty, the *matutine* deserted.
  Who are these that walk by the shore of the salt sea water?
Here in the dusky eve, on the road by the salt sea water?
  Who are these? and where? it is no sweet seclusion;
Blank hill-sides slope down to a salt sea loch at their bases,
Scored by runnels, that fringe ere they end with rowan and alder;
Cottages here and there outstanding bare on the mountain,
Peat-roofed, windowless, white; the road underneath by the water.
  There on the blank hill-side, looking down through the loch to
    the ocean,   11
There with a runnel beside, and pine-trees twain before it,
There with the road underneath, and in sight of coaches and
    steamers,
Dwelling of David Mackaye and his daughters Elspie and Bella,
Sends up a column of smoke the Bothie of Tober-na-vuolich.
  And of the older twain, the elder was telling the younger,
How on his pittance of soil he lived, and raised potatoes,
Barley, and oats, in the bothie where lived his father before him;
Yet was smith by trade, and had travelled making horse-shoes
Far; in the army had seen some service with brave Sir Hector,   20
Wounded soon, and discharged, disabled as smith and soldier;
He had been many things since that,—drover, schoolmaster,
Whitesmith,—but when his brother died childless came up hither;
And although he could get fine work that would pay, in the city,
Still was fain to abide where his father abode before him.
And the lassies are bonnie,—I'm father and mother to them,—
Bonnie and young; they're healthier here, I judge, and safer:
I myself find time for their reading, writing, and learning.
  So on the road they walk by the shore of the salt sea water,
Silent a youth and maid, and elders twain conversing.   30

This was the letter that came when Adam was leaving the cottage.
If you can manage to see me before going off to Dartmoor,
Come by Tuesday's coach through Glencoe (you have not seen it),
Stop at the ferry below, and ask your way (you will wonder,
There however I am) to the Bothie of Tober-na-vuolich.
  And on another scrap, of next day's date, was written:
It was by accident purely I lit on the place; I was returning,
Quietly, travelling homeward, by one of these wretched coaches;
One of the horses cast a shoe; and a farmer passing
Said, Old David's your man; a clever fellow at shoeing   40
Once; just here by the firs; they call it Tober-na-vuolich.
So I saw and spoke with David Mackaye, our acquaintance.
When we came to the journey's end, some five miles further,
In my unoccupied evening I walked back again to the bothie.
  But on a final crossing, still later in date, was added:
Come as soon as you can; be sure and do not refuse me.
Who would have guessed I should find my haven and end of my
      travel,
Here, by accident too, in the bothie we laughed about so?
Who would have guessed that here would be she whose glance at
      Rannoch
Turned me in that mysterious way; yes, angels conspiring,   50
Slowly drew me, conducted me, home, to herself; the needle
Which in the shaken compass flew hither and thither, at last, long
Quivering, poises to north. I think so. But I am cautious;
More, at least, than I was in the old silly days when I left you.
  Not at the bothie now; at the changehouse in the clachan;[1]
Why I delay my letter is more than I can tell you.

  There was another scrap, without or date or comment,
Dotted over with various observations, as follows:
Only think, I had danced with her twice, and did not remember.
I was as one that sleeps on the railway; one, who dreaming   60
Hears thro' his dream the name of his home shouted out; hears and
      hears not,—

      [1] Public-house in the hamlet.

Faint, and louder again, and less loud, dying in distance;
Dimly conscious, with something of inward debate and choice,—and
Sense of claim and reality present, anon relapses
Nevertheless, and continues the dream and fancy, while forward
Swiftly, remorseless, the car presses on, he knows not whither.

Handsome who handsome is, who handsome does is more so;
Pretty is all very pretty, it's prettier far to be useful.
No, fair Lady Maria, I say not that; but I *will* say,
Stately is service accepted, but lovelier service rendered,   70
Interchange of service the law and condition of beauty:
Any way beautiful only to be the thing one is meant for.
I, I am sure, for the sphere of mere ornament am not intended:
No, nor she, I think, thy sister at Tober-na-vuolich.

This was the letter of Philip, and this had brought the Tutor:
This is why tutor and pupil are walking with David and Elspie.—

When for the night they part, and these, once more together,
Went by the lochside along to the changehouse near in the clachan,
Thus to his pupil anon commenced the grave man Adam.

Yes, she is beautiful, Philip, beautiful even as morning: 80
Yes, it is that which I said, the Good and not the Attractive!
Happy is he that finds, and finding does not leave it!

Ten more days did Adam with Philip abide at the changehouse,
Ten more nights they met, they walked with father and daughter.
Ten more nights, and night by night more distant away were
Philip and she; every night less heedful, by habit, the father.
Happy ten days, most happy; and, otherwise than intended,
Fortunate visit of Adam, companion and friend to David.
Happy ten days, be ye fruitful of happiness! Pass o'er them slowly,
Slowly; like cruse of the prophet be multiplied, even to ages!   90
Pass slowly o'er them ye days of October; ye soft misty mornings,
Long dusky eves; pass slowly; and thou great Term-Time of Oxford,
Awful with lectures and books, and Little-goes and Great-goes,
Till but the sweet bud be perfect, recede and retire for the lovers,
Yea, for the sweet love of lovers, postpone thyself even to doomsday!

Pass o'er them slowly, ye hours! Be with them, ye Loves and
   Graces!

Indirect and evasive no longer, a cowardly bather,
Clinging to bough and to rock, and sidling along by the edges,
In your faith, ye Muses and Graces, who love the plain present,
Scorning historic abridgement and artifice anti-poetic,   100
In your faith, ye Muses and Loves, ye Loves and Graces,
I will confront the great peril, and speak with the mouth of the
    lovers,
As they spoke by the alders, at evening, the runnel below them,
Elspie a diligent knitter, and Philip her fingers watching.

VII

Vesper adest, juvenes, consurgite; Vesper Olympo
Expectata diu vix tandem lumina tollit.

FOR she confessed, as they sat in the dusk, and he saw not her
blushes,
Elspie confessed at the sports long ago with her father she saw him,
When at the door the old man had told him the name of the bothie;
There after that at the dance; yet again at a dance in Rannoch—
And she was silent, confused. Confused much rather Philip
Buried his face in his hands, his face that with blood was bursting.
Silent, confused, yet by pity she conquered her fear, and continued.
Katie is good and not silly; be comforted, Sir, about her;
Katie is good and not silly; tender, but not like many
Carrying off, and at once for fear of being seen, in the bosom   10
Locking-up as in a cupboard the pleasure that any man gives them,
Keeping it out of sight as a prize they need be ashamed of;
That is the way, I think, Sir, in England more than in Scotland;
No, she lives and takes pleasure in all, as in beautiful weather,
Sorry to lose it, but just as we would be to lose fine weather.
And she is strong to return to herself and feel undeserted.
Oh, she is strong, and not silly; she thinks no further about you;
She has had kerchiefs before from gentle, I know, as from simple.
Yes, she is good and not silly; yet were you wrong, Mr. Philip,
Wrong, for yourself perhaps more than for her.
                                        But Philip replied not,   20
Raised not his eyes from the hands on his knees.
                                        And Elspie continued.
That was what gave me much pain, when I met you that dance at
Rannoch,
Dancing myself too with you, while Katie danced with Donald;
That was what gave me such pain; I thought it all a mistaking,
All a mere chance, you know, and accident,—not proper choosing,—
There were at least five or six—not there, no, that I don't say,
But in the country about,—you might just as well have been courting.

That was what gave me much pain, and (you won't remember that,
    though,)
Three days after, I met you, beside my uncle's, walking,
And I was wondering much, and hoped you wouldn't notice,   30
So as I passed I couldn't help looking. You didn't know me.
But I was glad, when I heard next day you were gone to the teacher.
    And uplifting his face at last, with eyes dilated,
Large as great stars in mist, and dim, with dabbled lashes,
Philip, with new tears starting,
                          You think I do not remember,
Said,—suppose that I did not observe! Ah me, shall I tell you?
Elspie, it was your look that sent me away from Rannoch.
It was your glance, that, descending, an instant revelation,
Showed me where I was, and whitherward going; recalled me,
Sent me, not to my books, but to wrestlings of thought in the
    mountains.   40
Yes, I have carried your glance within me undimmed, unaltered,
As a lost boat the compass some passing ship has lent her,
Many a weary mile on road, and hill, and moorland:
And you suppose, that I do not remember, I had not observed it!
O, did the sailor bewildered observe when they told him his bearings?
O, did he cast overboard, when they parted, the compass they
    gave him?
    And he continued more firmly, although with stronger emotion:
    Elspie, why should I speak it? you cannot believe it, and should
    not:
Why should I say that I love, which I all but said to another?
Yet should I dare, should I say, O Elspie, you only I love; you, 50
First and sole in my life that has been and surely that shall be;
Could—O, could you believe it, O Elspie, believe it and spurn not!
Is it—possible,—possible, Elspie?
                          Well,—she answered,
And she was silent some time, and blushed all over, and answered
Quietly, after her fashion, still knitting, Maybe, I think of it,
Though I don't know that I did: and she paused again; but it may be,
Yes,—I don't know, Mr. Philip,—but only it feels to me strangely

Like to the high new bridge, they used to build at, below there,
Over the burn and glen on the road. You won't understand me.
But I keep saying in my mind—this long time slowly with trouble 60
I have been building myself, up, up, and toilfully raising,
Just like as if the bridge were to do it itself without masons,
Painfully getting myself upraised one stone on another,
All one side I mean; and now I see on the other
Just such another fabric uprising, better and stronger,
Close to me, coming to join me: and then I sometimes fancy,—
Sometimes I find myself dreaming at nights about arches and
    bridges,—
Sometimes I dream of a great invisible hand coming down, and
Dropping the great key-stone in the middle: there in my dreaming,
There I feel the great key-stone coming in, and through it   70
Feel the other part—all the other stones of the archway,
Joined into mine with a strange happy sense of completeness. But,
    dear me,
This is confusion and nonsense. I mix all the things I can think of.
And you won't understand, Mr. Philip.
                                    But while she was speaking,
So it happened, a moment she paused from her work, and, pondering,
Laid her hand on her lap: Philip took it: she did not resist:
So he retained her fingers, the knitting being stopped. But emotion
Came all over her more and yet more, from his hand, from her
    heart, and
Most from the sweet idea and image her brain was renewing.
So he retained her hand, and, his tears down-dropping on it,   80
Trembling a long time, kissed it at last. And she ended.
And as she ended, uprose he; saying, What have I heard? Oh,
What have I done, that such words should be said to me? Oh, I see it,
See the great key-stone coming down from the heaven of heavens!
And he fell at her feet, and buried his face in her apron.

   But as under the moon and stars they went to the cottage,
Elspie sighed and said, Be patient, dear Mr. Philip,
Do not do anything hasty. It is all so soon, so sudden.
Do not say anything yet to any one.

> Elspie, he answered,
> Does not my friend go on Friday? I then shall see nothing of you: 90
> Do not I go myself on Monday?
>   But oh, he said, Elspie;
> Do as I bid you, my child; do not go on calling me Mr.;
> Might I not just as well be calling you Miss Elspie?
> Call me, this heavenly night, for once, for the first time, Philip.
>   Philip, she said and laughed, and said she could not say it;
> Philip, she said; he turned, and kissed the sweet lips as they said it.

> But on the morrow Elspie kept out of the way of Philip;
> And at the evening seat, when he took her hand by the alders,
> Drew it back, saying, almost peevishly,
>   No, Mr. Philip,
> I was quite right, last night; it is too soon, too sudden.   100
> What I told you before was foolish perhaps, was hasty.
> When I think it over, I am shocked and terrified at it.
> Not that at all I unsay it; that is, I know I said it,
> And when I said it, felt it. But oh, we must wait, Mr. Philip!
> We mustn't pull ourselves at the great key-stone of the centre;
> Some one else up above must hold it, fit it, and fix it;
> If we try ourselves, we shall only damage the archway,
> Damage all our own work that we wrought, our painful upbuilding.
> When, you remember, you took my hand last evening, talking,
> I was all over a tremble: and as you pressed the fingers   110
> After, and afterwards kissed it, I could not speak. And then, too,
> As we went home, you kissed me for saying your name. It was
>   dreadful.
> I have been kissed before, she added, blushing slightly,
> I have been kissed more than once by Donald my cousin, and others;
> It is the way of the lads, and I make up my mind not to mind it;
> But, Mr. Philip, last night, and from you, it was different quite, Sir.
> When I think of all that, I am shocked and terrified at it.
> Yes, it is dreadful to me.
>   She paused, but quickly continued,
> Smiling almost fiercely, continued, looking upward.

You are too strong, you see, Mr. Philip! just like the sea there, 120
Which *will* come, through the straits and all between the mountains,
Forcing its great strong tide into every nook and inlet,
Getting far in, up the quiet stream of sweet inland water,
Sucking it up, and stopping it, turning it, driving it backward,
Quite preventing its own quiet running: and then, soon after,
Back it goes off, leaving weeds on the shore, and wrack and un-
      cleanness:
And the poor burn in the glen tries again its peaceful running,
But it is brackish and tainted, and all its banks in disorder.
That was what I dreamt all last night. I was the burnie,
Trying to get along through the tyrannous brine, and could not; 130
I was confined and squeezed in the coils of the great salt tide, that
Would mix-in itself with me, and change me; I felt myself changing;
And I struggled, and screamed, I believe, in my dream. It was
      dreadful.
You are too strong, Mr. Philip! I am but a poor slender burnie,
Used to the glens and the rocks, the rowan and birch of the woodies,
Quite unused to the great salt sea; quite afraid and unwilling.
   Ere she had spoken two words, had Philip released her fingers:
As she went on, he recoiled, fell back, and shook, and shivered;
There he stood, looking pale and ghastly; when she had ended,
Answering in hollow voice,   140
                        It is true; oh quite true, Elspie;
Oh, you are always right; oh, what, what have I been doing!
I will depart to-morrow. But oh, forget me not wholly,
Wholly, Elspie, nor hate me, no, do not hate me, my Elspie.
   But a revulsion passed through the brain and bosom of Elspie;
And she got up from her seat on the rock, putting by her knitting;
Went to him, where he stood, and answered:
                                        No, Mr. Philip,
No, you are good, Mr. Philip, and gentle; and I am the foolish;
No, Mr. Philip, forgive me.
                        She stepped right to him, and boldly
Took up his hand, and placed it in hers; he daring no movement;
Took up the cold hanging hand, up-forcing the heavy elbow.   150

I am afraid, she said, but I will! and kissed the fingers.
And he fell on his knees and kissed her own past counting.

  But a revulsion wrought in the brain and bosom of Elspie;
And the passion she just had compared to the vehement ocean,
Urging in high spring-tide its masterful way through the mountains,
Forcing and flooding the silvery stream, as it runs from the inland;
That great power withdrawn, receding here and passive,
Felt she in myriad springs, her sources, far in the mountains,
Stirring, collecting, rising, upheaving, forth-outflowing,
Taking and joining, right welcome, that delicate rill in the valley, 160
Filling it, making it strong, and still descending, seeking,
With a blind forefeeling descending ever, and seeking,
With a delicious forefeeling, the great still sea before it;
There deep into it, far, to carry, and lose in its bosom,
Waters that still from their sources exhaustless are fain to be added.
  As he was kissing her fingers, and knelt on the ground before her,
Yielding backward she sank to her seat, and of what she was doing
Ignorant, bewildered, in sweet multitudinous vague emotion,
Stooping, knowing not what, put her lips to the hair on his forehead:
And Philip, raising himself, gently, for the first time, round her 170
Passing his arms, close, close, enfolded her, close to his bosom.
  As they went home by the moon, Forgive me, Philip, she
· whispered;
I have so many things to think of, all of a sudden;
I who had never once thought a thing,—in my ignorant Highlands.

VIII

Jam veniet virgo, jam dicetur hymenæus

BUT a revulsion again came over the spirit of Elspie,
When she thought of his wealth, his birth and education:
Wealth indeed but small, though to her a difference truly;
Father nor mother had Philip, a thousand pounds his portion,
Somewhat impaired in a world where nothing is had for nothing;
Fortune indeed but small, and prospects plain and simple.
  But the many things that he knew, and the ease of a practised
Intellect's motion, and all those indefinable graces
(Were they not hers, too, Philip?) to speech, and manner, and
    movement,
Lent by the knowledge of self, and wisely-instructed feeling— 10
When she thought of these, and these contemplated daily,
Daily appreciating more, and more exactly appraising,—
With these thoughts, and the terror withal of a thing she could not
Estimate, and of a step (such a step!) in the dark to be taken,
Terror nameless and ill-understood of deserting her station,—
Daily heavier, heavier upon her pressed the sorrow,
Daily distincter, distincter within her arose the conviction,
He was too high, too perfect, and she so unfit, so unworthy,
(Ah me! Philip, that ever a word such as that should be written!)
It would do neither for him nor for her; she also was something, 20
Not much indeed, it was true, yet not to be lightly extinguished.
Should *he—he*, she said, have a wife beneath him? herself be
An inferior there where only equality can be?
It would do neither for him nor for her.
                                     Alas for Philip!
Many were tears and great was perplexity. Nor had availed then
All his prayer and all his device. But much was spoken
Now, between Adam and Elspie; companions were they hourly:
Much by Elspie to Adam, enquiring, anxiously seeking,
From his experience seeking impartial accurate statement
What it was to do this or do that, go hither or thither,   30

How in the after life would seem what now seeming certain
Might so soon be reversed; in her quest and obscure exploring
Still from that quiet orb soliciting light to her footsteps;
Much by Elspie to Adam, enquiring, eagerly seeking:
Much by Adam to Elspie, informing, reassuring,
Much that was sweet to Elspie, by Adam heedfully speaking,
Quietly, indirectly, in general terms, of Philip,
Gravely, but indirectly, not as incognisant wholly,
But as suspending until she should seek it, direct intimation;
Much that was sweet in her heart of what he was and would be, 40
Much that was strength to her mind, confirming beliefs and insights
Pure and unfaltering, but young and mute and timid for action;
Much of relations of rich and poor, and of true education.
  It was on Saturday eve, in the gorgeous bright October,
Then when brackens are changed, and heather blooms are faded,
And amid russet of heather and fern green trees are bonnie;
Alders are green, and oaks; the rowan scarlet and yellow;
One great glory of broad gold pieces appears the aspen,
And the jewels of gold that were hung in the hair of the birch-tree,
Pendulous, here and there, her coronet, necklace, and ear-rings, 50
Cover her now, o'er and o'er; she is weary and scatters them from her.
There, upon Saturday eve, in the gorgeous bright October,
Under the alders knitting, gave Elspie her troth to Philip.
For as they talked, anon she said,
                                    It is well, Mr. Philip.
Yes, it is well: I have spoken, and learnt a deal with the teacher.
At the last I told him all, I could not help it;
And it came easier with him than could have been with my father;
And he calmly approved, as one that had fully considered.
Yes, it is well, I have hoped, though quite too great and sudden;
I am so fearful, I think it ought not to be for years yet.   60
I am afraid; but believe in you; and I trust to the teacher:
You have done all things gravely and temperate, not as in passion;
And the teacher is prudent, and surely can tell what is likely.
What my father will say, I know not; we will obey him:
But for myself, I could dare to believe all well, and venture.

O Mr. Philip, may it never hereafter seem to be different!
And she hid her face—

          Oh, where, but in Philip's bosom!

After some silence, some tears too perchance, Philip laughed, and
    said to her,
  So, my own Elspie, at last you are clear that I'm bad enough for
    you.
Ah, but your father won't make one half the question about it   70
You have—he'll think me, I know, nor better nor worse than
    Donald,
Neither better nor worse for my gentlemanship and book-work,
Worse, I fear, as he knows me an idle and vagabond fellow,
Though he allows, but he'll think it was all for your sake, Elspie,
Though he allows I did some good at the end of the shearing.
But I had thought in Scotland you didn't care for this folly.
How I wish, he said, you had lived all your days in the Highlands!
This is what comes of the year you spent in our foolish England.
You do not all of you feel these fancies.

                No, she answered,
And in her spirit the freedom and ancient joy was reviving,   80
No, she said, and uplifted herself, and looked for her knitting,
No, nor do *I*, dear Philip, I don't myself feel always,
As I have felt, more sorrow for me, these four days lately,
Like the Peruvian Indians I read about last winter,
Out in America there, in somebody's life of Pizarro;
Who were as good perhaps as the Spaniards; only weaker;
And that the one big tree might spread its root and branches,
All the lesser about it must even be felled and perish.
No, I feel much more as if I, as well as you, were,
Somewhere, a leaf on the one great tree, that, up from old time   90
Growing, contains in itself the whole of the virtue and life of
Bygone days, drawing now to itself all kindreds and nations,
And must have for itself the whole world for its root and branches.
No, I belong to the tree, I shall not decay in the shadow;
Yes, and I feel the life-juices of all the world and the ages

Coming to me as to you, more slowly no doubt and poorer;
You are more near, but then you will help to convey them to me.
No, don't smile, Philip, now, so scornfully!—While you look so
Scornful and strong, I feel as if I were standing and trembling,
Fancying the burn in the dark a wide and rushing river;   100
And I feel coming unto me from you, or it may be from elsewhere,
Strong contemptuous resolve; I forget, and I bound as across it.
But after all, you know, it may be a dangerous river.

   Oh, if it were so, Elspie, he said, I can carry you over.
Nay, she replied, you would tire of having me for a burden.

   O sweet burden, he said, and are you not light as a feather?
But it is deep, very likely, she said, over head and ears too.

   O let us try, he answered, the waters themselves will support us,
Yea, very ripples and waves will form to a boat underneath us;
There is a boat, he said, and a name is written upon it,   110
Love, he said, and kissed her.—
                        But I will read your books, though,
Said she, you'll leave me some, Philip.
                        Not I, replied he, a volume.
This is the way with you all, I perceive, high and low together.
Women must read,—as if they didn't know all beforehand:
Weary of plying the pump, we turn to the running water,
And the running spring will needs have a pump built upon it.
Weary and sick of our books, we come to repose in your eye-light,
As to the woodland and water, the freshness and beauty of Nature,
Lo, you will talk, forsooth, of the things we are sick to the death of.

   What, she said, and if I have let you become my sweetheart, 120
I am to read no books! but you may go your ways then,
And I will read, she said, with my father at home as I used to.

   If you must have it, he said, I myself will read them to you.

   Well, she said, but no, I will read to myself, when I choose it;
What, you suppose we never read anything here in our Highlands,
Bella and I with the father, in all our winter evenings!
But we must go, Mr. Philip—
                        I shall not go at all, said
He, if you call me Mr. Thank heaven! that's over for ever.

No, but it's not, she said, it is not over, nor will be.
Was it not then, she asked, the name I called you first by?   130
No, Mr. Philip, no—you have kissed me enough for two nights;
No—come, Philip, come, or I'll go myself without you.
    You never call me Philip, he answered, until I kiss you.
    As they went home by the moon that waning now rose later,
Stepping through mossy stones by the runnel under the alders,
Loitering unconsciously, Philip, she said, I will not be a lady,
We will do work together, you do not wish me a lady;
It is a weakness perhaps and a foolishness; still it is so;
I have been used all my life to help myself and others;
I could not bear to sit and be waited upon by footmen,   140
No, not even by women—
                                                And, God forbid, he answered,
God forbid you should ever be aught but yourself, my Elspie!
As for service, I love it not, I; your weakness is mine too,
I am sure Adam told you as much as that about me.
    I am sure, she said, he called you wild and flighty.
    That was true, he said, till my wings were clipped. But, my Elspie,
You will at least just go and see my uncle and cousins,
Sister, and brother, and brother's wife. You should go, if you liked it,
Just as you are; just what you are, at any rate, my Elspie.
Yes, we will go, and give the old solemn gentility stage-play   150
One little look, to leave it with all the more satisfaction.
    That may be, my Philip, she said; you are good to think of it.
But we are letting our fancies run-on indeed; after all, it
May all come, you know, Mr. Philip, to nothing whatever,
There is so much that needs to be done, so much that may happen.
    All that needs to be done, said he, shall be done, and quickly.

    And on the morrow he took good heart and spoke with David;
Not unwarned the father, nor had been unperceiving;
Fearful much, but in all from the first reassured by the Tutor.
And he remembered how he had fancied the lad from the first;
        and   160
Then, too, the old man's eye was much more for inner than outer,

And the natural tune of his heart without misgiving
Went to the noble words of that grand song of the Lowlands,
Rank is the guinea stamp, but the man's a man for a' that.

   Still he was doubtful, would hear nothing of it now, but insisted
Philip should go to his books; if he chose, he might write; if after
Chose to return, might come; he truly believed him honest.
But a year must elapse, and many things might happen.
Yet at the end he burst into tears, called Elspie, and blessed them;
Elspie, my bairn, he said, I thought not, when at the doorway 170
Standing with you, and telling the young man where he would
     find us,
I did not think he would one day be asking me here to surrender
What is to me more than wealth in my Bothie of Tober-na-vuolich.

IX

Arva, beata Petamus arva!

So on the morrow's morrow, with Term-time dread returning,
Philip returned to his books, and read, and remained at Oxford,
All the Christmas and Easter remained and read at Oxford.
  Great was wonder in College when postman showed to butler
Letters addressed to David Mackaye, at Tober-na-vuolich,
Letter on letter, at least one a week, one every Sunday:
  Great at that Highland post was wonder too and conjecture,
When the postman showed letters to wife, and wife to the lassies,
And the lassies declared they couldn't be really to David;
Yes, they could see inside a paper with E. upon it.   10
  Great was surmise in College at breakfast, wine, and supper,
Keen the conjecture and joke; but Adam kept the secret,
Adam the secret kept, and Philip read like fury.
  This is a letter written by Philip at Christmas to Adam.
There may be beings, perhaps, whose vocation it is to be idle,
Idle, sumptuous even, luxurious, if it must be:
Only let each man seek to be that for which nature meant him.
If you were meant to plough, Lord Marquis, out with you, and do it;
If you were meant to be idle, O beggar, behold, I will feed you.
If you were born for a groom, and you seem, by your dress, to
      believe so,   20
Do it like a man, Sir George, for pay, in a livery stable;
Yes, you may so release that slip of a boy at the corner,
Fingering books at the window, misdoubting the eighth com-
      mandment.
Ah, fair Lady Maria, God meant you to live, and be lovely;
Be so then, and I bless you. But ye, ye spurious ware, who
Might be plain women, and can be by no possibility better!
—Ye unhappy statuettes, and miserable trinkets,
Poor alabaster chimney-piece ornaments under glass cases,
Come, in God's name, come down! the very French clock by you
Puts you to shame with ticking; the fire-irons deride you.   30

You, young girl, who have had such advantages, learnt so quickly,
Can you not teach? O yes, and she likes Sunday school extremely,
Only it's soon in the morning. Away! if to teach be your calling,
It is no play, but a business: off! go teach and be paid for it.
Lady Sophia's so good to the sick, so firm and so gentle.
Is there a nobler sphere than of hospital nurse and matron?
Hast thou for cooking a turn, little Lady Clarissa? in with them,
In with your fingers! their beauty it spoils, but your own it enhances;
For it is beautiful only to do the thing we are meant for.
   This was the answer that came from the Tutor, the grave man,
     Adam.   40
When the armies are set in array, and the battle beginning,
Is it well that the soldier whose post is far to the leftward
Say, I will go to the right, it is there I shall do best service?
There is a great Field-Marshal, my friend, who arrays our battalions;
Let us to Providence trust, and abide and work in our stations.
   This was the final retort from the eager, impetuous Philip.
I am sorry to say your Providence puzzles me sadly;
Children of Circumstance are we to be? you answer, On no wise!
Where does Circumstance end, and Providence where begins it?
What are we to resist, and what are we to be friends with?   50
If there is battle, 'tis battle by night: I stand in the darkness,
Here in the mêlée of men, Ionian and Dorian on both sides,
Signal and password known; which is friend and which is foeman?
Is it a friend? I doubt, though he speak with the voice of a brother.
Still you are right, I suppose; you always are, and will be;
Though I mistrust the Field-Marshal, I bow to the duty of order.
Yet is my feeling rather to ask, where *is* the battle?
Yes, I could find in my heart to cry, notwithstanding my Elspie,
O that the armies indeed were arrayed! O joy of the onset!
Sound, thou Trumpet of God, come forth, Great Cause, to array us,
King and leader appear, thy soldiers sorrowing seek thee.   61
Would that the armies indeed were arrayed, O where is the battle!
Neither battle I see, nor arraying, nor King in Israel,
Only infinite jumble and mess and dislocation,
Backed by a solemn appeal, 'For God's sake do not stir, there!'

Yet you are right, I suppose; if you don't attack my conclusion,
Let us get on as we can, and do the thing we are fit for;
Every one for himself, and the common success for us all, and
Thankful, if not for our own, why then for the triumph of others,
Get along, each as we can, and do the thing we are meant for.   70
That isn't likely to be by sitting still, eating and drinking.
    These are fragments again without date addressed to Adam.
    As at return of tide the total weight of ocean,
Drawn by moon and sun from Labrador and Greenland,
Sets-in amain, in the open space betwixt Mull and Scarba,
Heaving, swelling, spreading, the might of the mighty Atlantic;
There into cranny and slit of the rocky, cavernous bottom
Settles down, and with dimples huge the smooth sea-surface
Eddies, coils, and whirls; by dangerous Corryvreckan:
So in my soul of souls through its cells and secret recesses,   80
Comes back, swelling and spreading, the old democratic fervour.
    But as the light of day enters some populous city,
Shaming away, ere it come, by the chilly day-streak signal,
High and low, the misusers of night, shaming out the gas lamps—
All the great empty streets are flooded with broadening clearness,
Which, withal, by inscrutable simultaneous access
Permeates far and pierces to the very cellars lying in
Narrow high back-lane, and court, and alley of alleys:—
He that goes forth to his walks, while speeding to the suburb,
Sees sights only peaceful and pure; as labourers settling   90
Slowly to work, in their limbs the lingering sweetness of slumber;
Humble market-carts, coming-in, bringing-in, not only
Flower, fruit, farm-store, but sounds and sights of the country
Dwelling yet on the sense of the dreamy drivers; soon after
Half-awake servant-maids unfastening drowsy shutters
Up at the windows, or down, letting-in the air by the doorway;
School-boys, school-girls soon, with slate, portfolio, satchel,
Hampered as they haste, those running, these others maidenly
    tripping;
Early clerk anon turning out to stroll, or it may be
Meet his sweetheart—waiting behind the garden gate there;   100

171

Merchant on his grass-plat haply, bare-headed; and now by this
  time
Little child bringing breakfast to 'father' that sits on the timber
There by the scaffolding; see, she waits for the can beside him;
Meantime above purer air untarnished of new-lit fires:
So that the whole great wicked artificial civilised fabric—
All its unfinished houses, lots for sale, and railway outworks—
Seems reaccepted, resumed to Primal Nature and Beauty:—
—Such—in me, and to me, and on me the love of Elspie!

Philip returned to his books, but returned to his Highlands after;
Got a first, 'tis said; a winsome bride, 'tis certain.   110
There while courtship was ending, nor yet the wedding appointed,
Under her father he studied the handling of hoe and of hatchet:
Thither that summer succeeding came Adam and Arthur to see him
Down by the lochs from the distant Glenmorison; Adam the tutor,
Arthur, and Hope; and the Piper anon who was there for a visit;
He had been into the schools; plucked almost; all but a *gone-coon*;
So he declared; never once had brushed up his *hairy* Aldrich;
Into the great might-have-been upsoaring sublime and ideal
Gave to historical questions a free poetical treatment;
Leaving vocabular ghosts undisturbed in their lexicon-limbo,   120
Took Aristophanes up at a shot; and the whole three last weeks
Went, in his life and the sunshine rejoicing, to Nuneham and
  Godstowe:
What were the claims of Degree to those of life and the sunshine?
There did the four find Philip, the poet, the speaker, the chartist,
Delving at Highland soil, and railing at Highland landlords,
Railing, but more, as it seemed, for the fun of the Piper's fury.
There saw they David and Elspie Mackaye, and the Piper was almost,
Almost deeply in love with Bella the sister of Elspie;
But the good Adam was heedful; they did not go too often.
There in the bright October, the gorgeous bright October,   130
When the brackens are changed, and heather blooms are faded,
And amid russet of heather and fern green trees are bonnie,
Alders are green, and oaks, the rowan scarlet and yellow,
Heavy the aspen, and heavy with jewels of gold the birch-tree,

There, when shearing had ended, and barley-stooks were garnered,
David gave Philip to wife his daughter, his darling Elspie;
Elspie the quiet, the brave, was wedded to Philip the poet.

So won Philip his bride. They are married and gone—But oh, Thou
Mighty one, Muse of great Epos, and Idyll the playful and tender,
Be it recounted in song, ere we part, and thou fly to thy Pindus,   140
(Pindus is it, O Muse, or Ætna, or even Ben-nevis?)
Be it recounted in song, O Muse of the Epos and Idyll,
Who gave what at the wedding, the gifts and fair gratulations.

Adam, the grave careful Adam, a medicine chest and tool-box,
Hope a saddle, and Arthur a plough, and the Piper a rifle,
Airlie a necklace for Elspie, and Hobbes a Family Bible,
Airlie a necklace, and Hobbes a Bible and iron bedstead.

What was the letter, O Muse, sent withal by the corpulent hero?
This is the letter of Hobbes the kilted and corpulent hero.

So the last speech and confession is made, O my eloquent
   speaker!   150
So *the good time* is *coming*,[1] or come is it? O my chartist!
So the Cathedral is finished at last, O my Pugin of Women;
Finished, and now, is it true? to be taken out whole to New Zealand!
Well, go forth to thy field, to thy barley, with Ruth, O Boaz,
Ruth, who for thee hath deserted her people, her gods, her mountains.
Go, as in Ephrath of old, in the gate of Bethlehem said they,
Go, be the wife in thy house both Rachel and Leah unto thee!
Be thy wedding of silver, albeit of iron thy bedstead!
Yea, to the full golden fifty renewed be! and fair memoranda
Happily fill the fly-leaves duly left in the Family Bible.   160
Live, and when Hobbes is forgotten, may'st thou, an unroasted
   Grandsire,
See thy children's children, and Democracy upon New Zealand!
This was the letter of Hobbes, and this the postscript after.
Wit in the letter will prate, but wisdom speaks in a postscript;
Listen to wisdom—*Which things*—you perhaps didn't know, my
   dear fellow,
I have reflected; *Which things are an allegory*, Philip.

---

[1] 'The Good Time Coming.'—Chartist Song.

For this Rachel-and-Leah is marriage; which, I have seen it,
Lo, and have known it, is always, and must be, bigamy only,
Even in noblest kind a duality, compound, and complex,
One part heavenly-ideal, the other vulgar and earthy: 170
For this Rachel-and-Leah is marriage, and Laban their father
Circumstance, chance, the world, our uncle and hard taskmaster.
Rachel we found as we fled from the daughters of Heth by the desert;
Rachel we met at the well; we came, we saw, we kissed her;
Rachel we serve-for, long years,—that seem as a few days only,
E'en for the love we have to her,—and win her at last of Laban.
Is it not Rachel we take in our joy from the hand of her father?
Is it not Rachel we lead in the mystical veil from the altar?
Rachel we dream-of at night: in the morning, behold, it is Leah.
'Nay, it is custom,' saith Laban, the Leah indeed is the elder.   180
Happy and wise who consents to redouble his service to Laban,
So, fulfilling her week, he may add to the elder the younger,
Not repudiates Leah, but wins the Rachel unto her!
Neither hate thou thy Leah, my Jacob, she also is worthy;
So, many days shall thy Rachel have joy, and survive her sister;
Yea, and her children—*Which things are an allegory*, Philip,
Aye, and by Origen's head with a vengeance truly, a long one!

This was a note from the Tutor, the grave man, nicknamed Adam.
I shall see you of course, my Philip, before your departure;
Joy be with you, my boy, with you and your beautiful Elspie.
Happy is he that found, and finding was not heedless;   191 .
Happy is he that found, and happy the friend that was with him.
So won Philip his bride:—
                    They are married, and gone to New Zealand.
Five hundred pounds in pocket, with books, and two or three pictures,
Tool-box, plough, and the rest, they rounded the sphere to New
     Zealand.
There he hewed, and dug; subdued the earth and his spirit;
There he built him a home; there Elspie bare him his children,
David and Bella; perhaps ere this too an Elspie or Adam;
There hath he farmstead and land, and fields of corn and flax fields;
And the Antipodes too have a Bothie of Tober-na-vuolich.   200

AMOURS DE VOYAGE

Oh, you are sick of self-love, Malvolio,
And taste with a distempered appetite!
SHAKSPEARE

Il doutait de tout, même de l'amour.
FRENCH NOVEL

Solvitur ambulando.
SOLUTIO SOPHISMATUM

Flevit amores
Non elaboratum ad pedem.
HORACE

AMOURS DE VOYAGE

CANTO I

Over the great windy waters, and over the clear-crested summits,
  Unto the sun and the sky, and unto the perfecter earth,
Come, let us go,—to a land wherein gods of the old time wandered,
  Where every breath even now changes to ether divine.
Come, let us go; though withal a voice whisper, 'The world that we
    live in,
  Whithersoever we turn, still is the same narrow crib;
'Tis but to prove limitation, and measure a cord, that we travel;
  Let who would 'scape and be free go to his chamber and think;
'Tis but to change idle fancies for memories wilfully falser;
  'Tis but to go and have been.'—Come, little bark! let us go.   10

I. CLAUDE TO EUSTACE

DEAR EUSTATIO, I write that you may write me an answer,
Or at the least to put us again *en rapport* with each other.
Rome disappoints me much,—St. Peter's, perhaps, in especial;
Only the Arch of Titus and view from the Lateran please me:
This, however, perhaps, is the weather, which truly is horrid.
Greece must be better, surely; and yet I am feeling so spiteful,
That I could travel to Athens, to Delphi, and Troy, and Mount Sinai,
Though but to see with my eyes that these are vanity also.
  Rome disappoints me much; I hardly as yet understand, but
Rubbishy seems the word that most exactly would suit it.   20
All the foolish destructions, and all the sillier savings,
All the incongruous things of past incompatible ages,
Seem to be treasured up here to make fools of present and future.
Would to Heaven the old Goths had made a cleaner sweep of it!
Would to Heaven some new ones would come and destroy these
    churches!
However, one can live in Rome as also in London.
Rome is better than London, because it is other than London.

It is a blessing, no doubt, to be rid, at least for a time, of
All one's friends and relations,—yourself (forgive me!) included,—
All the *assujettissement* of having been what one has been,   30
What one thinks one is, or thinks that others suppose one;
Yet, in despite of all, we turn like fools to the English.
Vernon has been my fate; who is here the same that you knew him,—
Making the tour, it seems, with friends of the name of Trevellyn.

II. CLAUDE TO EUSTACE

ROME disappoints me still; but I shrink and adapt myself to it.
Somehow a tyrannous sense of a superincumbent oppression
Still, wherever I go, accompanies ever, and makes me
Feel like a tree (shall I say?) buried under a ruin of brickwork.
Rome, believe me, my friend, is like its own Monte Testaceo,
Merely a marvellous mass of broken and castaway wine-pots.   40
Ye gods! what do I want with this rubbish of ages departed,
Things that nature abhors, the experiments that she has failed in?
What do I find in the Forum? An archway and two or three pillars.
Well, but St. Peter's? Alas, Bernini has filled it with sculpture!
No one can cavil, I grant, at the size of the great Coliseum.
Doubtless the notion of grand and capacious and massive amusement,
This the old Romans had; but tell me, is this an idea?
Yet of solidity much, but of splendour little is extant:
'Brickwork I found thee, and marble I left thee!' their Emperor
     vaunted;
'Marble I thought thee, and brickwork I find thee!' the Tourist may
     answer.   50

III. GEORGINA TREVELLYN TO LOUISA ——

AT last, dearest Louisa, I take up my pen to address you.
Here we are, you see, with the seven-and-seventy boxes,
Courier, Papa and Mamma, the children, and Mary and Susan:
Here we all are at Rome, and delighted of course with St. Peter's,
And very pleasantly lodged in the famous Piazza di Spagna.
Rome is a wonderful place, but Mary shall tell you about it;
Not very gay, however; the English are mostly at Naples;

There are the A.s, we hear, and most of the W. party.
George, however, is come; did I tell you about his mustachios?
Dear, I must really stop, for the carriage, they tell me, is waiting; 60
Mary will finish; and Susan is writing, they say, to Sophia.
Adieu, dearest Louise,—evermore your faithful Georgina.
Who can a Mr. Claude be whom George has taken to be with?
Very stupid, I think, but George says so *very* clever.

IV. CLAUDE TO EUSTACE

No, the Christian faith, as at any rate I understood it,
With its humiliations and exaltations combining,
Exaltations sublime, and yet diviner abasements,
Aspirations from something most shameful here upon earth and
In our poor selves to something most perfect above in the heavens,—
No, the Christian faith, as I, at least, understood it,   70
Is not here, O Rome, in any of these thy churches;
Is not here, but in Freiburg, or Rheims, or Westminster Abbey.
What in thy Dome I find, in all thy recenter efforts,
Is a something, I think, more *rational* far, more earthly,
Actual, less ideal, devout not in scorn and refusal,
But in a positive, calm, Stoic-Epicurean acceptance.
This I begin to detect in St. Peter's and some of the churches,
Mostly in all that I see of the sixteenth-century masters;
Overlaid of course with infinite gauds and gewgaws,
Innocent, playful follies, the toys and trinkets of childhood,   80
Forced on maturer years, as the serious one thing needful,
By the barbarian will of the rigid and ignorant Spaniard.
    Curious work, meantime, re-entering society: how we
Walk a livelong day, great Heaven, and watch our shadows!
What our shadows seem, forsooth, we will ourselves be.
Do I look like that? you think me that: then I *am* that.

V. CLAUDE TO EUSTACE

LUTHER, they say, was unwise; like a half-taught German, he could
    not
See that old follies were passing most tranquilly out of remembrance;

Leo the Tenth was employing all efforts to clear out abuses;
Jupiter, Juno, and Venus, Fine Arts, and Fine Letters, the Poets, 90
Scholars, and Sculptors, and Painters, were quietly clearing away the
Martyrs, and Virgins, and Saints, or at any rate Thomas Aquinas:
He must forsooth make a fuss and distend his huge Wittenberg
    lungs, and
Bring back Theology once yet again in a flood upon Europe:
Lo you, for forty days from the windows of heaven it fell; the
Waters prevail on the earth yet more for a hundred and fifty;
Are they abating at last? the doves that are sent to explore are
Wearily fain to return, at the best with a leaflet of promise,—
Fain to return, as they went, to the wandering wave-tost vessel,—
Fain to re-enter the roof which covers the clean and the unclean,—
Luther, they say, was unwise; he didn't see how things were going;
Luther was foolish,—but, O great God! what call you Ignatius? 102
O my tolerant soul, be still! but you talk of barbarians,
Alaric, Attila, Genseric;—why, they came, they killed, they
Ravaged, and went on their way; but these vile, tyrannous Spaniards,
These are here still,—how long, O ye heavens, in the country of
    Dante?
These, that fanaticized Europe, which now can forget them, re-
    lease not
This, their choicest of prey, this Italy; here you see them,—
Here, with emasculate pupils and gimcrack churches of Gesu,
Pseudo-learning and lies, confessional-boxes and postures,—   110
Here, with metallic beliefs and regimental devotions,—
Here, overcrusting with slime, perverting, defacing, debasing,
Michael Angelo's dome, that had hung the Pantheon in heaven,
Raphael's Joys and Graces, and thy clear stars, Galileo!

VI. CLAUDE TO EUSTACE

WHICH of three Misses Trevellyn it is that Vernon shall marry
Is not a thing to be known; for our friend is one of those natures
Which have their perfect delight in the general tender-domestic,
So that he trifles with Mary's shawl, ties Susan's bonnet,
Dances with all, but at home is most, they say, with Georgina,

Who is, however, *too* silly in my apprehension for Vernon.   120
I, as before when I wrote, continue to see them a little;
Not that I like them much or care a *bajocco* for Vernon,
But I am slow at Italian, have not many English acquaintance,
And I am asked, in short, and am not good at excuses.
Middle-class people these, bankers very likely, not wholly
Pure of the taint of the shop; will at table d'hôte and restaurant
Have their shilling's worth, their penny's pennyworth even:
Neither man's aristocracy this, nor God's, God knoweth!
Yet they are fairly descended, they give you to know, well connected;
Doubtless somewhere in some neighbourhood have, and are careful
    to keep, some   130
Threadbare-genteel relations, who in their turn are enchanted
Grandly among county people to introduce at assemblies
To the unpennied cadets our cousins with excellent fortunes.
Neither man's aristocracy this, nor God's, God knoweth!

VII. CLAUDE TO EUSTACE

AH, what a shame, indeed, to abuse these most worthy people!
Ah, what a sin to have sneered at their innocent rustic pretensions!
Is it not laudable really, this reverent worship of station?
Is it not fitting that wealth should tender this homage to culture?
Is it not touching to witness these efforts, if little availing,
Painfully made, to perform the old ritual service of manners?   140
Shall not devotion atone for the absence of knowledge? and fervour
Palliate, cover, the fault of a superstitious observance?
Dear, dear, what do I say? but, alas, just now, like Iago,
I can be nothing at all, if it is not critical wholly;
So in fantastic height, in coxcomb exaltation,
Here in the Garden I walk, can freely concede to the Maker
That the works of his hand are all very good: his creatures,
Beast of the field and fowl, he brings them before me; I name them;
That which I name them, they are,—the bird, the beast, and the
    cattle.
But for Adam,—alas, poor critical coxcomb Adam!   150
But for Adam there is not found an help-meet for him.

VIII. CLAUDE TO EUSTACE

No, great Dome of Agrippa, thou art not Christian! canst not,
Strip and replaster and daub and do what they will with thee, be so!
Here underneath the great porch of colossal Corinthian columns,
Here as I walk, do I dream of the Christian belfries above them?
Or on a bench as I sit and abide for long hours, till thy whole vast
Round grows dim as in dreams to my eyes, I repeople thy niches,
Not with the Martyrs, and Saints, and Confessors, and Virgins, and
　　children,
But with the mightier forms of an older, austerer worship;
And I recite to myself, how　　　　　　　　　　　　　　　160
　　　　　　　　Eager for battle here
　　　　Stood Vulcan, here matronal Juno,
　　　　　　And with the bow to his shoulder faithful
　　　　He who with pure dew laveth of Castaly
　　　　His flowing locks, who holdeth of Lycia
　　　　The oak forest and the wood that bore him,
　　　　　　Delos' and Patara's own Apollo.[1]

IX. CLAUDE TO EUSTACE

YET it is pleasant, I own it, to be in their company; pleasant,
Whatever else it may be, to abide in the feminine presence.
Pleasant, but wrong, will you say? But this happy, serene coexistence
Is to some poor soft souls, I fear, a necessity simple,　　　　171
Meat and drink and life, and music, filling with sweetness,
Thrilling with melody sweet, with harmonies strange overwhelming,
All the long-silent strings of an awkward, meaningless fabric.
Yet as for that, I could live, I believe, with children; to have those
Pure and delicate forms encompassing, moving about you,

[1] Hic avidus stetit
　　Vulcanus, hic matrona Juno, et
　　　Nunquam humeris positurus arcum,
　　Qui rore puro Castaliæ lavit
　　Crines solutos, qui Lyciæ tenet
　　　Dumeta natalemque silvam,
　　　　Delius et Patareus Apollo.

This were enough, I could think; and truly with glad resignation
Could from the dream of romance, from the fever of flushed
    adolescence,
Look to escape and subside into peaceful avuncular functions.
Nephews and nieces! alas, for as yet I have none! and, moreover, 180
Mothers are jealous, I fear me, too often, too rightfully; fathers
Think they have title exclusive to spoiling their own little darlings;
And by the law of the land, in despite of Malthusian doctrine,
No sort of proper provision is made for that most patriotic,
Most meritorious subject, the childless and bachelor uncle.

X. CLAUDE TO EUSTACE

YE, too, marvellous Twain, that erect on the Monte Cavallo
Stand by your rearing steeds in the grace of your motionless move-
    ment,
Stand with your upstretched arms and tranquil regardant faces,
Stand as instinct with life in the might of immutable manhood,—
O ye mighty and strange, ye ancient divine ones of Hellas,   190
Are ye Christian too? to convert and redeem and renew you,
Will the brief form have sufficed, that a Pope has set up on the apex
Of the Egyptian stone that o'ertops you, the Christian symbol?
    And ye, silent, supreme in serene and victorious marble,
Ye that encircle the walls of the stately Vatican chambers,
Juno and Ceres, Minerva, Apollo, the Muses and Bacchus,
Ye unto whom far and near come posting the Christian pilgrims,
Ye that are ranged in the halls of the mystic Christian Pontiff,
Are ye also baptized? are ye of the kingdom of Heaven?
Utter, O some one, the word that shall reconcile Ancient and
    Modern!   200
Am I to turn me for this unto thee, great Chapel of Sixtus?

XI. CLAUDE TO EUSTACE

THESE are the facts. The uncle, the elder brother, the squire (a
Little embarrassed, I fancy), resides in the family place in
Cornwall, of course; 'Papa is in business,' Mary informs me;
He's a good sensible man, whatever his trade is. The mother

Is—shall I call it fine?—herself she would tell you refined, and
Greatly, I fear me, looks down on my bookish and maladroit manners;
Somewhat affecteth the blue; would talk to me often of poets;
Quotes, which I hate, Childe Harold; but also appreciates Words-
    worth;
Sometimes adventures on Schiller; and then to religion diverges; 210
Questions me much about Oxford; and yet, in her loftiest flights still
Grates the fastidious ear with the slightly mercantile accent.

Is it contemptible, Eustace—I'm perfectly ready to think so,—
Is it,—the horrible pleasure of pleasing inferior people?
I am ashamed my own self; and yet true it is, if disgraceful,
That for the first time in life I am living and moving with freedom.
I, who never could talk to the people I meet with my uncle,—
I, who have always failed,—I, trust me, can suit the Trevellyns;
I, believe me,—great conquest,—am liked by the country bankers.
And I am glad to be liked, and like in return very kindly.   220
So it proceeds; *Laissez faire, laissez aller,*—such is the watchword.
Well, I know there are thousands as pretty and hundreds as pleasant,
Girls by the dozen as good, and girls in abundance with polish
Higher and manners more perfect than Susan or Mary Trevellyn.
Well, I know, after all, it is only juxtaposition,—
Juxtaposition, in short; and what is juxtaposition?

XII. CLAUDE TO EUSTACE

But I am in for it now,—*laissez faire,* of a truth, *laissez aller.*
Yes, I am going,—I feel it, I feel and cannot recall it,—
Fusing with this thing and that, entering into all sorts of relations,
Tying I know not what ties, which, whatever they are, I know one
    thing,   230
Will, and must, woe is me, be one day painfully broken,—
Broken with painful remorses, with shrinkings of soul, and relentings,
Foolish delays, more foolish evasions, most foolish renewals.
But I have made the step, have quitted the ship of Ulysses;
Quitted the sea and the shore, passed into the magical island;

Yet on my lips is the *moly*, medicinal, offered of Hermes.
I have come into the precinct, the labyrinth closes around me,
Path into path rounding slyly; I pace slowly on, and the fancy,
Struggling awhile to sustain the long sequences, weary, bewildered,
Fain must collapse in despair; I yield, I am lost, and know nothing;
Yet in my bosom unbroken remaineth the clue; I shall use it.   241
Lo, with the rope on my loins I descend through the fissure; I
    sink, yet
Inly secure in the strength of invisible arms up above me;
Still, wheresoever I swing, wherever to shore, or to shelf, or
Floor of cavern untrodden, shell-sprinkled, enchanting, I know l
Yet shall one time feel the strong cord tighten about me,—
Feel it, relentless, upbear me from spots I would rest in; and
    though the
Rope sway wildly, I faint, crags wound me, from crag unto crag re-
Bounding, or, wide in the void, I die ten deaths, ere the end I
Yet shall plant firm foot on the broad lofty spaces I quit, shall   250
Feel underneath me again the great massy strengths of abstraction,
Look yet abroad from the height o'er the sea whose salt wave I have
    tasted.

XIII. GEORGINA TREVELLYN TO LOUISA ——

DEAREST LOUISA,—Inquire, if you please, about Mr. Claude ——.
He has been once at R., and remembers meeting the H.s.
Harriet L., perhaps, may be able to tell you about him.
It is an awkward youth, but still with very good manners;
Not without prospects, we hear; and, George says, highly connected.
Georgy declares it absurd, but Mamma is alarmed and insists he has
Taken up strange opinions, and may be turning a Papist.
Certainly once he spoke of a daily service he went to.   260
'Where?' we asked, and he laughed and answered, 'At the Pantheon.'
This was a temple, you know, and now is a Catholic church; and
Though it is said that Mazzini has sold it for Protestant service,
Yet I suppose this change can hardly as yet be effected.
Adieu again,—evermore, my dearest, your loving Georgina.

P.S. BY MARY TREVELLYN

I AM to tell you, you say, what I think of our last new acquaintance.
Well, then, I think that George has a very fair right to be jealous.
I do not like him much, though I do not dislike being with him.
He is what people call, I suppose, a superior man, and
Certainly seems so to me; but I think he is terribly selfish.   270

Alba, thou findest me still, and, Alba, thou findest me ever,
   Now from the Capitol steps, now over Titus's Arch,
Here from the large grassy spaces that spread from the Lateran portal,
   Towering o'er aqueduct lines lost in perspective between,
Or from a Vatican window, or bridge, or the high Coliseum,
   Clear by the garlanded line cut of the Flavian ring.
Beautiful can I not call thee, and yet thou hast power to o'ermaster.
   Power of mere beauty; in dreams, Alba, thou hauntest me still.
Is it religion? I ask me; or is it a vain superstition?
   Slavery abject and gross? service, too feeble, of truth?   280
Is it an idol I bow to, or is it a god that I worship?
   Do I sink back on the old, or do I soar from the mean?
So through the city I wander and question, unsatisfied ever,
   Reverent so I accept, doubtful because I revere.

CANTO II

Is it illusion? or does there a spirit from perfecter ages,
   Here, even yet, amid loss, change, and corruption abide?
Does there a spirit we know not, though seek, though we find, compre-
      hend not,
   Here to entice and confuse, tempt and evade us, abide?
Lives in the exquisite grace of the column disjointed and single,
   Haunts the rude masses of brick garlanded gayly with vine,
E'en in the turret fantastic surviving that springs from the ruin,
   E'en in the people itself? is it illusion or not?
Is it illusion or not that attracteth the pilgrim transalpine,
   Brings him a dullard and dunce hither to pry and to stare?   10
Is it illusion or not that allures the barbarian stranger,
   Brings him with gold to the shrine, brings him in arms to the gate?

I. CLAUDE TO EUSTACE

WHAT do the people say, and what does the government do?—you
Ask, and I know not at all. Yet fortune will favour your hopes; and
I, who avoided it all, am fated, it seems, to describe it.
I, who nor meddle nor make in politics,—I who sincerely
Put not my trust in leagues nor any suffrage by ballot,
Never predicted Parisian millenniums, never beheld a
New Jerusalem coming down dressed like a bride out of heaven
Right on the Place de la Concorde,—I, nevertheless, let me say it,   20
Could in my soul of souls, this day, with the Gaul at the gates, shed
One true tear for thee, thou poor little Roman Republic!
What, with the German restored, with Sicily safe to the Bourbon,
Not leave one poor corner for native Italian exertion?
France, it is foully done! and you, poor foolish England,—
You, who a twelvemonth ago said nations must choose for them-
      selves, you
Could not, of course, interfere,—you, now, when a nation has
      chosen——

Pardon this folly! *The Times* will, of course, have announced the
   occasion,
Told you the news of to-day; and although it was slightly in error
When it proclaimed as a fact the Apollo was sold to a Yankee,   30
You may believe when it tells you the French are at Civita Vecchia.

II. CLAUDE TO EUSTACE

DULCE it is, and *decorum*, no doubt, for the country to fall,—to
Offer one's blood an oblation to Freedom, and die for the Cause; yet
Still, individual culture is also something, and no man
Finds quite distinct the assurance that he of all others is called on,
Or would be justified, even, in taking away from the world that
Precious creature, himself. Nature sent him here to abide here,
Else why sent him at all? Nature wants him still, it is likely.
On the whole, we are meant to look after ourselves; it is certain
Each has to eat for himself, digest for himself, and in general   40
Care for his own dear life, and see to his own preservation;
Nature's intentions, in most things uncertain, in this are decisive;
Which, on the whole, I conjecture the Romans will follow, and I
   shall.
   So we cling to our rocks like limpets; Ocean may bluster,
Over and under and round us; we open our shells to imbibe our
Nourishment, close them again, and are safe, fulfilling the purpose
Nature intended,—a wise one, of course, and a noble, we doubt not.
Sweet it may be and decorous, perhaps, for the country to die; but,
On the whole, we conclude the Romans won't do it, and I shan't.

III. CLAUDE TO EUSTACE

WILL they fight? They say so. And will the French? I can hardly,   50
Hardly think so; and yet——He is come, they say, to Palo,
He is passed from Monterone, at Santa Severa
He hath laid up his guns. But the Virgin, the Daughter of Roma,
She hath despised thee and laughed thee to scorn,—the Daughter of
   Tiber,
She hath shaken her head and built barricades against thee!
Will they fight? I believe it. Alas! 'tis ephemeral folly,

Vain and ephemeral folly, of course, compared with pictures,
Statues, and antique gems!—Indeed: and yet indeed too,
Yet, methought, in broad day did I dream,—tell it not in St. James's,
Whisper it not in thy courts, O Christ Church!—yet did I, waking,
Dream of a cadence that sings, *Si tombent nos jeunes héros, la*   61
Terre en produit de nouveaux contre vous tous prêts à se battre;
Dreamt of great indignations and angers transcendental,
Dreamt of a sword at my side and a battle-horse underneath me.

IV. CLAUDE TO EUSTACE

Now supposing the French or the Neapolitan soldier
Should by some evil chance come exploring the Maison Serny
(Where the family English are all to assemble for safety),
Am I prepared to lay down my life for the British female?
Really, who knows? One has bowed and talked, till, little by little,
All the natural heat has escaped of the chivalrous spirit.   70
Oh, one conformed, of course; but one doesn't die for good manners,
Stab or shoot, or be shot, by way of a graceful attention.
No, if it should be at all, it should be on the barricades there;
Should I incarnadine ever this inky pacifical finger,
Sooner far should it be for this vapour of Italy's freedom,
Sooner far by the side of the d——d and dirty plebeians.
Ah, for a child in the street I could strike; for the full-blown lady——
Somehow, Eustace, alas! I have not felt the vocation.
Yet these people of course will expect, as of course, my protection,
Vernon in radiant arms stand forth for the lovely Georgina,   80
And to appear, I suppose, were but common civility. Yes, and
Truly I do not desire they should either be killed or offended.
Oh, and of course you will say, 'When the time comes, you will be
    ready.'
Ah, but before it comes, am I to presume it will be so?
What I cannot feel now, am I to suppose that I shall feel?
Am I not free to attend for the ripe and indubious instinct?
Am I forbidden to wait for the clear and lawful perception?
Is it the calling of man to surrender his knowledge and insight
For the mere venture of what may, perhaps, be the virtuous action?

Must we, walking our earth, discerning a little, and hoping   90
Some plain visible task shall yet for our hands be assigned us,—
Must we abandon the future for fear of omitting the present,
Quit our own fireside hopes at the alien call of a neighbour,
To the mere possible shadow of Deity offer the victim?
And is all this, my friend, but a weak and ignoble refining,
Wholly unworthy the head or the heart of Your Own Correspondent?

V. CLAUDE TO EUSTACE

YES, we are fighting at last, it appears. This morning as usual,
Murray, as usual, in hand, I enter the Caffè Nuovo;
Seating myself with a sense as it were of a change in the weather,
Not understanding, however, but thinking mostly of Murray,   100
And, for to-day is their day, of the Campidoglio Marbles,
Caffè-latte! I call to the waiter,—and *Non c' è latte*,
This is the answer he makes me, and this the sign of a battle.
So I sit; and truly they seem to think anyone else more
Worthy than me of attention. I wait for my milkless *nero*,
Free to observe undistracted all sorts and sizes of persons,
Blending civilian and soldier in strangest costume, coming in, and
Gulping in hottest haste, still standing, their coffee,—withdrawing
Eagerly, jangling a sword on the steps, or jogging a musket
Slung to the shoulder behind. They are fewer, moreover, than usual,
Much, and silenter far; and so I begin to imagine   III
Something is really afloat. Ere I leave, the Caffè is empty,
Empty too the streets, in all its length the Corso
Empty, and empty I see to my right and left the Condotti.
   Twelve o'clock, on the Pincian Hill, with lots of English,
Germans, Americans, French,—the Frenchmen, too, are pro-
      tected,—
So we stand in the sun, but afraid of a probable shower;
So we stand and stare, and see, to the left of St. Peter's,
Smoke, from the cannon, white,—but that is at intervals only,—
Black, from a burning house, we suppose, by the Cavalleggieri; 120
And we believe we discern some lines of men descending
Down through the vineyard-slopes, and catch a bayonet gleaming.

Every ten minutes, however,—in this there is no misconception,—
Comes a great white puff from behind Michael Angelo's dome, and
After a space the report of a real big gun,—not the Frenchman's?—
That must be doing some work. And so we watch and conjecture.

Shortly, an Englishman comes, who says he has been to St. Peter's,
Seen the Piazza and troops, but that is all he can tell us;
So we watch and sit, and, indeed, it begins to be tiresome.—
All this smoke is outside; when it has come to the inside,   130
It will be time, perhaps, to descend and retreat to our houses.

Half-past one, or two. The report of small arms frequent,
Sharp and savage indeed; that cannot all be for nothing:
So we watch and wonder; but guessing is tiresome, very.
Weary of wondering, watching, and guessing, and gossiping idly,
Down I go, and pass through the quiet streets with the knots of
National Guards patrolling, and flags hanging out at the windows,
English, American, Danish,—and, after offering to help an
Irish family moving *en masse* to the Maison Serny,
After endeavouring idly to minister balm to the trembling   140
Quinquagenarian fears of two lone British spinsters,
Go to make sure of my dinner before the enemy enter.
But by this there are signs of stragglers returning; and voices
Talk, though you don't believe it, of guns and prisoners taken;
And on the walls you read the first bulletin of the morning.—
This is all that I saw, and all I know of the battle.

VI. CLAUDE TO EUSTACE

VICTORY! VICTORY!—Yes! ah, yes, thou republican Zion,
Truly the kings of the earth are gathered and gone by together;
Doubtless they marvelled to witness such things, were astonished,
    and so forth.
Victory! Victory! Victory!—Ah, but it is, believe me,   150
Easier, easier far, to intone the chant of the martyr
Than to indite any pæan of any victory. Death may
Sometimes be noble; but life, at the best, will appear an illusion.
While the great pain is upon us, it is great; when it is over,
Why, it is over. The smoke of the sacrifice rises to heaven,

Of a sweet savour, no doubt, to Somebody; but on the altar,
Lo, there is nothing remaining but ashes and dirt and ill odour.

　So it stands, you perceive; the labial muscles that swelled with
Vehement evolution of yesterday Marseillaises,
Articulations sublime of defiance and scorning, to-day col-　160
Lapse and languidly mumble, while men and women and papers
Scream and re-scream to each other the chorus of Victory. Well, but
I am thankful they fought, and glad that the Frenchmen were beaten.

VII. CLAUDE TO EUSTACE

So, I have seen a man killed! An experience that, among others!
Yes, I suppose I have; although I can hardly be certain,
And in a court of justice could never declare I had seen it.
But a man was killed, I am told, in a place where I saw
Something; a man was killed, I am told, and I saw something.

　I was returning home from St. Peter's; Murray, as usual,
Under my arm, I remember; had crossed the St. Angelo bridge;
　　and　170
Moving towards the Condotti, had got to the first barricade, when
Gradually, thinking still of St. Peter's, I became conscious
Of a sensation of movement opposing me,—tendency this way
(Such as one fancies may be in a stream when the wave of the tide is
Coming and not yet come,—a sort of poise and retention);
So I turned, and, before I turned, caught sight of stragglers
Heading a crowd, it is plain, that is coming behind that corner.
Looking up, I see windows filled with heads; the Piazza,
Into which you remember the Ponte St. Angelo enters,　179
Since I passed, has thickened with curious groups; and now the
Crowd is coming, has turned, has crossed that last barricade, is
Here at my side. In the middle they drag at something. What is it?
Ha! bare swords in the air, held up! There seem to be voices
Pleading and hands putting back; official, perhaps; but the swords
　　are
Many, and bare in the air. In the air? They descend; they are smiting,
Hewing, chopping—At what? In the air once more upstretched!
　　And

Is it blood that's on them? Yes, certainly blood! Of whom, then?
Over whom is the cry of this furor of exultation?
　While they are skipping and screaming, and dancing their caps on
　　the points of
Swords and bayonets, I to the outskirts back, and ask a　　　　190
Mercantile-seeming bystander, 'What is it?' and he, looking always
That way, makes me answer, 'A Priest, who was trying to fly to
The Neapolitan army,'—and thus explains the proceeding.
　You didn't see the dead man? No;—I began to be doubtful;
I was in black myself, and didn't know what mightn't happen;—
But a National Guard close by me, outside of the hubbub,
Broke his sword with slashing a broad hat covered with dust,—and
Passing away from the place with Murray under my arm, and
Stooping, I saw through the legs of the people the legs of a body.
　You are the first, do you know, to whom I have mentioned the
　　matter.　　　　　　　　　　　　　　　　　　　　　200
Whom should I tell it to, else?—these girls?—the Heavens forbid
　it!—
Quidnuncs at Monaldini's?—idlers upon the Pincian?
　If I rightly remember, it happened on that afternoon when
Word of the nearer approach of a new Neapolitan army
First was spread. I began to bethink me of Paris Septembers,
Thought I could fancy the look of the old 'Ninety-two. On that
　　evening
Three or four, or, it may be, five, of these people were slaughtered.
Some declare they had, one of them, fired on a sentinel; others
Say they were only escaping; a Priest, it is currently stated,
Stabbed a National Guard on the very Piazza Colonna:　　　210
History, Rumour of Rumours, I leave it to thee to determine!
　But I am thankful to say the government seems to have strength to
Put it down; it has vanished, at least; the place is most peaceful.
Through the Trastevere walking last night, at nine of the clock, I
Found no sort of disorder; I crossed by the Island-bridges,
So by the narrow streets to the Ponte Rotto, and onwards
Thence by the Temple of Vesta, away to the great Coliseum,
Which at the full of the moon is an object worthy a visit.

VIII. GEORGINA TREVELLYN TO LOUISA ——

ONLY think, dearest Louisa, what fearful scenes we have witnessed!—

*   *   *   *   *   *   *   *

George has just seen Garibaldi, dressed up in a long white cloak, on
Horseback, riding by, with his mounted negro behind him: 221
This is a man, you know, who came from America with him,
Out of the woods, I suppose, and uses a *lasso* in fighting,
Which is, I don't quite know, but a sort of noose, I imagine;
This he throws on the heads of the enemy's men in a battle,
Pulls them into his reach, and then most cruelly kills them:
Mary does not believe, but we heard it from an Italian.
Mary allows she was wrong about Mr. Claude *being selfish*;
He was *most* useful and kind on the terrible thirtieth of April.
Do not write here any more; we are starting directly for Florence:
We should be off to-morrow, if only Papa could get horses;   231
All have been seized everywhere for the use of this dreadful Mazzini.

P.S.
   Mary has seen thus far.—I am really so angry, Louisa,—
Quite out of patience, my dearest! What can the man be intending?
I am quite tired; and Mary, who might bring him to in a moment,
Lets him go on as he likes, and neither will help nor dismiss him.

IX. CLAUDE TO EUSTACE

IT is most curious to see what a power a few calm words (in
Merely a brief proclamation) appear to possess on the people.
Order is perfect, and peace; the city is utterly tranquil;
And one cannot conceive that this easy and *nonchalant* crowd, that
Flows like a quiet stream through street and market-place, entering
Shady recesses and bays of church, *osteria*, and *caffè*,   242
Could in a moment be changed to a flood as of molten lava,
Boil into deadly wrath and wild homicidal delusion.
   Ah, 'tis an excellent race,—and even in old degradation,
Under a rule that enforces to flattery, lying, and cheating,
E'en under Pope and Priest, a nice and natural people.

Oh, could they but be allowed this chance of redemption!—but
    clearly
That is not likely to be. Meantime, notwithstanding all journals,
Honour for once to the tongue and the pen of the eloquent writer!
Honour to speech! and all honour to thee, thou noble Mazzini! 251

X. CLAUDE TO EUSTACE

I AM in love, meantime, you think; no doubt you would think so.
I am in love, you say; with those letters, of course, you would say so.
I am in love, you declare. I think not so; yet I grant you
It is a pleasure indeed to converse with this girl. Oh, rare gift,
Rare felicity, this! she can talk in a rational way, can
Speak upon subjects that really are matters of mind and of thinking,
Yet in perfection retain her simplicity; never, one moment,
Never, however you urge it, however you tempt her, consents to
Step from ideas and fancies and loving sensations to those vain 260
Conscious understandings that vex the minds of man-kind.
No, though she talk, it is music; her fingers desert not the keys; 'tis
Song, though you hear in the song the articulate vocables sounded,
Syllabled singly and sweetly the words of melodious meaning.
    I am in love, you say: I do not think so, exactly.

XI. CLAUDE TO EUSTACE

THERE are two different kinds, I believe, of human attraction:
One which simply disturbs, unsettles, and makes you uneasy,
And another that poises, retains, and fixes and holds you.
I have no doubt, for myself, in giving my voice for the latter.
I do not wish to be moved, but growing where I was growing, 270
There more truly to grow, to live where as yet I had languished.
I do not like being moved: for the will is excited; and action
Is a most dangerous thing; I tremble for something factitious,
Some malpractice of heart and illegitimate process;
We are so prone to these things with our terrible notions of duty.

XII. CLAUDE TO EUSTACE

AH, let me look, let me watch, let me wait, unhurried, unprompted!

Bid me not venture on aught that could alter or end what is present!
Say not, Time flies, and Occasion, that never returns, is departing!
Drive me not out, ye ill angels with fiery swords, from my Eden,
Waiting, and watching, and looking! Let love be its own inspiration!
Shall not a voice, if a voice there must be, from the airs that environ,
Yea, from the conscious heavens, without our knowledge or effort,
Break into audible words? And love be its own inspiration?   283

XIII. CLAUDE TO EUSTACE

WHEREFORE and how I am certain, I hardly can tell; but it *is* so.
She doesn't like me, Eustace; I think she never will like me.
Is it my fault, as it is my misfortune, my ways are not her ways?
Is it my fault, that my habits and modes are dissimilar wholly?
'Tis not her fault, 'tis her nature, her virtue, to misapprehend them:
'Tis not her fault, 'tis her beautiful nature, not ever to know me.
Hopeless it seems,—yet I cannot, though hopeless, determine to
     leave it: 290
She goes,—therefore I go; she moves,—I move, not to lose her.

XIV. CLAUDE TO EUSTACE

OH, 'tisn't manly, of course, 'tisn't manly, this method of wooing;
'Tisn't the way very likely to win. For the woman, they tell you,
Ever prefers the audacious, the wilful, the vehement hero;
She has no heart for the timid, the sensitive soul; and for know-
     ledge,—
Knowledge, O ye Gods!—When did they appreciate knowledge?
Wherefore should they, either? I am sure I do not desire it.
   Ah, and I feel too, Eustace, she cares not a tittle about me!
(Care about me, indeed! and do I really expect it?)
But my manner offends; my ways are wholly repugnant;   300
Every word that I utter estranges, hurts, and repels her;
Every moment of bliss that I gain, in her exquisite presence,
Slowly, surely, withdraws her, removes her, and severs her from me.
Not that I care very much!—any way, I escape from the boy's own
Folly, to which I am prone, of loving where it is easy.

Not that I mind very much! Why should I? I am not in love, and
Am prepared, I think, if not by previous habit,
Yet in the spirit beforehand for this and all that is like it;
It is an easier matter for us contemplative creatures,
Us, upon whom the pressure of action is laid so lightly;   310
We, discontented indeed with things in particular, idle,
Sickly, complaining, by faith in the vision of things in general
Manage to hold on our way without, like others around us,
Seizing the nearest arm to comfort, help, and support us.
Yet, after all, my Eustace, I know but little about it,
All I can say for myself, for present alike and for past, is,
Mary Trevellyn, Eustace, is certainly worth your acquaintance.
You couldn't come, I suppose, as far as Florence to see her?

XV. GEORGINA TREVELLYN TO LOUISA ——

. . . . . . , TO-MORROW we're starting for Florence,
Truly rejoiced, you may guess, to escape from republican terrors;
Mr. C. and Papa to escort us; we by *vettura*   321
Through Siena, and Georgy to follow and join us by Leghorn.
Then——Ah, what shall I say, my dearest? I tremble in thinking!
You will imagine my feelings,—the blending of hope and of sorrow!
How can I bear to abandon Papa and Mamma and my Sisters?
Dearest Louisa, indeed it is very alarming; but trust me
Ever, whatever may change, to remain your loving Georgina.

P.S. BY MARY TREVELLYN

. . . . . . 'Do I like Mr. Claude any better?'
I am to tell you,—and, 'Pray, is it Susan or I that attract him?'
This he never has told, but Georgina could certainly ask him.   330
All I can say for myself is, alas! that he rather repels me.
There! I think him agreeable, but also a little repulsive.
So be content, dear Louisa; for one satisfactory marriage
Surely will do in one year for the family you would establish;
Neither Susan nor I shall afford you the joy of a second.

P.S. BY GEORGINA TREVELLYN

MR. CLAUDE, you must know, is behaving a little bit better;
He and Papa are great friends; but he really is too *shilly-shally,*—
So unlike George! Yet I hope that the matter is going on fairly.
I shall, however, get George, before he goes, to say something.
Dearest Louise, how delightful to bring young people together! 340

Is it to Florence we follow, or are we to tarry yet longer,
  E'en amid clamour of arms, here in the city of old,
Seeking from clamour of arms in the Past and the Arts to be hidden,
  Vainly 'mid Arts and the Past seeking one life to forget?
Ah, fair shadow, scarce seen, go forth! for anon he shall follow,—
  He that beheld thee, anon, whither thou leadest, must go!
Go, and the wise, loving Muse, she also will follow and find thee!
  She, should she linger in Rome, were not dissevered from thee!

CANTO III

Yet to the wondrous St. Peter's, and yet to the solemn Rotonda,
Mingling with heroes and gods, yet to the Vatican walls,
Yet may we go, and recline, while a whole mighty world seems above us
Gathered and fixed to all time into one roofing supreme;
Yet may we, thinking on these things, exclude what is meaner around us;
Yet, at the worst of the worst, books and a chamber remain;
Yet may we think, and forget, and possess our souls in resistance.—
Ah, but away from the stir, shouting, and gossip of war,
Where, upon Apennine slope, with the chestnut the oak-trees immingle,
Where amid odorous copse bridle-paths wander and wind, 10
Where under mulberry-branches the diligent rivulet sparkles,
Or amid cotton and maize peasants their water-works ply,
Where, over fig-tree and orange in tier upon tier still repeated,
Garden on garden upreared, balconies step to the sky,—
Ah, that I were, far away from the crowd and the streets of the city,
Under the vine-trellis laid, O my beloved, with thee!

I. MARY TREVELLYN TO MISS ROPER,—*on the way to Florence*

WHY doesn't Mr. Claude come with us? you ask.—We don't know.
You should know better than we. He talked of the Vatican marbles;
But I can't wholly believe that this was the actual reason,—
He was so ready before, when we asked him to come and escort us.
Certainly he is odd, my dear Miss Roper. To change so 21
Suddenly, just for a whim, was not quite fair to the party,—
Not quite right. I declare, I really almost am offended:
I, his great friend, as you say, have doubtless a title to be so.
Not that I greatly regret it, for dear Georgina distinctly
Wishes for nothing so much as to show her adroitness. But, oh, my
Pen will not write any more;—let us say nothing further about it.

    *   *   *   *   *   *   *   *

Yes, my dear Miss Roper, I certainly called him repulsive;
So I think him, but cannot be sure I have used the expression

Quite as your pupil should; yet he does most truly repel me.   30
Was it to you I made use of the word? or who was it told you?
Yes, repulsive; observe, it is but when he talks of ideas
That he is quite unaffected, and free, and expansive, and easy;
I could pronounce him simply a cold intellectual being.—
When does he make advances?—He thinks that women should
     woo him;
Yet, if a girl should do so, would be but alarmed and disgusted.
She that should love him must look for small love in return,—like
     the ivy
On the stone wall, must expect but a rigid and niggard support, and
E'en to get that must go searching all round with her humble
     embraces.

II. CLAUDE TO EUSTACE,—*from Rome*

TELL me, my friend, do you think that the grain would sprout in the
     furrow,   40
Did it not truly accept as its *summum* and *ultimum bonum*
That mere common and may-be indifferent soil it is set in?
Would it have force to develop and open its young cotyledons,
Could it compare, and reflect, and examine one thing with another?
Would it endure to accomplish the round of its natural functions,
Were it endowed with a sense of the general scheme of existence?
   While from Marseilles in the steamer we voyaged to Civita
     Vecchia,
Vexed in the squally seas as we lay by Capraja and Elba,
Standing, uplifted, alone on the heaving poop of the vessel,
Looking around on the waste of the rushing incurious billows,   50
'This is Nature,' I said: 'we are born as it were from her waters,
Over her billows that buffet and beat us, her offspring uncared-for,
Casting one single regard of a painful victorious knowledge,
Into her billows that buffet and beat us we sink and are swallowed.'
This was the sense in my soul, as I swayed with the poop of the
     steamer;
And as unthinking I sat in the hall of the famed Ariadne,
Lo, it looked at me there from the face of a Triton in marble.

It is the simpler thought, and I can believe it the truer.
Let us not talk of growth; we are still in our Aqueous Ages.

III. CLAUDE TO EUSTACE

FAREWELL, Politics, utterly! What can I do? I cannot   60
Fight, you know; and to talk I am wholly ashamed. And although I
Gnash my teeth when I look in your French or your English papers,
What is the good of that? Will swearing, I wonder, mend matters?
Cursing and scolding repel the assailants? No, it is idle;
No, whatever befalls, I will hide, will ignore or forget it.
Let the tail shift for itself; I will bury my head. And what's the
Roman Republic to me, or I to the Roman Republic?
    Why not fight?—In the first place, I haven't so much as a musket;
In the next, if I had, I shouldn't know how I should use it;
In the third, just at present I'm studying ancient marbles;   70
In the fourth, I consider I owe my life to my country;
In the fifth,—I forget, but four good reasons are ample.
Meantime, pray, let 'em fight, and be killed. I delight in devotion.
So that I 'list not, hurrah for the glorious army of martyrs!
Sanguis martyrum semen Ecclesiæ; though it would seem this
Church is indeed of the purely Invisible, Kingdom-come kind:
Militant here on earth! Triumphant, of course, then, elsewhere!
Ah, good Heaven, but I would I were out far away from the pother!

IV. CLAUDE TO EUSTACE

NOT, as we read in the words of the olden-time inspiration,
Are there two several trees in the place we are set to abide in;   80
But on the apex most high of the Tree of Life in the Garden,
Budding, unfolding, and falling, decaying and flowering ever,
Flowering is set and decaying the transient blossom of Knowledge,—
Flowering alone, and decaying, the needless, unfruitful blossom.
    Or as the cypress-spires by the fair-flowing stream Hellespontine,
Which from the mythical tomb of the godlike Protesilaüs
Rose sympathetic in grief to his love-lorn Laodamia,
Evermore growing, and, when in their growth to the prospect
    attaining,

Over the low sea-banks, of the fatal Ilian city,
Withering still at the sight which still they upgrow to encounter. 90
   Ah, but ye that extrude from the ocean your helpless faces,
Ye over stormy seas leading long and dreary processions,
Ye, too, brood of the wind, whose coming is whence we discern not,
Making your nest on the wave, and your bed on the crested billow,
Skimming rough waters, and crowding wet sands that the tide shall
    return to,
Cormorants, ducks, and gulls, fill ye my imagination!
Let us not talk of growth; we are still in our Aqueous Ages.

V. MARY TREVELLYN TO MISS ROPER,—*from Florence*

DEAREST MISS ROPER,—Alas! we are all at Florence quite safe, and
You, we hear, are shut up! indeed, it is sadly distressing!
We were most lucky, they say, to get off when we did from the
    troubles. 100
Now you are really besieged! they tell us it soon will be over;
Only I hope and trust without any fight in the city.
Do you see Mr. Claude?—I thought he might do something for you.
I am quite sure on occasion he really would wish to be useful.
What is he doing? I wonder;—still studying Vatican marbles?
Letters, I hope, pass through. We trust your brother is better.

VI. CLAUDE TO EUSTACE

JUXTAPOSITION, in fine; and what is juxtaposition?
Look you, we travel along in the railway-carriage, or steamer,
And, *pour passer le temps*, till the tedious journey be ended,
Lay aside paper or book, to talk with the girl that is next one; 110
And, *pour passer le temps*, with the terminus all but in prospect,
Talk of eternal ties and marriages made in heaven.
   Ah, did we really accept with a perfect heart the illusion!
Ah, did we really believe that the Present indeed is the Only!
Or through all transmutation, all shock and convulsion of passion,
Feel we could carry undimmed, unextinguished, the light of our
    knowledge!
   But for his funeral train which the bridegroom sees in the distance,

Would he so joyfully, think you, fall in with the marriage-procession?
But for that final discharge, would he dare to enlist in that service?
But for that certain release, ever sign to that perilous contract?   120
But for that exit secure, ever bend to that treacherous doorway?—
Ah, but the bride, meantime,—do you think she sees it as he does?
  But for the steady fore-sense of a freer and larger existence,
Think you that man could consent to be circumscribed here into
    action?
But for assurance within of a limitless ocean divine, o'er
Whose great tranquil depths unconscious the wind-tost surface
Breaks into ripples of trouble that come and change and endure
    not,—
But that in this, of a truth, we have our being, and know it,
Think you we men could submit to live and move as we do here?
Ah, but the women,—God bless them! they don't think at all
    about it.   130
  Yet we must eat and drink, as you say. And as limited beings
Scarcely can hope to attain upon earth to an Actual Abstract,
Leaving to God contemplation, to His hands knowledge confiding,
Sure that in us if it perish, in Him it abideth and dies not,
Let us in His sight accomplish our petty particular doings,—
Yes, and contented sit down to the victual that He has provided.
Allah is great, no doubt, and Juxtaposition his prophet.
Ah, but the women, alas! they don't look at it in that way.
  Juxtaposition is great;—but, my friend, I fear me, the maiden
Hardly would thank or acknowledge the lover that sought to
    obtain her,   140
Not as the thing he would wish, but the thing he must even put up
    with,—
Hardly would tender her hand to the wooer that candidly told her
That she is but for a space, an *ad-interim* solace and pleasure,—
That in the end she shall yield to a perfect and absolute something,
Which I then for myself shall behold, and not another,—
Which, amid fondest endearments, meantime I forget not, for-
    sake not.
Ah, ye feminine souls, so loving and so exacting,

Since we cannot escape, must we even submit to deceive you?
Since so cruel is truth, sincerity shocks and revolts you,
Will you have us your slaves to lie to you, flatter and—leave you? 150

VII. CLAUDE TO EUSTACE

JUXTAPOSITION is great,—but, you tell me, affinity greater.
Ah, my friend, there are many affinities, greater and lesser,
Stronger and weaker; and each, by the favour of juxtaposition,
Potent, efficient, in force,—for a time; but none, let me tell you,
Save by the law of the land and the ruinous force of the will, ah,
None, I fear me, at last quite sure to be final and perfect.
Lo, as I pace in the street, from the peasant-girl to the princess,
Homo sum, nihil humani a me alienum puto,—
Vir sum, nihil fœminei,—and e'en to the uttermost circle,
All that is Nature's is I, and I all things that are Nature's.   160
Yes, as I walk, I behold, in a luminous, large intuition,
That I can be and become anything that I meet with or look at:
I am the ox in the dray, the ass with the garden-stuff panniers;
I am the dog in the doorway, the kitten that plays in the window,
On sunny slab of the ruin the furtive and fugitive lizard,
Swallow above me that twitters, and fly that is buzzing about me;
Yea, and detect, as I go, by a faint but a faithful assurance,
E'en from the stones of the street, as from rocks or trees of the forest,
Something of kindred, a common, though latent vitality, greet me;
And, to escape from our strivings, mistakings, misgrowths, and
     perversions,   170
Fain could demand to return to that perfect and primitive silence,
Fain be enfolded and fixed, as of old, in their rigid embraces.

VIII. CLAUDE TO EUSTACE

AND as I walk on my way, I behold them consorting and coupling;
Faithful it seemeth, and fond, very fond, very probably faithful;
All as I go on my way, with a pleasure sincere and unmingled.

  Life is beautiful, Eustace, entrancing, enchanting to look at;
As are the streets of a city we pace while the carriage is changing,
As is a chamber filled-in with harmonious, exquisite pictures,

Even so beautiful Earth; and could we eliminate only
This vile hungering impulse, this demon within us of craving,   180
Life were beatitude, living a perfect divine satisfaction.

IX. CLAUDE TO EUSTACE

MILD monastic faces in quiet collegiate cloisters:
So let me offer a single and celibatarian phrase, a
Tribute to those whom perhaps you do not believe I can honour.
But, from the tumult escaping, 'tis pleasant, of drumming and
    shouting,
Hither, oblivious awhile, to withdraw, of the fact or the falsehood,
And amid placid regards and mildly courteous greetings
Yield to the calm and composure and gentle abstraction that reign o'er
Mild monastic faces in quiet collegiate cloisters.

  Terrible word, Obligation! You should not, Eustace, you should
    not,   190
No, you should not have used it. But, oh, great Heavens, I repel it!
Oh, I cancel, reject, disavow, and repudiate wholly
Every debt in this kind, disclaim every claim, and dishonour,
Yea, my own heart's own writing, my soul's own signature! Ah, no!
I will be free in this; you shall not, none shall, bind me.
No, my friend, if you wish to be told, it was this above all things,
This that charmed me, ah, yes, even this, that she held me to nothing.
No, I could talk as I pleased; come close; fasten ties, as I fancied;
Bind and engage myself deep;—and lo, on the following morning
It was all e'en as before, like losings in games played for nothing. 200
Yes, when I came, with mean fears in my soul, with a semi-per-
    formance
At the first step breaking down in its pitiful rôle of evasion,
When to shuffle I came, to compromise, not meet, engagements,
Lo, with her calm eyes there she met me and knew nothing of it,—
Stood unexpecting, unconscious. *She* spoke not of obligations,
Knew not of debt,—ah, no, I believe you, for excellent reasons.

X. CLAUDE TO EUSTACE

HANG this thinking, at last! what good is it? oh, and what evil!

Oh, what mischief and pain! like a clock in a sick man's chamber,
Ticking and ticking, and still through each covert of slumber pursuing.
What shall I do to thee, O thou Preserver of Men? Have compassion; 210
Be favourable, and hear! Take from me this regal knowledge;
Let me, contented and mute, with the beasts of the field, my brothers,
Tranquilly, happily lie,—and eat grass, like Nebuchadnezzar!

XI. CLAUDE TO EUSTACE

TIBUR is beautiful, too, and the orchard slopes, and the Anio
Falling, falling yet, to the ancient lyrical cadence;
Tibur and Anio's tide; and cool from Lucretilis ever,
With the Digentian stream, and with the Bandusian fountain,
Folded in Sabine recesses, the valley and villa of Horace:—
So not seeing I sang; so seeing and listening say I,
Here as I sit by the stream, as I gaze at the cell of the Sibyl, 220
Here with Albunea's home and the grove of Tiburnus beside me;[1]
Tivoli beautiful is, and musical, O Teverone,
Dashing from mountain to plain, thy parted impetuous waters!
Tivoli's waters and rocks; and fair under Monte Gennaro
(Haunt even yet, I must think, as I wander and gaze, of the shadows,
Faded and pale, yet immortal, of Faunus, the Nymphs, and the Graces),
Fair in itself, and yet fairer with human completing creations,
Folded in Sabine recesses the valley and villa of Horace:—
So not seeing I sang; so now—Nor seeing, nor hearing,
Neither by waterfall lulled, nor folded in sylvan embraces, 230
Neither by cell of the Sibyl, nor stepping the Monte Gennaro,
Seated on Anio's bank, nor sipping Bandusian waters,
But on Montorio's height, looking down on the tile-clad streets, the
Cupolas, crosses, and domes, the bushes and kitchen-gardens,

[1] —— domus Albuneæ resonantis,
Et præceps Anio, et Tiburni lucus, et uda
Mobilibus pomaria rivis.

Which, by the grace of the Tiber, proclaim themselves Rome of the
    Romans,—
But on Montorio's height, looking forth to the vapoury mountains,
Cheating the prisoner Hope with illusions of vision and fancy,—
But on Montorio's height, with these weary soldiers by me,
Waiting till Oudinot enter, to reinstate Pope and Tourist.

XII. MARY TREVELLYN TO MISS ROPER

DEAR MISS ROPER,—It seems, George Vernon, before we left Rome,
    said   240
Something to Mr. Claude about what they call his attentions.
Susan, two nights ago, for the first time, heard this from Georgina.
It is *so* disagreeable and *so* annoying to think of!
If it could only be known, though we may never meet him again, that
It was all George's doing, and we were entirely unconscious,
It would extremely relieve—Your ever affectionate Mary.
P.S. (1)
  Here is your letter arrived this moment, just as I wanted.
So you have seen him,—indeed,—and guessed,—how dreadfully
    clever!
What did he really say? and what was your answer exactly?
Charming!—but wait for a moment, for I haven't read through the
    letter.   250
P.S. (2)
  Ah, my dearest Miss Roper, do just as you fancy about it.
If you think it sincerer to tell him I know of it, do so.
Though I should most extremely dislike it, I know I could manage.
It is the simplest thing, but surely wholly uncalled for.
Do as you please; you know I trust implicitly to you.
Say whatever is right and needful for ending the matter.
Only don't tell Mr. Claude, what I will tell you as a secret,
That I should like very well to show him myself I forget it.
P.S. (3)
  I am to say that the wedding is finally settled for Tuesday.
Ah, my dear Miss Roper, you surely, surely can manage   260

Not to let it appear that I know of that odious matter.
It would be pleasanter far for myself to treat it exactly
As if it had not occurred: and I do not think he would like it.
I must remember to add, that as soon as the wedding is over
We shall be off, I believe, in a hurry, and travel to Milan,
There to meet friends of Papa's, I am told, at the Croce di Malta;
Then I cannot say whither, but not at present to England.

XIII. CLAUDE TO EUSTACE

YES, on Montorio's height for a last farewell of the city,—
So it appears; though then I was quite uncertain about it.
So, however, it was. And now to explain the proceeding. 270
    I was to go, as I told you, I think, with the people to Florence.
Only, the day before, the foolish family Vernon
Made some uneasy remarks, as we walked to our lodging together,
As to intentions, forsooth, and so forth. I was astounded,
Horrified quite; and obtaining just then, as it happened, an offer
(No common favour) of seeing the great Ludovisi collection,
Why, I made this a pretence, and wrote that they must excuse me.
How could I go? Great Heavens! to conduct a permitted flirtation
Under those vulgar eyes, the observed of such observers!
Well, but I now, by a series of fine diplomatic inquiries, 280
Find from a sort of relation, a good and sensible woman,
Who is remaining at Rome with a brother too ill for removal,
That it was wholly unsanctioned, unknown,—not, I think, by
    Georgina:
She, however, ere this,—and that is the best of the story,—
She and the Vernon, thank Heaven, are wedded and gone—honey-
    mooning.
So—on Montorio's height for a last farewell of the city.
Tibur I have not seen, nor the lakes that of old I had dreamt of;
Tibur I shall not see, nor Anio's waters, nor deep en-
Folded in Sabine recesses the valley and villa of Horace;
Tibur I shall not see;—but something better I shall see. 290
    Twice I have tried before, and failed in getting the horses;
Twice I have tried and failed: this time it shall not be a failure.

Therefore farewell, ye hills, and ye, ye envineyarded ruins!
Therefore farewell, ye walls, palaces, pillars, and domes!
Therefore farewell, far seen, ye peaks of the mythic Albano,
Seen from Montorio's height, Tibur and Æsula's hills!
Ah, could we once, ere we go, could we stand, while, to ocean descending,
Sinks o'er the yellow dark plain slowly the yellow broad sun,
Stand, from the forest emerging at sunset, at once in the champaign,
Open, but studded with trees, chestnuts umbrageous and old,   300
E'en in those fair open fields that incurve to thy beautiful hollow,
Nemi, imbedded in wood, Nemi, inurned in the hill!—
Therefore farewell, ye plains, and ye hills, and the City Eternal!
Therefore farewell! We depart, but to behold you again!

CANTO IV

Eastward, or Northward, or West? I wander and ask as I wander,
  Weary, yet eager and sure, Where shall I come to my love?
Whitherward hasten to seek her? Ye daughters of Italy, tell me,
  Graceful and tender and dark, is she consorting with you?
Thou that out-climbest the torrent, that tendest thy goats to the summit,
  Call to me, child of the Alp, has she been seen on the heights?
Italy, farewell I bid thee! for whither she leads me, I follow.
  Farewell the vineyard! for I, where I but guess her, must go.
Weariness welcome, and labour, wherever it be, if at last it
  Bring me in mountain or plain into the sight of my love.   10

I. CLAUDE TO EUSTACE,—*from Florence*

GONE from Florence; indeed; and that is truly provoking;—
Gone to Milan, it seems; then I go also to Milan.
Five days now departed; but they can travel but slowly;—
I quicker far; and I know, as it happens, the house they will go to.—
Why, what else should I do? Stay here and look at the pictures,
Statues, and churches? Alack, I am sick of the statues and pictures!—
No, to Bologna, Parma, Piacenza, Lodi, and Milan,
Off go we to-night,—and the Venus go to the Devil!

II. CLAUDE TO EUSTACE,—*from Bellaggio*

GONE to Como, they said; and I have posted to Como.
There was a letter left; but the *cameriere* had lost it.   20
Could it have been for me? They came, however, to Como,
And from Como went by the boat,—perhaps to the Splügen,—
Or to the Stelvio, say, and the Tyrol; also it might be
By Porlezza across to Lugano, and so to the Simplon
Possibly, or the St. Gothard,—or possibly, too, to Baveno,
Orta, Turin, and elsewhere. Indeed, I am greatly bewildered.

III. CLAUDE TO EUSTACE,—*from Bellaggio*

I HAVE been up the Splügen, and on the Stelvio also:
Neither of these can I find they have followed; in no one inn, and

This would be odd, have they written their names. I have been to
    Porlezza;
There they have not been seen, and therefore not at Lugano.   30
What shall I do? Go on through the Tyrol, Switzerland, Deutschland,
Seeking, an inverse Saul, a kingdom, to find only asses?
    There is a tide, at least, in the *love* affairs of mortals,
Which, when taken at flood, leads on to the happiest fortune,—
Leads to the marriage-morn and the orange-flowers and the altar,
And the long lawful line of crowned joys to crowned joys suc-
    ceeding.—
Ah, it has ebbed with me! Ye gods, and when it was flowing,
Pitiful fool that I was, to stand fiddle-faddling in that way!

IV. CLAUDE TO EUSTACE,—*from Bellaggio*

I HAVE returned and found their names in the book at Como.
Certain it is I was right, and yet I am also in error.   40
Added in feminine hand, I read, *By the boat to Bellaggio.*—
So to Bellaggio again, with the words of her writing to aid me.
Yet at Bellaggio I find no trace, no sort of remembrance.
So I am here, and wait, and know every hour will remove them.

V. CLAUDE TO EUSTACE,—*from Bellaggio*

I HAVE but one chance left,—and that is going to Florence.
But it is cruel to turn. The mountains seem to demand me,—
Peak and valley from far to beckon and motion me onward.
Somewhere amid their folds she passes whom fain I would follow;
Somewhere among those heights she haply calls me to seek her.
Ah, could I hear her call! could I catch the glimpse of her raiment!
Turn, however, I must, though it seem I turn to desert her;   51
For the sense of the thing is simply to hurry to Florence,
Where the certainty yet may be learnt, I suppose, from the Ropers.

VI. MARY TREVELLYN, *from Lucerne,*
TO MISS ROPER, *at Florence*

DEAR MISS ROPER,—By this you are safely away, we are hoping,
Many a league from Rome; ere long we trust we shall see you.

How have you travelled? I wonder;—was Mr. Claude your com-
    panion?
As for ourselves, we went from Como straight to Lugano;
So by the Mount St. Gothard; we meant to go by Porlezza,
Taking the steamer, and stopping, as you had advised, at Bellaggio,
Two or three days or more; but this was suddenly altered,   60
After we left the hotel, on the very way to the steamer.
So we have seen, I fear, not one of the lakes in perfection.
    Well, he is not come; and now, I suppose, he will not come.
What will you think, meantime?—and yet I must really confess it;—
What will you say? I wrote him a note. We left in a hurry,
Went from Milan to Como, three days before we expected.
But I thought, if he came all the way to Milan, he really
Ought not to be disappointed: and so I wrote three lines to
Say I had heard he was coming, desirous of joining our party;—
If so, then I said, we had started for Como, and meant to   70
Cross the St. Gothard, and stay, we believed, at Lucerne, for the
    summer.
Was it wrong? and why, if it was, has it failed to bring him?
Did he not think it worth while to come to Milan? He knew (you
Told him) the house we should go to. Or may it, perhaps, have mis-
    carried?
Any way, now, I repent, and am heartily vexed that I wrote it.

There is a home on the shore of the Alpine sea, that upswelling
    High up the mountain-sides spreads in the hollow between;
Wilderness, mountain, and snow from the land of the olive conceal it;
    Under Pilatus's hill low by its river it lies:
Italy, utter the word, and the olive and vine will allure not,—   80
    Wilderness, forest, and snow will not the passage impede;
Italy, unto thy cities receding, the clue to recover,
    Hither, recovered the clue, shall not the traveller haste?

CANTO V

There is a city, upbuilt on the quays of the turbulent Arno,
Under Fiesole's heights,—thither are we to return?
There is a city that fringes the curve of the inflowing waters,
Under the perilous hill fringes the beautiful bay,—
Parthenope do they call thee?—the Siren, Neapolis, seated
Under Vesevus's hill,—are we receding to thee?—
Sicily, Greece, will invite, and the Orient;—or are we to turn to
England, which may after all be for its children the best?

I. MARY TREVELLYN, *at Lucerne,* TO MISS ROPER, *at Florence*

So you are really free, and living in quiet at Florence;
That is delightful news; you travelled slowly and safely;   10
Mr. Claude got you out; took rooms at Florence before you;
Wrote from Milan to say so; had left directly for Milan,
Hoping to find us soon;—*if he could, he would, you are certain.—*
Dear Miss Roper, your letter has made me exceedingly happy.
    You are quite sure, you say, he asked you about our intentions;
You had not heard as yet of Lucerne, but told him of Como.—
Well, perhaps he will come; however, I will not expect it.
Though you say you are sure,—*if he can, he will, you are certain.*
O my dear, many thanks from your ever affectionate Mary.

II. CLAUDE TO EUSTACE

Florence.

ACTION will furnish belief,—but will that belief be the true one? 20
This is the point, you know. However, it doesn't much matter.
What one wants, I suppose, is to predetermine the action,
So as to make it entail, not a chance-belief, but the true one.
Out of the question, you say; *if a thing isn't wrong, we may do it.*
Ah! but this *wrong,* you see—but I do not know that it matters.
Eustace, the Ropers are gone, and no one can tell me about them.

Pisa.

Pisa, they say they think, and so I follow to Pisa,

213

Hither and thither enquiring. I weary of making enquiries.
I am ashamed, I declare, of asking people about it.—
Who are your friends? You said you had friends who would certainly
   know them.   30

                                         Florence.

But it is idle, moping, and thinking, and trying to fix her
Image more and more in, to write the old perfect inscription
Over and over again upon every page of remembrance.
   I have settled to stay at Florence to wait for your answer.
Who are your friends? Write quickly and tell me. I wait for your
   answer.

III. MARY TREVELLYN TO MISS ROPER, *at Lucca Baths*

You are at Lucca Baths, you tell me, to stay for the summer;
Florence was quite too hot; you can't move further at present.
Will you not come, do you think, before the summer is over?
   Mr. C. got you out with very considerable trouble;
And he was useful and kind, and seemed so happy to serve you. 40
Didn't stay with you long, but talked very openly to you;
Made you almost his confessor, without appearing to know it,—
What about?—and you say you didn't need his confessions.
O my dear Miss Roper, I dare not trust what you tell me!
   Will he come, do you think? I am really so sorry for him!
They didn't give him my letter at Milan, I feel pretty certain.
You had told him Bellaggio. We didn't go to Bellaggio;
So he would miss our track, and perhaps never come to Lugano,
Where we were written in full, *To Lucerne across the St. Gothard.*
But he could write to you;—you would tell him where you were
   going.   50

IV. CLAUDE TO EUSTACE

Let me, then, bear to forget her. I will not cling to her falsely:
Nothing factitious or forced shall impair the old happy relation.
I will let myself go, forget, not try to remember;
I will walk on my way, accept the chances that meet me,

Freely encounter the world, imbibe these alien airs, and
Never ask if new feelings and thoughts are of her or of others.
Is she not changing, herself?—the old image would only delude me.
I will be bold, too, and change,—if it must be. Yet if in all things,
Yet if I do but aspire evermore to the Absolute only,
I shall be doing, I think, somehow, what she will be doing;—   60
I shall be thine, O my child, some way, though I know not in what
    way.
Let me submit to forget her; I must; I already forget her.

V. CLAUDE TO EUSTACE

UTTERLY vain is, alas! this attempt at the Absolute,—wholly!
I, who believed not in her, because I would fain believe nothing,
Have to believe as I may, with a wilful, unmeaning acceptance.
I, who refused to enfasten the roots of my floating existence
In the rich earth, cling now to the hard, naked rock that is left me.—
Ah! she was worthy, Eustace,—and that, indeed, is my comfort,—
Worthy a nobler heart than a fool such as I could have given.

YES, it relieves me to write, though I do not send, and the chance
    that   70
Takes may destroy my fragments. But as men pray, without asking
Whether One really exist to hear or do anything for them,—
Simply impelled by the need of the moment to turn to a Being
In a conception of whom there is freedom from all limitation,—
So in your image I turn to an *ens rationis* of friendship,
Even so write in your name I know not to whom nor in what wise.

THERE was a time, methought it was but lately departed,
When, if a thing was denied me, I felt I was bound to attempt it;
Choice alone should take, and choice alone should surrender.
There was a time, indeed, when I had not retired thus early,   80
Languidly thus, from pursuit of a purpose I once had adopted.
But it is over, all that! I have slunk from the perilous field in

Whose wild struggle of forces the prizes of life are contested.
It is over, all that! I am a coward, and know it.
Courage in me could be only factitious, unnatural, useless.

COMFORT has come to me here in the dreary streets of the city,
Comfort—how do you think?—with a barrel-organ to bring it.
Moping along the streets, and cursing my day, as I wandered,
All of a sudden my ear met the sound of an English psalm-tune.
Comfort me it did, till indeed I was very near crying.   90
Ah, there is some great truth, partial, very likely, but needful,
Lodged, I am strangely sure, in the tones of the English psalm-tune.
Comfort it was at least; and I must take without question
Comfort, however it come, in the dreary streets of the city.

WHAT with trusting myself and seeking support from within me,
Almost I could believe I had gained a religious assurance,
Found in my own poor soul a great moral basis to rest on.
Ah, but indeed I see, I feel it factitious entirely;
I refuse, reject, and put it utterly from me;
I will look straight out, see things, not try to evade them;   100
Fact shall be fact for me, and the Truth the Truth as ever,
Flexible, changeable, vague, and multiform, and doubtful.—
Off, and depart to the void, thou subtle, fanatical tempter!

I SHALL behold thee again (is it so?) at a new visitation,
O ill genius thou! I shall, at my life's dissolution,
(When the pulses are weak, and the feeble light of the reason
Flickers, an unfed flame retiring slow from the socket),
Low on a sick-bed laid, hear one, as it were, at the doorway,
And looking up see thee, standing by, looking emptily at me;
I shall entreat thee then, though now I dare to refuse thee,—   110
Pale and pitiful now, but terrible then to the dying.—
Well, I will see thee again: and while I can, will repel thee.

VI. CLAUDE TO EUSTACE

ROME is fallen, I hear, the gallant Medici taken,
Noble Manara slain, and Garibaldi has lost *il Moro*;—
Rome is fallen; and fallen, or falling, heroical Venice.
I, meanwhile, for the loss of a single small chit of a girl, sit
Moping and mourning here,—for her, and myself much smaller.
   Whither depart the souls of the brave that die in the battle,
Die in the lost, lost fight, for the cause that perishes with them?
Are they upborne from the field on the slumberous pinions of angels
Unto a far-off home, where the weary rest from their labour,   121
And the deep wounds are healed, and the bitter and burning moisture
Wiped from the generous eyes? or do they linger, unhappy,
Pining, and haunting the grave of their by-gone hope and endeavour?
   All declamation, alas! though I talk, I care not for Rome, nor
Italy; feebly and faintly, and but with the lips, can lament the
Wreck of the Lombard youth, and the victory of the oppressor.
Whither depart the brave?—God knows; I certainly do not.

VII. MARY TREVELLYN TO MISS ROPER

HE has not come as yet; and now I must not expect it.
You have written, you say, to friends at Florence, to see him,   130
If he perhaps should return;—but that is surely unlikely.
Has he not written to you?—he did not know your direction.
Oh, how strange never once to have told him where you were going!
Yet if he only wrote to Florence, that would have reached you.
If what you say he said was true, why has he not done so?
Is he gone back to Rome, do you think, to his Vatican marbles?—
O my dear Miss Roper, forgive me! do not be angry!—
You have written to Florence;—your friends would certainly
     find him.
Might you not write to him?—but yet it is so little likely!
I shall expect nothing more.—Ever yours, your affectionate Mary.

VIII. CLAUDE TO EUSTACE

I CANNOT stay at Florence, not even to wait for a letter.   141
Galleries only oppress me. Remembrance of hope I had cherished

(Almost more than as hope, when I passed through Florence the
    first time)
Lies like a sword in my soul. I am more a coward than ever,
Chicken-hearted, past thought. The *caffès* and waiters distress me.
All is unkind, and, alas! I am ready for anyone's kindness.
Oh, I knew it of old, and knew it, I thought, to perfection,
If there is any one thing in the world to preclude all kindness,
It is the need of it,—it is this sad, self-defeating dependence.
Why is this, Eustace? Myself, were I stronger, I think I could tell
    you.   150
But it is odd when it comes. So plumb I the deeps of depression,
Daily in deeper, and find no support, no will, no purpose.
All my old strengths are gone. And yet I shall have to do something.
Ah, the key of our life, that passes all wards, opens all locks,
Is not *I will*, but *I must*. I must,—I must,—and I do it.

AFTER all, do I know that I really cared so about her?
Do whatever I will, I cannot call up her image;
For when I close my eyes, I see, very likely, St. Peter's,
Or the Pantheon façade, or Michael Angelo's figures,
Or at a wish, when I please, the Alban hills and the Forum,— 160
But that face, those eyes,—ah no, never anything like them;
Only, try as I will, a sort of featureless outline,
And a pale blank orb, which no recollection will add to.
After all perhaps there was something factitious about it;
I have had pain, it is true: have wept; and so have the actors.

AT the last moment I have your letter, for which I was waiting;
I have taken my place, and see no good in enquiries.
Do nothing more, good Eustace, I pray you. It only will vex me.
Take no measures. Indeed, should we meet, I could not be certain;
All might be changed, you know. Or perhaps there was nothing to
    be changed.   170
It is a curious history, this; and yet I foresaw it;
I could have told it before. The Fates, it is clear, are against us;

For it is certain enough I met with the people you mention;
They were at Florence the day I returned there, and spoke to me
      even;
Stayed a week, saw me often; departed, and whither I know not.
Great is Fate, and is best. I believe in Providence partly.
What is ordained is right, and all that happens is ordered.
Ah, no, that isn't it. But yet I retain my conclusion.
I will go where I am led, and will not dictate to the chances.
Do nothing more, I beg. If you love me, forbear interfering.   180

IX. CLAUDE TO EUSTACE

SHALL we come out of it all, some day, as one does from a tunnel?
Will it be all at once, without our doing or asking,
We shall behold clear day, the trees and meadows about us,
And the faces of friends, and the eyes we loved looking at us?
Who knows? Who can say? It will not do to suppose it.

X. CLAUDE TO EUSTACE,—*from Rome*

ROME will not suit me, Eustace; the priests and soldiers possess it;
Priests and soldiers:—and, ah! which is worst, the priest or the
      soldier?
    Politics, farewell, however! For what could I do? with inquiring,
Talking, collating the journals, go fever my brain about things o'er
Which I can have no control. No, happen whatever may happen, 190
Time, I suppose, will subsist; the earth will revolve on its axis;
People will travel; the stranger will wander as now in the city;
Rome will be here, and the Pope the *custode* of Vatican marbles.
    I have no heart, however, for any marble or fresco;
I have essayed it in vain; 'tis vain as yet to essay it:
But I may haply resume some day my studies in this kind;
Not as the Scripture says, is, I think, the fact. Ere our death-day,
Faith, I think, does pass, and Love; but Knowledge abideth.
Let us seek Knowledge;—the rest may come and go as it happens.
Knowledge is hard to seek, and harder yet to adhere to. 200
Knowledge is painful often; and yet when we know, we are happy.
Seek it, and leave mere Faith and Love to come with the chances.

As for Hope,—to-morrow I hope to be starting for Naples.
Rome will not do, I see, for many very good reasons.
  Eastward, then, I suppose, with the coming of winter, to Egypt.

XI. MARY TREVELLYN TO MISS ROPER

You have heard nothing; of course, I know you can have heard
    nothing.
Ah, well, more than once I have broken my purpose, and sometimes,
Only too often, have looked for the little lake-steamer to bring him.
But it is only fancy,—I do not really expect it.
Oh, and you see I know so exactly how he would take it: 210
Finding the chances prevail against meeting again, he would banish
Forthwith every thought of the poor little possible hope, which
I myself could not help, perhaps, thinking only too much of;
He would resign himself, and go. I see it exactly.
So I also submit, although in a different manner.
  Can you not really come? We go very shortly to England.

So go forth to the world, to the good report and the evil!
  Go, little book! thy tale, is it not evil and good?
Go, and if strangers revile, pass quietly by without answer.
  Go, and if curious friends ask of thy rearing and age,   220
Say, 'I am flitting about many years from brain unto brain of
  Feeble and restless youths born to inglorious days:
But,' so finish the word, 'I was writ in a Roman chamber,
  When from Janiculan heights thundered the cannon of France.'

DIPSYCHUS

PROLOGUE

'I HOPE it is in good plain verse', said my uncle; 'none of your hurry-scurry anapæsts, as you call them, in lines which sober people are reading for plain heroics. Nothing is more disagreeable than to say a line over two, or, it may be, three or four times, and at last not be sure that there are not three or four ways of reading, each as good and as much intended as another. *Simplex duntaxat et unum.* But you young people think Horace and your uncles old fools.'

'Certainly, my dear sir,' said I; 'that is, I mean, Horace and my uncle are perfectly right. Still, there is an instructed ear and an uninstructed. A rude taste for identical recurrences would exact singsong from "Paradise Lost", and grumble because "Il Penseroso" doesn't run like a nursery rhyme.'

'Well, well,' said my uncle, '*sunt certi denique fines*, no doubt. So commence, my young Piso, while Aristarchus is tolerably wakeful, and do not waste by your logic the fund you will want for your poetry.'

DIPSYCHUS

SCENE I

Dipsychus

THE scene is different, and the place; the air
Tastes of the nearer North: the people too
Not perfect southern lightness. Wherefore then
Should those old verses come into my mind
I made last year at Naples? O poor fool,
Still nesting on thyself!

'Through the great sinful streets of Naples as I past,
With fiercer heat than flamed above my head
My heart was hot within; the fire burnt, and at last
My brain was lightened when my tongue had said,   10
   Christ is not risen!'

Spirit

Christ is not risen? Oh indeed!
Wasn't aware that was your creed.

Dipsychus

So it goes on. Too lengthy to repeat—
   'Christ is not risen.'

Spirit

   Dear, how odd!
He'll tell us next there is no God.
I thought 'twas in the Bible plain,
On the third day he rose again.

Dipsychus

Ashes to Ashes, Dust to Dust;
As of the Unjust also of the Just—   20
   Yea, of that Just One too!

Is He not risen, and shall we not rise?
O we unwise!

Spirit

H'm! and the tone then after all
Something of the ironical?
Sarcastic, say; or were it fitter
To style it the religious bitter?

Dipsychus

Interpret it I cannot. I but wrote it—
At Naples, truly, as the preface tells,
Last year in the Toledo; it came on me,   30
And did me good at once. At Naples then,
At Venice now. Ah! and I think at Venice
Christ is not risen either.

Spirit

                    Nay—
T'was well enough once in a way;
Such things don't fall out every day.
Having once happened, as we know,
In Palestine so long ago,
How should it now at Venice here?
Where people, true enough, appear
To appreciate more and understand   40
Their ices, and their Austrian band,
And dark-eyed girls—

Dipsychus

        The whole great square they fill,
From the red flaunting streamers on the staffs,
And that barbaric portal of St. Mark's,
To where, unnoticed, at the darker end,
I sit upon my step. One great gay crowd.
The Campanile to the silent stars

Goes up, above—its apex lost in air.
While these—do what?

Spirit

Enjoy the minute,   50
And the substantial blessings in it;
Ices, *par exemple*; evening air;
Company, and this handsome square;
Some pretty faces here and there;
Music! Up, up; it isn't fit
With beggars here on steps to sit.
Up—to the café! Take a chair
And join the wiser idlers there.
Aye! what a crowd! and what a noise!
With all these screaming half-breeched boys.   60
Partout dogs, boys, and women wander—
And see, a fellow singing yonder;
Singing, ye gods, and dancing too—
Tooraloo, tooraloo, tooraloo, loo;
Fiddle di, diddle di, diddle di da
Figaro sù, Figaro giù—
Figaro quà, Figaro là!
How he likes doing it! Ah, ha, ha!

Dipsychus

While these do what—ah heaven!

Spirit

If you want to pray   70
I'll step aside a little way.
Eh? But I will not be far gone;
You may be wanting me anon.
Our lonely pious altitudes
Are followed quick by prettier moods.
Who knows not with what ease devotion
Slips into earthlier emotion?

Dipsychus

While these do what? Ah, heaven, too true, at Venice
Christ is not risen either!

SCENE II—THE PUBLIC GARDEN

Dipsychus

Assuredly, a lively scene!
And, ah, how pleasant, something green!
With circling heavens one perfect rose
Each smoother patch of water glows,
Hence to where, o'er the full tide's face,
We see the Palace and the Place,
And the White dome. Beauteous but hot.
Where in the meantime is the spot,
My favourite, where by masses blue
And white cloud-folds, I follow true   10
The great Alps, rounding grandly o'er,
Huge arc, to the Dalmatian shore?

Spirit

This rather stupid place to-day,
It's true, is most extremely gay;
And rightly—the Assunzione
Was always a *gran' funzione*.

Dipsychus

What is this persecuting voice that haunts me?
What? whence? of whom? How am I to detect?
Myself or not myself? My own bad thoughts,
Or some external agency at work,   20
To lead me who knows whither?

Spirit
                    Eh?
We're certainly in luck to-day:

What lots of boats before us plying—
Gay parties, singing, shouting, crying,
Saluting others past them flying!
What numbers at the landing lying!
What lots of pretty girls, too, hieing
Hither and thither—coming, going,
And with what satisfaction showing,
To our male eyes unveiled and bare   30
Their dark exuberance of hair,
Black eyes, rich tints, and sundry graces
Of classic pure Italian faces!

Dipsychus

Off, off! Oh heaven, depart, depart, depart!
Oh me! the toad sly-sitting at Eve's ear
Whispered no dream more poisonous than this!

Spirit

A perfect show of girls I see it is.
Ah, what a charming foot, ye deities!
In that attraction as one fancies
Italy's not so rich as France is;   40
In Paris—

Dipsychus

Cease, cease, cease!
I will not hear this. Leave me!

Spirit

So!
How do those pretty verses go?

Ah comme je regrette
Mon bras si dodu,
Ma jambe bien faite
Et le temps perdu!
Et le temps perdu!

227

'Tis here, I see, the custom too
For damsels eager to be lovered   50
To go about with arms uncovered;
And doubtless there's a special charm
In looking at a well-shaped arm.
In Paris, I was saying—

Dipsychus

                    Ah me, me!
Clear stars above, thou roseate westward sky,
Take up my being into yours; assume
My sense to own you only; steep my brain
In your essential purity. Or, great Alps,
That wrapping round your heads in solemn clouds
Seem sternly to sweep past our vanities,   60
Lead me with you—take me away; preserve me!
—Ah, if it must be, look then, foolish eyes—
Listen fond ears; but, oh, poor mind, stand fast!

Spirit

In Paris, at the Opera
In the *coulisses*—but ah, aha!
There was a glance, I saw you spy it—
So! shall we follow suit and try it?
Pooh! what a goose you are! quick, quick!
This hesitation makes me sick.
You simpleton! what's your alarm?   70
She'd merely thank you for your arm.

Dipsychus

Sweet thing! ah well! but yet I am not sure.
Ah no. I think she did not mean it. No.

Spirit

Plainly, unless I much mistake,
She likes a something in your make:

228

She turned her head—another glance—
She really gives you every chance.

Dipsychus

Ah, pretty thing—well, well. Yet should I go?
Alas, I cannot say. What should I do?

Spirit

What should you do? Well, that is funny!   80
I think you are supplied with money.

Dipsychus

No, no—it may not be. I could, I would—
And yet I would not—cannot. To what end?

Spirit

Trust her for teaching! Go but you,
She'll quickly show you what to do.
Well, well! It's too late now—they're gone;
Some wiser youth is coming on.

SCENE II A—THE QUAYS

*   *   *   *

Dipsychus

O moon and stars forgive! And thou, clear heaven,
Look pureness back into me. O great God,
Why, why in wisdom and in grace's name,
And in the name of saints and saintly thoughts,
Of mothers, and of sisters, and chaste wives,
And angel woman-faces we have seen,
And angel woman-spirits we have guessed,
And innocent sweet children, and pure love,

Why did I ever one brief moment's space
To this insidious lewdness lend chaste ears,   10
Or parley with this filthy Belial?

*   *   *   *

Spirit

O yes, you dream of sin and shame—
Trust me, it leaves one much the same.
'Tisn't Elysium any more
Than what comes after or before:
But heavens! as innocent a thing
As picking strawberries in spring.
You think I'm anxious to allure you—
My object is much more to cure you.

*   *   *   *

I know it's mainly your temptation   20
To think the thing a revelation,
A mystic mouthful that will give
Knowledge and death—none know and live!
I tell you plainly that it brings
Some ease; but the emptiness of things
(That one old sermon Earth still preaches
Until we practise what she teaches)
Is the sole lesson you'll learn by it—
Still you undoubtedly should try it.
'Try all things'—bad and good, no matter;   30
You can't till then hold fast the latter.
If not, this itch will stick and vex you
Your live long days till death unsex you—
Hide in your bones, for aught I know,
And with you to the next world go.
Briefly—you cannot rest, I'm certain,
Until your hand has drawn the curtain.
Once known the little lies behind it,
You'll go your way and never mind it.

Ill's only cure is, never doubt it,   40
To do—and think no more about it.

*   *   *   *

Dipsychus

Could I believe that any child of Eve
Were formed and fashioned, raised and reared for nought
But to be swilled with animal delight
And yield five minutes' pleasure to the male—

*   *   *   *

Spirit

It was a lover and his lass,
   With a hey and a ho, and a hey nonino!
Betwixt the acres of the rye,
   With a hey and a ho, and a hey nonino!
These pretty country folks would lie—   50
   In the spring time, the pretty spring time.

Dipsychus

And could I think I owed it not to her,
In virtue of our manhood's stronger sight,
Even against entreaty to forbear—

Spirit

O Joseph and Don Quixote! This
A chivalry of chasteness is,
That turns to nothing all, that story
Has made out of your ancient glory!

*   *   *   *

Dipsychus

Or could I think that it had been for nought
That from my boyhood until now, in spite   60
Of most misguiding theories, at the moment
Somewhat has ever stepped in to arrest

231

My ingress at the fatal-closing door,
That many and many a time my foolish foot
O'ertreading the dim sill, spite of itself
And spite of me, instinctively fell back.

Spirit

Like Balaam's ass, in spite of thwacking,
Against the wall his master backing,
Because of something hazy stalking
Just in the way they should be walking—   70
Soon after too, he took to talking!

Dipsychus

Backed, and refused my bidding—Could I think,
In spite of carnal understanding's sneers,
All this fortuitous only—all a chance?

Spirit

Ah, just what I was going to say;
An Angel met you in the way!
Cry mercy of his heavenly highness—
I took him for that cunning shyness.

*   *   *   *

Dipsychus

O welcome then, the sweet domestic bonds,
The matrimonial sanctities; the hopes   80
And cares of wedded life; parental thoughts,
The prattle of young children, the good word
Of fellow men, the sanction of the law,
And permanence and habit, that transmute
Grossness itself to crystal. O, why, why,
Why ever let this speculating brain
Rest upon other objects than on this?

Spirit

Well, well—if you must stick perforce
Unto the ancient holy course,
And map your life out on the plan   90
Of the connubial puritan,
For God's sake carry out your creed,
Go home and marry—and be d——d.
I'll help you.

Dipsychus

You!

Spirit

O never scout me;
I know you'll ne'er propose without me.

Dipsychus

I have talked o'ermuch. The Spirit passes from me.
O folly, folly, what have I done? Ah me!

Spirit

You'd like another turn, I see.
Yes, yes, a little quiet turn.
By all means let us live and learn.   100
Here's many a lady still waylaying,
And sundry gentlemen purveying.
And if 'twere only just to see
The room of an Italian *fille*,
'Twere worth the trouble and the money.
You'll like to find—I found it funny—
The chamber *où vous faites votre affaire*
Stand nicely fitted up for prayer;
While dim you trace along one end
The Sacred Supper's length extend.   110
The calm Madonna o'er your head
Smiles, *col bambino*, on the bed
Where—but your chaste ears I must spare—

233

Where, as we said, *vous faites votre affaire*.
They'll suit you, these Venetian pets!
So natural, not the least coquettes—
Really at times one quite forgets—
Well, would you like perhaps to arrive at
A pretty creature's home in private?
We can look in, just say goodnight,   120
And, if you like to stay, all right.
Just as you fancy—is it well?

Dipsychus

O folly, folly, folly! To the Hotel!

SCENE III—THE HOTEL

Dipsychus

And I half yielded—oh, unthinking I!
Oh weak, weak fool! Alas, how quietly
Out of our better into our worse selves,
Out of a true world which our reason knew
Into a false world which our fancies make
Down the swift spiral opening still the same
We slide and never notice. Oh weak fool!

Spirit

Well, well—I may have been a little strong,
Of course, I wouldn't have you do what's wrong.
But we who've lived out in the world, you know,   10
Don't see these little things precisely so.
You feel yourself—to shrink and yet be fain,
And still to move and still draw back again,
Is a proceeding wholly without end.
If the plebeian street don't suit my friend,
Why he must try the drawing room, one fancies,
And he shall run to concerts and to dances!
And, with my aid, go into good society.
Life little loves, 'tis true, this peevish piety;

E'en they with whom it thinks to be securest—   20
Your most religious, delicatest, purest—
Discern, and show as pious people can
Their feeling that you are not quite a man.
Still the thing has its place; and with sagacity,
Much might be done by one of your capacity.
A virtuous attachment formed judiciously
Would come, one sees, uncommonly propitiously:
Turn you but your affections the right way,
And what mayn't happen none of us can say;
For in despite of devils and of mothers,   30
Your good young men make catches, too, like others.
Oh yes; into society we go;
At worst, 'twill teach you much you ought to know.

Dipsychus

To herd with people that one owns no care for;
Friend it with strangers that one sees but once;
To drain the heart with endless complaisance;
To warp the unfashioned diction on the lip,
And twist one's mouth to counterfeit; enforce
Reluctant looks to falsehood; base-alloy
The ingenuous golden frankness of the past;   40
To calculate and plot; be rough and smooth,
Forward and silent; deferential, cool,
Not by one's humour, which is the safe truth,
But on consideration—

Spirit
                                    That is, act
On a dispassionate judgement of the fact;
Look all your data fairly in the face,
And rule your conduct simply by the case.

Dipsychus

On vile consideration. At the best,
With pallid hotbed courtesies forestall

235

The green and vernal spontaneity,   50
And waste the priceless moments of the man
In regulating manner. Whether these things
Be right, I do not know: I only know 'tis
To lose one's youth too early. Oh, not yet,
Not yet I make this sacrifice.

Spirit
Du tout!
To give up nature's just what wouldn't do.
By all means keep your sweet ingenuous graces,
And use them at the proper times and places.
For work, for play, for business, talk, and love,
I own as wisdom truly from above   60
That scripture of the serpent and the dove;
Nor's aught so perfect for the world's affairs
As the old parable of wheat and tares;
What we all love is good touched up with evil—
Religion's self must have a spice of devil.

Dipsychus
                    Let it be enough
That in our needful mixture with the world,
On each new morning with the rising sun
Our rising heart, fresh from the seas of sleep,
Scarce o'er the level lifts his purer orb   70
Ere lost and sullied with polluting smoke—
A noonday coppery disk. Lo, scarce come forth,
Some vagrant miscreant meets, and with a look
Transmutes me his, and for a whole sick day
Lepers me.

Spirit
                    Why the one thing, I assure you,
From which good company can't but secure you.
About the individuals 't'an't so clear,
But who can doubt the general atmosphere?

Dipsychus

Ay truly, who at first? But in a while—

Spirit

O really, your discernment makes me smile—   80
Do you pretend to tell me you can see
Without one touch of melting sympathy
Those lovely, stately flowers, that fill with bloom
The brilliant season's gay *parterre*-like room,
Moving serene yet swiftly through the dances;
Those graceful forms and perfect countenances,
Whose every fold and line in all their dresses
Something refined and exquisite expresses?
To see them smile and hear them talk so sweetly
In me destroys all grosser thoughts completely.   90
I really seem without exaggeration
To experience the True Regeneration;
One's own dress too, one's manner, what one's doing
And saying, all assist to one's renewing—
I love to see in these their fitting places
The bows, and forms, and all you call grimaces.
I heartily could wish we'd kept some more of them,
However much they talk about the bore of them.
Fact is, your awkward parvenus are shy at it,
Afraid to look like waiters if they try at it.   100
'Tis sad to what democracy is leading;
Give me your Eighteenth Century for high breeding.
Though I can put up gladly with the present,
And quite can think our modern parties pleasant.
One shouldn't analyse the thing too nearly;
The main effect is admirable clearly.
Good manners, said our great aunts, next to piety;
And so, my friend, hurrah for good society.
For, mind you, if you don't do this, you still
Have got to tell me what it is you will.   110

SCENE IV—IN A GONDOLA

Dipsychus

Per ora. To the Grand Canal.
Afterwards e'en as fancy shall.

Afloat; we move. Delicious! Ah,
What else is like the gondola?
This level floor of liquid glass
Begins beneath it swift to pass.
It goes as though it went alone
By some impulsion of its own.
How light it moves, how softly! Ah,
Were all things like the gondola!   10

How light it moves, how softly! Ah,
Could life, as does our gondola,
Unvexed with quarrels, aims, and cares,
And moral duties and affairs,
Unswaying, noiseless, swift, and strong,
For ever thus—thus glide along!
How light we move, how softly! Ah,
Were all things like the gondola!

With no more motion than should bear
A freshness to the languid air;   20
With no more effort than exprest
The need and naturalness of rest,
Which we beneath a grateful shade
Should take on peaceful pillows laid—
How light we move, how softly! Ah,
Were all things like the gondola!

In one unbroken passage borne
To closing night from opening morn,
Uplift at whiles slow eyes to mark
Some palace front, some passing bark;   30
Through windows catch the varying shore,
And hear the soft turns of the oar—

How light we move, how softly! Ah,
Were all things like the gondola!

So live, nor need to call to mind
Our slaving brother set behind!

Spirit

Pooh! Nature meant him for no better
Than our most humble menial debtor;
Who thanks us for his day's employment,
As we our purse for our enjoyment.   40

Dipsychus

To make one's fellow-man an instrument—

Spirit

Is just the thing that makes him most content.

Dipsychus

Our gaieties, our luxuries,
    Our pleasures and our glee,
Mere insolence and wantonries,
    Alas! they feel to me.

How shall I laugh and sing and dance?
    My very heart recoils,
While here to give my mirth a chance
    A hungry brother toils.   50

The joy that does not spring from joy
    Which I in others see,
How can I venture to employ,
    Or find it joy for me?

Spirit

Oh come, come, come! By Him that set us here,
Who's to enjoy at all, pray let us hear?
You won't; he can't! Oh, no more fuss!
What's it to him, or he to us?

Sing, sing away, be glad and gay,
And don't forget that we shall pay.   60
How light we move, how softly! Ah,
Tra lal la la, the gondola!

Dipsychus

Yes, it is beautiful ever, let foolish men rail at it never.
Yes, it is beautiful truly, my brothers, I grant it you duly.
Wise are ye others that choose it, and happy ye all that can use it.
Life it is beautiful wholly, and could we eliminate only
This interfering, enslaving, o'ermastering demon of craving,
This wicked tempter inside us to ruin still eager to guide us,
Life were beatitude, action a possible pure satisfaction.

Spirit

(Hexameters, by all that's odious,   70
Beshod with rhyme to run melodious!)

Dipsychus

All as I go on my way I behold them consorting and coupling;
Faithful, it seemeth, and fond; very fond, very possibly faithful;
All as I go on my way with a pleasure sincere and unmingled.
Life it is beautiful truly, my brothers, I grant it you duly;
But for perfection attaining is one method only, abstaining;
Let us abstain, for we should so, if only we thought that we
    could so.

Spirit

(Bravo, bravissimo! this time though
You rather were run short for rhyme though;
Not that on that account your verse   80
Could be much better or much worse.)

Dipsychus

O let me love my love unto myself alone,
And know my knowledge to the world unknown;
No witness to the vision call,
Beholding, unbeheld of all;

And worship thee, with thee withdrawn, apart,
Whoe'er, whate'er thou art,
Within the closest veil of mine own inmost heart.

Better it were, thou sayest, to consent,
Feast while we may, and live ere life be spent;   90
Close up clear eyes, and call the unstable sure,
The unlovely lovely, and the filthy pure;
In self-belyings, self-deceivings roll,
And lose in Action, Passion, Talk, the soul.

Nay, better far to mark off thus much air
And call it heaven, place bliss and glory there;
Fix perfect homes in the unsubstantial sky,
And say, what is not, will be by-and-by;
What here exists not, must exist elsewhere.
But play no tricks upon thy soul, O man;   100
Let fact be fact, and life the thing it can.

Spirit

To these remarks so sage and clerkly,
Worthy of Malebranche or Berkeley,
I trust it won't be deemed a sin
If I too answer 'with a grin.'

These juicy meats, this flashing wine,
    May be an unreal mere appearance;
Only—for my inside, in fine,
    They have a singular coherence.

This lovely creature's glowing charms   110
    Are gross illusion, I don't doubt that;
But when I pressed her in my arms
    I somehow didn't think about that.

This world is very odd, we see;
    We do not comprehend it;
But in one fact can all agree
    God won't, and we can't mend it.

Being common sense, it can't be sin
    To take it as we find it;
The pleasure to take pleasure in;   120
    The pain, try not to mind it.

Dipsychus

Where are the great, whom thou would'st wish to praise thee?
Where are the pure, whom thou would'st choose to love thee?
Where are the brave, to stand supreme above thee,
Whose high commands would rouse, whose chiding raise thee?
    Seek, seeker, in thyself; submit to find
    In the stones, bread; and life in the blank mind.

    (Written in London, standing in the Park,
    An evening in July, just before dark.)

Spirit

As I sat at the café, I said to myself,   130
They may talk as they please about what they call pelf,
They may sneer as they like about eating and drinking,
But help it I cannot, I cannot help thinking
    How pleasant it is to have money, heigh ho!
    How pleasant it is to have money.

I sit at my table *en grand seigneur*,
And when I have done, throw a crust to the poor;
Not only the pleasure, one's self, of good living,
But also the pleasure of now and then giving.
    So pleasant it is to have money, heigh ho!   140
    So pleasant it is to have money.

It was but last winter I came up to Town,
But already I'm getting a little renown;
I make new acquaintance where'er I appear;
I am not too shy, and have nothing to fear.
    So pleasant it is to have money, heigh ho!
    So pleasant it is to have money.

I drive through the streets, and I care not a d—mn;
The people they stare, and they ask who I am;
And if I should chance to run over a cad,   150
I can pay for the damage if ever so bad.
  So pleasant it is to have money, heigh ho!
  So pleasant it is to have money.

We stroll to our box and look down on the pit,
And if it weren't low should be tempted to spit;
We loll and we talk until people look up,
And when it's half over we go out and sup.
  So pleasant it is to have money, heigh ho!
  So pleasant it is to have money.

The best of the tables and best of the fare—   160
And as for the others, the devil may care;
It isn't our fault if they dare not afford
To sup like a prince and be drunk as a lord.
  So pleasant it is to have money, heigh ho!
  So pleasant it is to have money.

We sit at our tables and tipple champagne;
Ere one bottle goes, comes another again;
The waiters they skip and they scuttle about,
And the landlord attends us so civilly out.
  So pleasant it is to have money, heigh ho!   170
  So pleasant it is to have money.

It was but last winter I came up to town,
But already I'm getting a little renown;
I get to good houses without much ado,
Am beginning to see the nobility too.
  So pleasant it is to have money, heigh ho!
  So pleasant it is to have money.

O dear! what a pity they ever should lose it!
For they are the gentry that know how to use it;
So grand and so graceful, such manners, such dinners,
But yet, after all, it is we are the winners.   181

So pleasant it is to have money, heigh ho!
So pleasant it is to have money.

Thus I sat at my table *en grand seigneur,*
And when I had done threw a crust to the poor;
Not only the pleasure, one's self, of good eating,
But also the pleasure of now and then treating.
So pleasant it is to have money, heigh ho!
So pleasant it is to have money.

They may talk as they please about what they call pelf,
And how one ought never to think of one's self,   191
And how pleasures of thought surpass eating and
    drinking—
My pleasure of thought is the pleasure of thinking
How pleasant it is to have money, heigh ho!
How pleasant it is to have money.

(Written in Venice, but for all parts true,
'Twas not a crust I gave him, but a sous.)

A gondola here, and a gondola there,
'Tis the pleasantest fashion of taking the air.
To right and to left; stop, turn, and go yonder,   200
And let us repeat, o'er the tide as we wander,
How pleasant it is to have money, heigh ho!
How pleasant it is to have money.

Come, leave your Gothic, worn-out story,
San Giorgio and the Redemptore;
I from no building, gay or solemn,
Can spare the shapely Grecian column.
'Tis not, these centuries four, for nought
Our European world of thought
Hath made familiar to its home   210
The classic mind of Greece and Rome;
In all new work that would look forth
To more than antiquarian worth,

Palladio's pediments and bases,
Or something such, will find their places:
Maturer optics don't delight
In childish dim religious light,
In evanescent vague effects
That shirk, not face, one's intellects;
They love not fancies fast betrayed,   220
And artful tricks of light and shade,
But pure form nakedly displayed,
And all things absolutely made.
The Doge's palace though, from hence,
In spite of Ruskin's d——d pretence,
The tide now level with the quay,
Is certainly a thing to see.
We'll turn to the Rialto soon;
One's told to see it by the moon.

A gondola here, and a gondola there,   230
'Tis the pleasantest fashion of taking the air.
To right and to left; stop, turn, and go yonder,
And let us repeat, o'er the flood as we wander,
  How pleasant it is to have money, heigh ho!
  How pleasant it is to have money.

Dipsychus

How light we go, how soft we skim,
And all in moonlight seem to swim!
The south side rises o'er our bark,
A wall impenetrably dark;
The north the while profusely bright.   240
The water—is it shade or light?
Say, gentle moon, which conquers now
The flood, those massy hulls, or thou?
How light we go, how softly! Ah,
Were life but as the gondola!
How light we go, how soft we skim,
And all in moonlight seem to swim!

245

In moonlight is it now,—or shade?
In planes of sure division made,
By angles sharp of palace walls   250
The clear light and the shadow falls;
O sight of glory, sight of wonder!
Seen, a pictorial portent, under,
O great Rialto, the vast round
Of thy thrice-solid arch profound!
How light we go, how softly! Ah,
Life should be as the gondola!

How light we go, how softly—

                    Spirit
                                    Nay;
'Fore heaven, enough of that to-day:
I'm deadly weary of your tune,   260
And half-*ennuyé* with the moon;
The shadows lie, the glories fall,
And are but moonshine after all.
It goes against my conscience really
To let myself feel so ideally.
Make me repose no power of man shall
In things so deucèd unsubstantial.
Come, for the Piazzetta steer;
'Tis nine o'clock or very near.
These airy blisses, skiey joys   270
Of vague romantic girls and boys,
Which melt the heart and the brain soften,
When not affected, as too often
They are, remind me, I protest,
Of nothing better at the best
Than Timon's feast to his ancient lovers,
Warm water under silver covers;
'Lap, dogs!' I think I hear him say;
And lap who will, so I'm away.

Dipsychus

How light we go, how soft we skim,   280
And all in open moonlight swim!
Bright clouds against, reclined I mark
The white dome now projected dark,
And, by o'er-brilliant lamps displayed,
The Doge's columns and arcade;
Over still waters mildly come
The distant laughter and the hum.
How light we go, how softly! Ah,
Life should be as the gondola!

Spirit

The Devil! we've had enough of you,   290
Quote us a little Wordsworth, do!
Those lines that are so just, they say:
'A something far more deeply' eh?
'Interfused'—what is it they tell us?
Which and the sunset are bedfellows.

Dipsychus

How light we go, how soft we skim,
And all in open moonlight swim!
Ah, gondolier, slow, slow, more slow!
We go; but wherefore thus should go?
Ah, let not muscle all too strong   300
Beguile, betray thee to our wrong!
On to the landing, onward. Nay,
Sweet dream, a little longer stay!
On to the landing; here. And, ah,
Life is not as the gondola!

Spirit

Tre ore. So. The Parthenone,
Is it, you haunt for your *limone*?
Let me induce you to join me
In *gramolata persici.*

SCENE V

Spirit

What now? the Lido shall it be?
That none may say we didn't see
The ground which Byron used to ride on,
And do I don't know what beside on.
Ho, barca! here! and this light gale
Will let us run it with a sail.

Dipsychus

I dreamt a dream; till morning light
A bell rang in my head all night,
Tinkling and tinkling first, and then
Tolling; and tinkling; tolling again.   10
So brisk and gay, and then so slow!
O joy, and terror! mirth, and woe!
Ting, ting, there is no God; ting, ting—
Dong, there is no God; dong,
There is no God; dong, dong!

Ting, ting, there is no God; ting, ting;
Come dance and play, and merrily sing—
Ting, ting a ding; ting, ting a ding!
O pretty girl who trippest along,
Come to my bed—it isn't wrong.   20
Uncork the bottle, sing the song!
Ting, ting a ding: dong, dong.
Wine has dregs; the song an end;
A silly girl is a poor friend
And age and weakness who shall mend?
Dong, there is no God; Dong!

Ting, ting a ding! Come dance and sing!
Staid Englishmen, who toil and slave
From your first breeching to your grave,
And seldom spend and always save,   30
And do your duty all your life

By your young family and wife;
Come, be't not said you ne'er had known
What earth can furnish you alone.
The Italian, Frenchman, German even,
Have given up all thoughts of heaven;
And you still linger—oh, you fool!—
Because of what you learnt at school.
You should have gone at least to college,
And got a little ampler knowledge.   40
Ah well, and yet—dong, dong, dong:
Do, if you like, as now you do;
If work's a cheat, so's pleasure too;
And nothing's new and nothing's true;
Dong, there is no God; dong!

O Rosalie, my precious maid,
I think thou thinkest love is true;
And on thy fragrant bosom laid
I almost could believe it too.
O in our nook, unknown, unseen,   50
We'll hold our fancy like a screen,
Us and the dreadful fact between.
And it shall yet be long, aye, long,
The quiet notes of our low song
Shall keep us from that sad dong, dong.
Hark, hark, hark! O voice of fear!
It reaches us here, even here!
Dong, there is no God; dong!

Ring ding, ring ding, tara, tara,
To battle, to battle—haste, haste—   60
To battle, to battle—aha, aha!
On, on, to the conqueror's feast.
From east and west, and south and north,
Ye men of valour and of worth,
Ye mighty men of arms, come forth,
And work your will, for that is just;

And in your impulse put your trust,
Beneath your feet the fools are dust.
Alas, alas! O grief and wrong,
The good are weak, the wicked strong;   70
And O my God, how long, how long?
Dong, there is no God; dong!

Ring, ting; to bow before the strong,
There is a rapture too in this;
Speak, outraged maiden, in thy wrong
Did terror bring no secret bliss?
Were boys' shy lips worth half a song
Compared to the hot soldier's kiss?
Work for thy master, work, thou slave
He is not merciful, but brave.   80
Be't joy to serve, who free and proud
Scorns thee and all the ignoble crowd;
Take that, 'tis all thou art allowed,
Except the snaky hope that they
May some time serve, who rule to-day,
When, by hell-demons, shan't they pay?
O wickedness, O shame and grief,
And heavy load, and no relief!
O God, O God! and which is worst,
To be the curser or the curst,   90
The victim or the murderer? Dong
Dong, there is no God; dong!

Ring ding, ring ding, tara, tara,
Away, and hush that preaching—fagh!
Ye vulgar dreamers about peace,
Who offer noblest hearts, to heal
The tenderest hurts honour can feel,
Paid magistrates and the Police!
O piddling merchant justice, go,
Exacter rules than yours we know;   100
Resentment's rule, and that high law

Of whoso best the sword can draw.
Ah well, and yet—dong, dong, dong.
Go on, my friends, as now you do;
Lawyers are villains, soldiers too;
And nothing's new and nothing's true.
Dong, there is no God; dong!

O Rosalie, my lovely maid,
I think thou thinkest love is true;
And on thy faithful bosom laid   110
I almost could believe it too.
The villainies, the wrongs, the alarms
Forget we in each other's arms.
No justice here, no God above;
But where we are, is there not love?
What? what? thou also go'st? For how
Should dead truth live in lover's vow?
What, thou? thou also lost? Dong
Dong, there is no God; dong!

I had a dream, from eve to light   120
A bell went sounding all the night.
Gay mirth, black woe, thin joys, huge pain:
I tried to stop it, but in vain.
It ran right on, and never broke;
Only when day began to stream
Through the white curtains to my bed,
And like an angel at my head
Light stood and touched me—I awoke,
And looked, and said, 'It is a dream.'

Spirit

Ah! not so bad. You've read, I see,   130
Your Béranger, and thought of me.
But really you owe some apology
For harping thus upon theology.
I'm not a judge, I own; in short,
Religion may not be my forte.

The Church of England I belong to,
But think Dissenters not far wrong too;
They're vulgar dogs; but for his *creed*
I hold that no man will be d——d.
My Establishment I much respect,   140
Her ordinances don't neglect;
Attend at Church on Sunday once,
And in the Prayer-book am no dunce;
Baptise my babies; nay, my wife
Would be churched too once in her life.
She's taken, I regret to state,
Rather a Puseyite turn of late.
To set the thing quite right, I went
At Easter to the Sacrament.
'Tis proper once a year or so   150
To do the civil thing and show—
But come and listen in your turn
And you shall hear and mark and learn.

   'There is no God,' the wicked saith,
     'And truly it's a blessing,
   For what he might have done with us
     It's better only guessing.'

   'There is no God,' a youngster thinks,
     'Or really, if there may be,
   He surely didn't mean a man   160
     Always to be a baby.'

   'There is no God, or if there is,'
     The tradesman thinks, ''twere funny
   If he should take it ill in me
     To make a little money.'

   'Whether there be,' the rich man says,
     'It matters very little,
   For I and mine, thank somebody,
     Are not in want of victual.'

Some others, also, to themselves   170
  Who scarce so much as doubt it,
Think there is none, when they are well,
  And do not think about it.

But country folks who live beneath
  The shadow of the steeple;
The parson and the parson's wife,
  And mostly married people;

Youths green and happy in first love,
  So thankful for illusion;
And men caught out in what the world   180
  Calls guilt, in first confusion;

And almost every one when age,
  Disease, or sorrows strike him,
Inclines to think there is a God,
  Or something very like Him.

But *eccoci!* with our *barchetta*,
Here at the Sant' Elisabetta.

Dipsychus

Vineyards and maize, that's pleasant for sore eyes.

Spirit

And on the island's other side,
The place where Murray's faithful Guide   190
Informs us Byron used to ride.

Dipsychus

These trellised vines! enchanting! Sandhills, ho!
The sea, at last the sea—the real broad sea—
Beautiful! and a glorious breeze upon it.

Spirit

Look back; one catches at this station
Lagoon and sea in combination.

Dipsychus

On her still lake the city sits,
Where bark and boat about her flits,
Nor dreams, her soft siesta taking,
Of Adriatic billows breaking.   200
I do; and see and hear them. Come! to the sea!

Spirit

The wind I think is the *sirocco*.
Yonder, I take it, is Malmocco.
Thank you! it never was my passion
To skip o'er sand-hills in that fashion.

Dipsychus

Oh, a grand surge! we'll bathe; quick, quick! undress!
Quick, quick! in, in!
We'll take the crested billows by their backs
And shake them. Quick! in, in!
And I will taste again the old joy   210
I gloried in so when a boy.

Spirit

Well; but it's not so pleasant for the feet;
We should have brought some towels and a sheet.

Dipsychus

In, in! I go. Ye great winds blow,
And break, thou curly waves, upon my breast.

Spirit

Hm! I'm undressing. Doubtless all is well—
I only wish these thistles were at hell.
By heaven, I'll stop before that bad yet worse is,
And take care of our watches—and our purses.

Dipsychus

Aha! come, come—great waters, roll!   220
Accept me, take me, body and soul!—
    Aha!

Spirit

Come, no more of that stuff,
I'm sure you've stayed in long enough.

Dipsychus

That's done me good. It grieves me though
I never came here long ago.

Spirit

Pleasant perhaps. However, no offence,
Animal spirits are not common sense.
You think perhaps I have outworn them—
Certainly I have learnt to scorn them;
They're good enough as an assistance,   230
But in themselves a poor existence.
But you—with this one bathe, no doubt,
Have solved all questions out and out.
'Tis Easter Day, and on the Lido
Lo, Christ the Lord is risen indeed, O!

SCENE VI

Spirit

Insulted! by the living Lord!
He laid his hand upon his sword.
Fort, did he say? a German brute,
With neither heart nor brains to shoot.

Dipsychus

What does he mean? he's wrong, I had done nothing.
'Twas a mistake—more his, I am sure, than mine.
He is quite wrong—I feel it. Come, let us go.

Spirit

Go up to him!—you must, that's flat.
Be threatened by a beast like that!

Dipsychus

He's violent: what can I do against him?   10
I neither wish to be killed nor to kill:
What's more, I never yet have touched a sword,
Nor fired, but twice, a pistol in my life.

Spirit

Oh, never mind, 'twon't come to fighting—
Only some verbal small requiting;
Or give your card—we'll do't by writing.
He'll not stick to it. Soldiers too
Are cowards, just like me or you.
What! not a single word to throw at
This snarling dog of a d——d Croat?   20

Dipsychus

My heaven! why should I care? he does not hurt me.
If he is wrong, it is the worse for him.
I certainly did nothing—I shall go.

Spirit

Did nothing! I should think not; no,
Nor ever will, I dare be sworn!
But, O my friend, well-bred, well-born—
You to behave so in these quarrels
Makes me half doubtful of your morals!
. . . . It were all one,
You had been some shopkeeper's son   30
Whose childhood ne'er was shown aught better
Than bills of creditor and debtor.

Dipsychus

By heaven, it falls from off me like the rain
From the oil-coat. I seem in spirit to see
How he and I at some great day shall meet
Before some awful judgement-seat of truth;
And I could deem that I behold him there

256

Come praying for the pardon I give now,
Did not I think these matters too, too small
For any record on the leaves of time.   40

Spirit

Oh Lord! and walking with your sister,
If some foul brute stept up and kissed her,
You'd leave that also, I dare say,
On account for the judgement day.

Dipsychus

Oh, these skin-bites, these airy words,
Which at the moment seem to pierce us through,
And one hour after are acknowledged nought;
These pricks of pride, these petty personal hurts,
O thou great Watcher of this noisy world,
What are they in thy sight? or what in his   50
Who finds some end of Action in his life?
What e'en in his whose sole permitted course
Is to pursue his peaceful byway walk,
And live his brief life purely in Thy sight,
And righteously towards his brother-men?

Spirit

And whether, so you're just and fair,
Other folks are so, you don't care;
You who profess more love than others
For your poor sinful human brothers.
But this anon we'll come, my friend, to,   60
My previous question first attend to.

Dipsychus

For grosser evils their gross remedies
The laws afford us; let us be content.
For finer wounds the law would, if it could,
Find medicine too; it cannot, let us bear;
For sufferance is the badge of all men's tribes.

Spirit

Because we can't do all we would,
Does it follow, to do nothing's good?
No way to help the law's rough sense
By equities of self-defence?   70

Dipsychus

Draw the line where you will, it will exclude
Much it should comprehend. I draw it here.

Spirit

Well, for yourself it may be nice
To serve vulgarity and vice:
Must sisters, too, and wives and mothers
Fare like their patient sons and brothers?

Dipsychus

He that loves sister, mother, more than me—

Spirit

But the injustice—the gross wrong!
To whom on earth does it belong
If not to you, to whom 'twas done,   80
Who see it plain as any sun,
To make the base and foul offender
Confess, and satisfaction render?
At least before the termination of it
Prove your own lofty reprobation of it.
Though gentleness, I know, was born in you,
Surely you have a little scorn in you?

Dipsychus

Heaven! to pollute one's fingers to pick up
The fallen coin of honour from the dirt—
Pure silver though it be, let it rather lie!   90
To take up any offence, where't may be said
That temper, vanity—I know not what—

Had led me on!
To enter the base crowd and bare one's flanks
To all ill voices of a blustering world,
To have so much as e'en half-felt of one
That ever one was angered for oneself!
Beyond suspicion Caesar's wife should be,
Beyond suspicion this bright honour shall.
Did he say scorn? I have some scorn, thank God.   100

Spirit

Certainly. Only if it's so,
Let us leave Italy, and go
Post-haste, to attend—you're ripe and rank for't—
The Great Peace-Meeting up at Frankfort.
Joy to the Croat! Take our lives,
Sweet friends, and please respect our wives.
Myself, a trifle quite, you slaughter;
But pray be decent with my daughter.
Joy to the Croat! Some fine day
He'll see the error of his way,   110
No doubt, and will repent and pray.
At any rate he'll open his eyes,
If not before, at the Last Assize.
Not, if I rightly understood you,
That even then, you'd punish, would you?
Nay, let the hapless soul escape.
Mere murder, robbery, and rape,
In whate'er station, age, or sex,
Your sacred spirit scarce can vex.
De minimis non curat lex.   120
To the Peace Congress—ring the bell!
Horses to Frankfort and to hell!

Dipsychus

I am not quite in union with myself
On this strange matter. I must needs confess
Instinct turns instinct in and out; and thought

259

Wheels round on thought. To bleed for other's wrongs
In vindication of a Cause, to draw
The sword of the Lord and Gideon—O, that seems
The flower and top of life! But fight because
Some poor misconstruing trifler haps to say   130
I lie, when I do not lie, or is rude
To some vain fashionable thing, some poor
Curl-paper of a doll that's set by chance
To dangle a dull hour on my vext arm,
Why should I? Call you this a Cause? I can't.
Oh he is wrong, no doubt. He misbehaves—
But is it worth so much as speaking loud?
And things more merely personal to myself
Of all earth's things do least affect myself.

Spirit

Sweet eloquence! at next May Meeting   140
How it would tell in the repeating!
I recognise, and kiss the rod—
The Methodistic 'voice of God';
I catch contrite that angel whine,
That snuffle human, yet divine.
The doctrine own, and no mistaker,
Of the bland Philanthropic Quaker.
O come, blest age, from bloodshed cease.
Bewildered brothers, dwell at peace.
This holy effluence from above   150
Shall fill your wildest hearts with love,
Shall bring the light of inward day
To Caffre fierce and sly Malay;
Soften hard pirates with a kiss
And melt barbarian isles with bliss—
Leaving, in lieu of war and robbing,
Only a little mild stock-jobbing:

O, doubtless! Let the simple heart
Mind her own business, do her part,

260

Her wrongs repel, maintain her honour—   160
O fiend and savage, out upon her!
Press, pulpit, from each other borrow
The terms of scandal, shame and sorrow;
Vulgarity shrieks out in fear of it,
And Piety turns sick to hear of it.
The downright things, twixt you and me,
The wrongs we really feel and see,
The hurts that actually try one,
Like common plain good deeds close by one,
Decidedly have no existence—   170
They are at such a little distance!
But to protect the lovely figures
Of your half ourang-outang niggers,
To preach the doctrine of the Cross
To worshippers in house of joss,
To take steps for the quick conversion
Of Turk, Armenian, Jew and Persian,
Or send up missions, per balloon,
To those poor heathens in the moon—
Oh that—But I'm afraid I storm;   180
I'm quite ashamed to be so warm.

Dipsychus

It may be I am somewhat a poltroon.
I never fought at school. Whether it be
Some native poorness in my spirit's blood,
Or that the holy doctrine of our faith
In too exclusive fervency possessed
My heart with feelings, with ideas my brain.

Spirit

Yes; you would argue that it goes
Against the Bible, I suppose.
But our revered religion—yes,   190
Our common faith—seems, I confess,

On these points to propose to address
The people more than you or me—
At best the vulgar bourgeoisie.
The sacred writers don't keep count,
But still the Sermon on the Mount
Must have been spoken, by what's stated,
To hearers by the thousands rated.
I cuff some fellow; mild and meek,
He should turn round the other cheek.   200
For him it may be right and good;
We are not all of gentle blood
Really, or as such understood.

Dipsychus

There are two kindreds upon earth, I know—
The oppressors and the oppressed. But as for me,
If I must choose to inflict wrong, or accept,
May my last end, and life too, be with these.
Yes, whatsoe'er the reason—want of blood,
Lymphatic humours, or my childhood's faith—
So is the thing, and be it well or ill,   210
I have no choice. I am a man of peace,
And the old Adam of the gentleman
Dares seldom in my bosom stir against
The good plebeian Christian seated there.

Spirit

Forgive me, if I name my doubt,
Whether you know '*fort*' means 'get out.'

SCENE VII—THE INTERIOR ARCADE OF THE DOGE'S
PALACE

Spirit

Thunder and rain! O dear, O dear!
But see, a noble shelter here,
This grand arcade where our Venetian

Has formed of Gothic and of Grecian
A combination strange, but striking,
And singularly to my liking.
Let moderns reap where ancients sowed—
I at least make it my abode.
And now let's hear your famous ode:
'Through the great sinful'—how d'ye go on?   10
For Principles of Art and so on
I care perhaps about three curses,
But hold myself a judge of verses.

Dipsychus

'My brain was lightened when my tongue had said,
          "Christ is not risen"'

          *   *   * ¹

Spirit

Well, now it's anything but clear
What is the tone that's taken here;
What is your logic? What's your theology?
Is it or is it not neology?
That's a great fault; you're this and that,   20
And here and there, and nothing flat.
Yet writing's golden word what is it,
But the three syllables, 'explicit'?
Say, if you cannot help it, less,
But what you do put, put express.
I fear that rule won't meet your feeling;
You think half-showing, half-concealing,
Is God's own method of revealing.

¹ Dipsychus is doubtless supposed, at this point, to say more of the 'Easter Day' Ode;
see pp. 54 ff.

Dipsychus

To please my own poor mind! To find repose;
To physic the sick soul; to furnish vent   30
To diseased humours in the moral frame.

Spirit

A sort of seton, I suppose,
A moral bleeding at the nose.

Dipsychus

Interpret it I cannot; I but wrote it.

Spirit

Perhaps; but none that read can doubt it,
There is a strong Strauss-smell about it.
Heavens! at your years your time to fritter
Upon a critical hair-splitter!
Take larger views (and quit your Germans)
From the Analogy and Sermons;   40
I fancied—you must doubtless know—
Butler had proved, an age ago,
That in religious as profane things
'Twas useless trying to explain things;
Men's business-wits the only sane things,
These and compliance are the main things.
God, Revelation, and the rest of it,
Bad at the best, we make the best of it.
Not quite the things we chose to think;
But neither is the World rose pink.   50
Yet *it* is fact as plain as day;
So may the rest be; who can say?
Thus life we see is wondrous odd,
And so, we argue, may be God.
At any rate, this rationalistic
Half-puritano-semitheistic
Cross of Neologist and Mystic

Is, of all doctrines, the least reasonable—
And of all topics most unseasonable.
Why should you fancy you know more of it   60
Than all the old folks that thought before of it?
Like a good subject and wise man,
Believe whatever things you can.
Take your religion as 'twas found you,
And say no more of it—confound you!
And now I think the rain has ended—
And the less said, the sooner mended.

SCENE VIII—THE ACADEMY

Dipsychus

A modern daub it was, perchance;
I know not; but I dare be sure
From Titian's hues no connoisseur
Had turned one condescending glance

Where Byron, somewhat drest-up, draws
His sword, impatient long, and speaks
Unto a tribe of motley Greeks
His pledge word unto their brave cause.

Not far, assumed to mystic bliss,
Behold the ecstatic Virgin rise!   10
Ah wherefore vainly to fond eyes
That melt to burning tears for this?

Yet if we *must* live, as would seem,
These peremptory heats to claim,—
Ah, not for profit, not for fame,
And not for pleasure's giddy dream,

And not for piping empty reeds,
And not for colouring idle dust,—
If live we positively must,
God's name be blest for noble deeds.   20

Verses! well, they are made, so let them go;
No more if I can help. This is one way
The procreant heat and fervour of our youth
Escapes, in puff, and smoke, and shapeless words
Of mere ejaculation, nothing worth,
Unless to make maturer years content
To slave in base compliance to the world.

I have scarce spoken yet to this strange follower
Whom I picked up—ye great gods, tell me where!
And when! for I remember such long years,   30
And yet he seems new come. I commune with myself;
He speaks, I hear him, and resume to myself;
Whate'er I think, he adds his comments to;
Which yet not interrupts me. Scarce I know
If ever once directly I addressed him.
Let me essay it now, for I have strength.
Yet what he wants, and what he fain would have,
O, I know all too surely; not in vain,
Although unnoticed, has he dogged my ear.
Come, we'll be definite, explicit, plain;   40
I can resist, I know; and 'twill be well
To have used for colloquy this manlier mood,
Which is to last, ye chances, say, how long?
How shall I call him? Mephistopheles?

Spirit

I come, I come.

Dipsychus

        So quick, so eager; ha!
Like an eaves-dropping menial on my thought,
With something of an exultation too, methinks,
Out-peeping in that springy, jaunty gait.
I doubt about it. Shall I do it? Oh! oh!
Shame on me! come! Should I, my follower,   50
Should I conceive (not that at all I do,

266

'Tis curiosity that prompts my speech)—
But should I form, a thing to be supposed,
A wish to bargain for your merchandise,
Say what were your demands? what were your terms?
What should I do? what should I cease to do?
What incense on what altars must I burn?
And what abandon? what unlearn, or learn?
Religion goes, I take it.

Spirit

                    Oh,
You'll go to church of course, you know;   60
Or at the least will take a pew
To send your wife and servants to.
Trust me, I make a point of that;
No infidelity, that's flat.

Dipsychus

Religion is not in a pew, say some;
Cucullus, *you* hold, *facit* monachum.

Spirit

Why, as to feelings of devotion,—
I interdict all vague emotion;
But if you will, for once and all
Compound with ancient Juvenal,   70
Orandum est, one perfect prayer
For *savoir-vivre, savoir-faire*.
    Theology—don't recommend you,
Unless, turned lawyer, Heaven should send you
In your profession's way a case
Of Baptism and Prevenient Grace;
But that's not likely. I'm inclined,
All circumstances borne in mind,
To think (to keep you in due borders)
You'd better enter holy orders.   80

Dipsychus

On that, my friend, you'd better not insist.

Spirit

Well, well, 'tis but a good thing missed.
The item's optional, no doubt;
But how to get you bread without?
You'll marry; I shall find the lady.
Make your proposal, and be steady.

Dipsychus

Marry, ill spirit! and at your sole choice?

Spirit

De rigueur! can't give you a voice.
What matter? Oh, trust one who knows you,
You'll make an admirable *sposo*.   90
Un' bella donn' un' gran' riposo.
As said the soldier in our carriage,
Although he didn't mean in marriage.
As to the rest I shall not quarrel,
You being, as it seems, *so* moral.
Though, orders laid upon the shelf,
In merest justice to myself,
But that I hate the pro and con of it,
I should have made a *sine-qua-non* of it.
Come, my dear boy, I will not bind you,   100
But scruples must be cast behind you.
All mawkish talking I dislike,
But when the iron *is* hot, strike!
Good God! to think of youthful bliss
Restricted to a sneaking kiss.

Dipsychus

Enough. But action—look to that well, mind me;
See that some not unworthy work you find me;
If man I be, then give the man expression.

268

Spirit

Of course you'll enter a profession;
If not the Church, why then the Law.   110
By Jove, we'll teach you how to draw!
Once in the way that you should go,
You'll do your business well, I know.
Besides, the best of the concern is
I'm hand and glove with the attorneys.
With them and me to help, don't doubt
But in due season you'll come out;
Leave Kelly, Cockburn, in the lurch.
And yet, do think about the Church.
By all that's rich 'twould do me good   120
To fig you out in robe and hood.
Wouldn't I give up wine and wench,
To mount you fairly on the bench!

Dipsychus

'Tis well, ill spirit, I admire your wit;
As for your wisdom, I shall think of it. .
And now farewell.

SCENE IX

Dipsychus

The Law! 'twere honester, if 'twere genteel,
To say the dung-cart. What! shall I go about,
And like the walking shoeblack roam the flags
With heedful eyes, down bent, and like a glass
In a sea-captain's hand sweeping all round,
To see whose boots are dirtiest? Oh, the luck
To stoop and clean a pair!
Religion:—if indeed it be in vain
To expect to find in this more modern time   10
That which the old world styled, in old-world phrase,
Walking with God. It seems His newer will

269   T

We should not think of Him at all, but trudge it,
And of the world He has assigned us make
What best we can.
                    Then love: I scarce can think
That these be-maddening discords of the mind
To pure melodious sequence could be changed,
And all the vext conundrums of our life
Prove to all time bucolically solved
By a new Adam and a second Eve
Set in a garden which no serpent seeks.   20
And yet I hold heart can beat true to heart:
And to hew down the tree which bears this fruit,
To do a thing which cuts me off from hope,
To falsify the movement of love's mind,
To seat some alien trifler on the throne
A queen may come to claim—that were ill done.
What! to the close hand of the clutching Jew
Hand up that rich reversion! and for what?
This would be hard, did I indeed believe
'Twould ever fall. But love, the large repose   30
Restorative, not to mere outside needs
Skin-deep, but throughly to the total man,
Exists, I will believe, but so, so rare,
So doubtful, so exceptional, hard to guess;
When guessed, so often counterfeit; in brief,
A thing not possibly to be conceived
An item in the reckonings of the wise.

Action, that staggers me. For I had hoped,
'Midst weakness, indolence, frivolity,
Irresolution, still had hoped: and this   40
Seems sacrificing hope. Better to wait:
The wise men wait; it is the foolish haste,
And ere the scenes are in their slides would play,
And while the instruments are tuning, dance.
    I see Napoleon on the heights, intent

To arrest that one brief unit of loose time
Which hands high Victory's thread; his Marshals fret,
His soldiers clamour low: the very guns
Seem going off of themselves; the cannon strain
Like hell-dogs in the leash. But he, he waits;   50
And lesser chances and inferior hopes
Meantime go pouring past. Men gnash their teeth;
The very faithful have begun to doubt;
But they molest not the calm eye that seeks
'Midst all this huddling silver little worth
The one thin piece that comes, pure gold. He waits,
O me, when the great deed e'en now has broke
Like a man's hand the horizon's level line,
So soon to fill the zenith with rich clouds;
Oh, in this narrow interspace, this moment,   60
This list and selvage of a glorious time,
To despair of the great and sell to the mean!
O thou of little faith, what hast thou done?
Yet if the occasion coming should find *us*
Undexterous, incapable? In light things
Prove thou the arms thou long'st to glorify,
Nor fear to work up from the lowest ranks
Whence come great Nature's captains. And high deeds
Haunt not the fringy edges of the fight,
But the pell-mell of men. Oh, what and if   70
E'en now by lingering here I let them slip,
Like an unpractised spyer through a glass,
Still pointing to the blank, too high! And yet,
In dead details to smother vital ends
Which should give life to them; in the deft trick
Of prentice-handling to forget great art,
To base mechanical adroitness yield
The Inspiration and the Hope, a slave!
Oh, and to blast that Innocence which, though
Here it may seem a dull unopening bud,   80
May yet bloom freely in celestial clime!

Were it not better done, then, to keep off
And see, not share, the strife; stand out the waltz
Which fools whirl dizzy in? Is it possible?
Contamination taints the idler first.
And without base compliance, e'en that same
Which buys bold hearts free course, Earth lends not these
Their pent and miserable standing-room.
Life loves no lookers-on at his great game,
And with boy's malice still delights to turn   90
The tide of sport upon the sitters-by,
And set observers scampering with their notes.
Oh, it is great to do and know not what,
Nor let it e'er be known. The dashing stream
Stays not to pick his steps among the rocks,
Or let his water-breaks be chronicled.
And though the hunter looks before he leap,
'Tis instinct rather than a shaped-out thought
That lifts him his bold way. Then, instinct, hail,
And farewell hesitation! If I stay,   100
I am not innocent; nor if I go—
E'en should I fall—beyond redemption lost.

Ah, if I had a course like a full stream,
If life were as the field of chase! No, no;
The age of instinct has, it seems, gone by,
And will not be forced back. And to live now
I must sluice out myself into canals,
And lose all force in ducts. The modern Hotspur
Shrills not his trumpet of 'To Horse, To Horse!'
But consults columns in a railway guide;   110
A demigod of figures; an Achilles
Of computation;
A verier Mercury, express come down
To *do* the world with swift arithmetic.
Well, one could bear with that; were the end ours,
One's choice and the correlative of the soul,

To drudge were then sweet service. But indeed
The earth moves slowly, if it move at all,
And by the general, not the single force.
At the [huge] members of the vast machine,   120
In all those crowded rooms of industry,
No individual soul has loftier leave
Than fiddling with a piston or a valve.
Well, one could bear that also: one could drudge
And do one's petty part, and be content
In base manipulation, solaced still
By thinking of the leagued fraternity,
And of co-operation, and the effect
Of the great engine. If indeed it work,
And is not a mere treadmill! Which it may be;   130
Who can confirm it is not? We ask Action,
And dream of arms and conflict; and string up
All self-devotion's muscles; and are set
To fold up papers. To what end? We know not.
Other folks do so; it is always done;
And it perhaps is right. And we are paid for it.
For nothing else we can be. He that eats
Must serve; and serve as other servants do:
And don the lacquey's livery of the house.
Oh, could I shoot my thought up to the sky,   140
A column of pure shape, for all to observe!
But I must slave, a meagre coral-worm,
To build beneath the tide with excrement
What one day will be island, or be reef,
And will feed men, or wreck them. Well, well, well.
Adieu, ye twisted thinkings. I submit.

Action is what one must get, it is clear,
And one could dream it better than one finds,
In its kind personal, in its motive not;
Not selfish as it now is, nor as now   150
Maiming the individual. If we had that,

273

It would cure all indeed. Oh, how would then
These pitiful rebellions of the flesh,
These caterwaulings of the effeminate heart,
These hurts of self-imagined dignity,
Pass like the seaweed from about the bows
Of a great vessel speeding straight to sea!
Yes, if we could have that; but I suppose
We shall not have it, and therefore I submit.

Spirit (from within)

Submit, submit!   160
'Tis common sense, and human wit
Can claim no higher name than it.
Submit, submit!

Devotion, and ideas, and love,
And beauty claim their place above;
But saint and sage and poet's dreams
Divide the light in coloured streams,
Which this alone gives all combined,
The *siccum lumen* of the mind
Called common sense: and no high wit   170
Gives better counsel than does it.
Submit, submit!

To see things simply as they are
Here, at our elbows, transcends far
Trying to spy out at midday
Some 'bright particular star,' which may,
Or not, be visible at night,
But clearly is not in daylight;
No inspiration vague outweighs
The plain good common sense that says,   180
Submit, submit!

'Tis common sense, and human wit
Can ask no higher name than it.
Submit, submit!

O did you think you were alone?
That I was so unfeeling grown
As not with joy to leave behind
My ninety-nine in hope to find
(How sweet the words my sense express!)
My lost sheep in the wilderness?   190

Scene X—The Piazza at Night

Dipsychus

There have been times, not many, but enough
To quiet all repinings of the heart;
There have been times, in which my [tranquil] soul,
No longer nebulous, sparse, errant, seemed
Upon its axis solidly to move,
Centred and fast; no mere chaotic blank
For random rays to traverse unretained,
But rounding luminous its fair ellipse
Around its central sun.
                              O happy hours!
O compensation ample for long days   10
Of what impatient tongues call wretchedness!
O beautiful, beneath the magic moon,
To walk the watery way of palaces!
O beautiful, o'ervaulted with gemmed blue,
This spacious court; with colour and with gold,
With cupolas, and pinnacles, and points,
And crosses multiplex, and tips and balls
(Wherewith the bright stars unreproving mix,
Nor scorn by hasty eyes to be confused);
Fantastically perfect this low pile   20
Of oriental glory; these long ranges
Of classic chiselling, this gay flickering crowd,
And the calm Campanile. Beautiful!
O beautiful! and that seemed more profound,

275

This morning by the pillar when I sat
Under the great arcade, at the review,
And took, and held, and ordered on my brain
The faces, and the voices, and the whole mass
O' the motley facts of existence flowing by!
O perfect, if 'twere all! But it is not;   30
Hints haunt me ever of a More beyond:
I am rebuked by a sense of the incomplete,
Of a completion over-soon assumed,
Of adding up too soon. What we call sin,
I could believe a painful opening out
Of paths for ampler virtue. The bare field,
Scant with lean ears of harvest, long had mocked
The vext laborious farmer. Came at length
The deep plough in the lazy undersoil
Down-driving; with a cry earth's fibres crack,   40
And a few months, and lo! the golden leas,
And autumn's crowded shocks and loaded wains.
Let us look back on life. Was any change,
Any now blest expansion, but at first
A pang, remorse-like, shot to the inmost seats
Of moral being? To do anything,
Distinct on any one thing to decide,
To leave the habitual and the old, and quit
The easy-chair of use and wont, seems crime
To the weak soul, forgetful how at first   50
Sitting down seemed so too. Oh, oh these qualms,
And oh these calls! And, oh! this woman's heart,
Fain to be forced, incredulous of choice,
And waiting a necessity for God.
    Yet I could think, indeed, the perfect call
Should force the perfect answer. If the voice
Ought to receive its echo from the soul,
Wherefore this silence? If it *should* rouse my being,
Why this reluctance? Have not I thought o'ermuch
Of other men, and of the ways of the world?   60

SCENE X DIPSYCHUS

But what they are, or have been, matters not.
To thine own self be true, the wise man says.
Are then my fears myself? O double self!
And I untrue to both. Oh, there are hours,
When love, and faith, and dear domestic ties,
And converse with old friends, and pleasant walks,
Familiar faces, and familiar books,
Study, and art, upliftings unto prayer,
And admiration of the noblest things,
Seem all ignoble only; all is mean,   70
And nought as I would have it. Then at others,
My mind is on her nest; my heart at home
In all around; my soul secure in place,
And the vext needle perfect to her poles.
Aimless and hopeless in my life I seem
To thread the winding byways of the town,
Bewildered, baffled, hurried hence and thence,
All at cross-purpose ever with myself,
Unknowing whence from whither. Then, in a moment,
At a step, I crown the Campanile's top,   80
And view all mapped below: islands, lagoon,
An hundred steeples and a million roofs,
The fruitful champaign, and the cloud-capt Alps,
And the broad Adriatic. Be it enough;
If I lose this, how terrible! No, no,
I am contented, and will not complain.
To the old paths, my soul! Oh, be it so!
I bear the workday burden of dull life
About these footsore flags of a weary world,
Heaven knows how long it has not been; at once,   90
Lo! I am in the Spirit on the Lord's day
With John in Patmos. Is it not enough,
One day in seven? and if this should go,
If this pure solace should desert my mind,
What were all else? I dare not risk this loss.
To the old paths, my soul!

Spirit

O yes.
To moon about religion; to inhume
Your ripened age in solitary walks,
For self-discussion; to debate in letters
Vext points with earnest friends; past other men   100
To cherish natural instincts, yet to fear them
And less than any use them. Oh, no doubt,
In a corner sit and mope, and be consoled
With thinking one is clever, while the room
Rings through with animation and the dance.
Then talk of old examples, and pervert
Ancient real facts to modern unreal dreams,
And build up baseless fabrics of romance
And heroism upon historic sand;
To burn, forsooth, for Action, yet despise   110
Its merest accidence and alphabet;
Cry out for service, and at once rebel
At the application of its plainest rules:
This you call life, my friend, reality;
Doing your duty unto God and man—
I know not what. Stay at Venice, if you will;
Sit musing in its churches hour on hour
Cross-kneed upon a bench; climb up at whiles
The neighbouring tower, and kill the lingering day
With old comparisons; when night succeeds,   120
Evading, yet a little seeking, what
You would and would not, turn your doubtful eyes
On moon and stars to help morality;
Once in a fortnight say, by lucky chance
Of happier-tempered coffee, gain (great Heaven!)
A pious rapture: is it not enough?
O that will keep you safe. Yet don't be sure—
Emotions are so slippery. Aye keep close
And burrow in your bedroom; pace up and down
A long half hour; with talking to yourself   130

Make waiters wonder; sleep a bit; write verse,
Burnt in disgust, then ill-restored, and left
Half-made, in pencil scrawl illegible.
Sink ere the end, most like, the hapless prey
Of some chance chambermaid, more sly than fair,
And in vain call for me. O well I know
You will not find, when I am not to help,
E'en so much face as hires a gondola.
Beware!—

Dipsychus

'Tis well; thou cursed spirit, go thy way!   140
I am in higher hands than yours. 'Tis well;
Who taught you menaces? Who told you, pray,
Because I asked you questions, and made show
Of hearing what you answered, therefore—

Spirit

                                        Oh,
As if I didn't know!

Dipsychus

                    Come, come, my friend,
I may have wavered, but I have thought better.
We'll say no more of it.

Spirit

                    Oh, I dare say:
But as you like; 'tis your own loss; once more,
Beware!

Dipsychus (alone)

Must it be then? So quick upon my thought   150
To follow the fulfilment and the deed?
I counted not on this; I counted ever
To hold and turn it over in my hands
Much longer, much. I took it up indeed,
For speculation rather; to gain thought,

New data. Oh, and now to be goaded on
By menaces, entangled amongst tricks!
That I won't suffer. Yet it is the law;
'Tis this makes action always. But for this
We ne'er should act at all; and act we must.   160
Why quarrel with the fashion of a fact
Which, one way, must be; one time, why not now?

Spirit

Submit, submit!
For tell me then, in earth's great laws
Have you found any saving clause,
Exemption special granted you
From doing what the rest must do?
Of Common Sense who made you quit,
And told you, you'd no need of it,
Nor to submit?   170

To move on angels' wings were sweet;
But who would therefore scorn his feet?
It cannot walk up to the sky;
It therefore will lie down and die.
Rich meats it don't obtain at call;
It therefore will not eat at all.
Poor babe, and yet a babe of wit!
But Common Sense? Not much of it,
Or 'twould submit.

Submit, submit!   180
As your good father did before you,
And as the mother who first bore you!
O yes! a child of heavenly birth!
But yet it *was* pupped too on earth.
Keep your new birth for that far day
When in the grave your bones you lay,
All with your kindred and connection,
In hopes of happy resurrection.

But how meantime to live is fit,
Ask Common Sense; and what says it?   190
Submit, submit!

'Tis Common Sense and human wit
Can find no higher name than it.
Submit, submit!

O I am with you, my sweet friend,
Yea, always, even to the end.

Scene XI

Dipsychus

'Tis gone, the fierce inordinate desire,
The burning thirst for Action—utterly;
Gone, like a ship that passes in the night
On the high seas; gone, yet will come again.
Gone, yet expresses something that exists.
Is it a thing ordained, then? is it a clue
For my life's conduct? is it a law for me
That opportunity shall breed distrust,
Not passing until that pass? Chance and resolve,
Like two loose comets wandering wide in space,   10
Crossing each other's orbits time on time,
Meet never. Void indifference and doubt
Let through the present boon, which ne'er turns back
To await the after sure-arriving wish.
How shall I then explain it to myself,
That in blank thought my purpose lives?
The uncharged cannon mocking still the spark
When come, which *ere* come it had loudly claimed.
Am I to let it be so still? For truly
The need exists, I know; the wish but sleeps   20
(Sleeps, and anon will wake and cry for food);
And to put by these unreturning gifts,
Because the feeling is not with me now

Which will I know be with me presently,
Seems folly more than merest babyhood's.
But must I then do violence to myself,
And push on nature, force desire (that's ill),
Because of knowledge? Which is great, but works
By rules of large exception; to tell which
Nought is less fallible than mere caprice.   30
To use knowledge well we must learn of ignorance:
To apply the rule forget the rule. Ah, but
I am compromised, you think. Oh, but indeed
I shan't do it more for that. No! nor refuse
To vindicate a scarce contested right
And certify vain independentness.

But what need is there? I am happy now,
I feel no lack—what cause is there for haste?
Am I not happy? is not that enough?

Spirit

O yes! O yes! and thought, no doubt,   40
'T had locked the very devil out.
He, he! He! he!—and didn't know
Through what small places we can go?
How do, my pretty dear? What! drying
It's pretty eyes? Has it been crying?

Dipsychus

Depart!

Spirit

O yes! you thought you had escaped, no doubt,
This worldly fiend that follows you about,
This compound of convention and impiety,
This mongrel of uncleanness and propriety.   50
What else were bad enough? but, let me say,
I too have my *grandes manières* in my way;
Could speak high sentiment as well as you,
And out-blank-verse you without much ado;

Have my religion also in my kind,
For dreaming unfit, because not designed.
What! you know not that I too can be serious,
Can speak big words, and use the tone imperious;
Can speak, not honeyedly of love and beauty,
But sternly of a something much like duty?   60
Oh, do you look surprised? were never told,
Perhaps, that all that glitters is not gold?
The Devil oft the Holy Scripture uses,
But God can act the Devil when He chooses.
Farewell! But, *verbum sapienti satis*—
I do not make this revelation gratis.
Farewell; beware!

Dipsychus

Ill spirits can quote holy books, I knew;
What will they *not* say? what not dare to do?

Spirit

Beware, beware!   70

Dipsychus

What, loitering still? Still, O foul spirit, there?
Go hence, I tell thee, go! I *will* beware.

(alone)

It must be then. I feel it in my soul;
The iron enters, sundering flesh and bone,
And sharper than the two-edged sword of God.
I come into deep waters—help, O help!
The floods run over me.

Therefore, farewell! a long and last farewell,
Ye pious sweet simplicities of life,
Good books, good friends, and holy moods, and all   80
That lent rough life sweet Sunday-seeming rests,
Making earth heaven-like. Welcome, wicked world,
The hardening heart, the calculating brain

Narrowing its doors to thought, the lying lips,
The calm-dissembling eyes; the greedy flesh,
The world, the Devil—welcome, welcome, welcome!

from within

This stern Necessity of things
On every side our being rings;
Our sallying eager actions fall
Vainly against that iron wall.   90
Where once her finger points the way,
The wise think only to obey;
Take life as she has ordered it,
And come what may of it, submit,
Submit, submit!

Who take implicitly her will,
For these her vassal-chances still
Bring store of joys, successes, pleasures;
But whoso ponders, weighs, and measures,
She calls her torturers up to goad   100
With spur and scourges on the road;
He does at last with pain whate'er
He spurned at first. Of such, beware,
Beware, beware!

Dipsychus

O God, O God! The great floods of the fiend
Flow over me! I come into deep waters
Where no ground is!

Spirit

Don't be the least afraid;
There's not the slightest reason for alarm.
I only meant by a perhaps rough shake
To rouse you from a dreamy, unhealthy sleep.   110
Up, then—up, and be going: the large world,
The thronged life waits us.

                                    Come, my pretty boy,
You have been making mows to the blank sky
Quite long enough for good. We'll put you up
Into the higher form. 'Tis time you learn
The Second Reverence, for things around.
Up, then, and go amongst them; don't be timid;
Look at them quietly a bit: by-and-by
Respect will come, and healthy appetite.
So let us go.
                        How now! not yet awake?   120
Oh, you will sleep yet, will you! Oh, you shirk,
You try and slink away! You cannot, eh?
Nay now, what folly's this? Why will you fool yourself?
Why will you walk about thus with your eyes shut,
Treating for facts the self-made hues that float
On tight-pressed pupils, which you know are not facts?
To use the undistorted light of the sun
Is not a crime; to look straight out upon
The big plain things that stare one in the face
Does not contaminate; to see pollutes not   130
What one must feel if one won't see; what *is*,
And will be too, howe'er we blink, and must
One way or other make itself observed.
Free walking's better than being led about; and
What will the blind man do, I wonder, if
Some one should cut the string of his dog? Just think,
What could you do, if I should go away?
   O, you have paths of your own before you, have you?
What shall it take to? literature, no doubt?
Novels, reviews? or poems! if you please!   140
The strong fresh gale of life will feel, no doubt,
The influx of your mouthful of soft air.
Well, make the most of that small stock of knowledge
You've condescended to receive from me;
That's your best chance. Oh, you despise that! Oh,
Prate then of passions you have known in dreams,

                        285   U

Of huge experience gathered by the eye;
Be large of aspiration, pure in hope,
Sweet in fond longings, but in all things vague.
Breathe out your dreamy scepticism, relieved   150
By snatches of old songs. People will like that, doubtless.
Or will you write about philosophy?
For a waste far-off *maybe* overlooking
The fruitful *is* close by, live in metaphysic,
With transcendental logic fill your stomach,
Schematise joy, effigiate meat and drink;
Or, let me see, a mighty Work, a Volume,
The Complemental of the inferior Kant,
The Critic of Pure Practic, based upon
The Antinomies of the Moral Sense: for, look you,   160
We cannot act without assuming x,
And at the same time y, its contradictory;
Ergo, to act. People will buy that, doubtless.
Or you'll perhaps teach youth (I do not question
Some downward turn you may find, some evasion
Of the broad highway's glaring white ascent),
Teach youth—in a small way; that is, always
So as to have much time left for yourself;
This you can't sacrifice, your leisure's precious.
Heartily you will not take to anything;   170
Will parents like that, think you? 'He writes poems,
He's odd opinions—hm!—and's not in Orders'—
For that you won't be. Well, old college fame,
The charity of some free-thinking merchant,
Or friendly intercession brings a first pupil;
And not a second. Oh, or if it should,
Whatever happen, don't I see you still,
Living no life at all? Even as now
An o'ergrown baby, sucking at the dugs
Of Instinct, dry long since. Come, come, you are old
     enough   180
For spoon-meat surely.

Will you go on thus
Until death end you? if indeed it does.
For what it does, none knows. Yet as for you,
You'll hardly have the courage to die outright;
You'll somehow halve even it. Methinks I see you,
Through everlasting limbos of void time,
Twirling and twiddling ineffectively,
And indeterminately swaying for ever.
Come, come, spoon-meat at any rate.
Well, well,
I will not persecute you more, my friend.   190
Only do think, as I observed before,
What *can* you do, if I should go away?

Dipsychus

Is the hour here, then? Is the minute come—
The irreprievable instant of stern time?
O for a few, few grains in the running glass,
Or for some power to hold them! O for a few
Of all that went so wastefully before!
It must be then, e'en now.

from within

It must, it must.
'Tis Common Sense! and human wit
Can claim no higher name than it.   200
Submit, submit!

Necessity! and who shall dare
Bring to *her* feet excuse or prayer?
Beware, beware!
We must, we must.
Howe'er we turn and pause and tremble—
Howe'er we shrink, deceive, dissemble—
Whate'er our doubting, grief, disgust,
The hand is on us, and we must,
We must, we must.   210

287

'Tis Common Sense! and human wit
Can find no better name than it.
Submit, submit!

Fear not, my lamb, whate'er men say,
I am the Shepherd; and the Way.

SCENE XII

Dipsychus

I had a vision; was it in my sleep?
And if it were, what then? But sleep or wake,
I saw a great light open o'er my head;
And sleep or wake, uplifted to that light,
Out of that light proceeding heard a voice
Uttering high words, which, whether sleep or wake,
In me were fixed, and in me must abide.

'When the enemy is near thee,
        Call on us!
In our hands we will upbear thee,   10
He shall neither scathe nor scare thee,
        Call on us!
Call when all good friends have left thee,
All good sights and sounds bereft thee;
Call when hope and heart are sinking,
And the brain is sick with thinking,
        Help, O help!
Call, and following close behind thee
There shall haste, and there shall find thee,
        Help, sure help.   20
When the panic comes upon thee,
When necessity seems on thee,
Hope and choice have all foregone thee,
Fate and force are closing o'er thee,

> And but one way stands before thee—
>   Call on us!
> Oh, and if thou dost not call,
> Be but faithful, that is all.
> Go right on, and close behind thee
> There shall follow still and find thee,   30
>   Help, sure help.'

Not for thy service, thou imperious fiend,
Not to do thy work, or the like of thine;
Not to please thee, O base and fallen spirit!
But One Most High, Most True, whom without thee
It seems I cannot.
               O the misery
That one must truck and practise with the world
To gain the 'vantage-ground to assail it from;
To set upon the giant one must first,
O perfidy! have eat the giant's bread.   40
If I submit, it is but to gain time
And arms and stature: 'tis but to lie safe
Until the hour strike to arise and slay:
'Tis the old story of the adder's brood
Feeding and nestling till the fangs be grown.
Were it not nobler done, then, to act fair,
To accept the service with the wages, do
Frankly the devil's work for the devil's pay?
Oh, but another my allegiance holds
Inalienably his. How much soe'er   50
I might submit, it must be to rebel.
Submit then sullenly, that's no dishonour.
Yet I could deem it better too to starve
And die untraitored. O, who sent me, though?
Some one, and to do something. O hard master!
To do a treachery. But indeed 'tis done:
I have already taken of the pay
And curst the payer; take I must, curse too.

Alas! the little strength that I possess
Derives, I think, of him. So still it is,   60
The timid child that clung unto her skirts,
A boy, will slight his mother, and, grown a man,
His father too. There's Scripture too for that!
Do we owe fathers nothing—mothers nought?
Is filial duty folly? Yet He says,
'He that loves father, mother more than me';
Yea, and 'the man his parents shall desert,'
The ordinance says, 'and cleave unto his wife.'
O man, behold thy wife, th' hard naked world;
Adam, accept thy Eve.
            So still it is,   70
The tree exhausts the soil; creepers kill it,
Their insects them: the lever finds its fulcrum
On what it then o'erthrows; the homely spade
In labour's hand unscrupulously seeks
Its first momentum on the very clod
Which next will be upturned. It seems a law.
And am not I, though I but ill recall
My happier age, a kidnapped child of Heaven,
Whom these uncircumcised Philistines
Have by foul play shorn, blinded, maimed, and kept   80
For what more glorious than to make them sport?
Wait, then, wait, O my soul! grow, grow, ye locks,—
Then perish they, and if need is, I too.

Spirit (aside)

A truly admirable proceeding!
Could there be finer special pleading
When scruples would be interceding?
There's no occasion I should stay;
He is working out, his own queer way,
The sum I set him; and this day
Will bring it, neither less nor bigger,   90
Exact to my predestined figure.

SCENE XIII

Dipsychus

Twenty-one past, twenty-five coming on;
One third of life departed, nothing done.
Out of the Mammon of Unrighteousness
That we make friends, the Scripture is express.
Mephisto, come; we will agree
Content; you'll take a moiety.

Spirit

A moiety, ye gods, he, he!

Dipsychus

Three quarters then. One eye you close,
And lay your finger to your nose.
Seven eighths? nine tenths? O griping beast!   10
Leave me a decimal at least.

Spirit

Oh, one of ten! to infect the nine
And make the devil a one be mine!
Oh, one! to jib all day, God wot,
When all the rest would go full trot!
One very little one, eh? to doubt with,
Just to pause, think, and look about with?
In course! you counted on no less—
You thought it likely I'd say yes!

Dipsychus

Be it then thus—since that it must, it seems.   20
Welcome, O world, henceforth; and farewell dreams!
Yet know, Mephisto, know, nor you nor I
Can in this matter either sell or buy;
For the fee simple of this trifling lot
To you or me, trust me, pertaineth not.

I can but render what is of my will,
And behind it somewhat remaineth still.
Oh, your sole chance was in the childish mind
Whose darkness dreamed that vows like this could bind;
Thinking all lost, it made all lost, and brought   30
In fact the ruin which had been but thought.
Thank Heaven (or you!) that's past these many years,
And we have knowledge wiser than our fears.
So your poor bargain take, my man,
And make the best of it you can.

Spirit

With reservations! oh, how treasonable!
When I had let you off so reasonable.
However, I don't fear; be it so!
Brutus is honourable, I know;
So mindful of the dues of others,   40
So thoughtful for his poor dear brothers,
So scrupulous, considerate, kind—
He wouldn't leave the devil behind
If he assured him he had claims
For his good company to hell-flames!
No matter, no matter, the bargain's made;
And I for my part will not be afraid.
Little Bo Peep, she lost her sheep
And knew not where to find them.
He, he! With reservations, Christo!   50
A child like you to cheat Mephisto!
With reservations! oh! ho, ho!
But time, my friend, has yet to show
Which of us two will closest fit
The proverb of the Biter Bit.
Little Bo Peep, she lost her sheep—

Dipsychus

Tell me thy name, now it is over.

Spirit

Oh!

Why, Mephistopheles, you know—
At least you've lately called me so;
Belial it was some days ago.   60
But take your pick; I've got a score—
Never a royal baby more.
For a brass plate upon a door
What think you of *Cosmocrator*?

Dipsychus

Τοὺς κοσμοκράτορας τοῦ αἰῶνος τούτου,
And that you are indeed, I do not doubt you.

Spirit

Ephesians, ain't it? near the end
You dropt a word to spare your friend.
What follows, too, in application
Would be absurd exaggeration.   70

Dipsychus

The Power of this World! hateful unto God!

Spirit

Cosmarchon's shorter, but sounds odd:
One wouldn't like, even if a true devil,
To be taken for a vulgar Jew devil.

Dipsychus

Yet in all these things we—'tis Scripture too—
Are more than conquerors, even over you.

Spirit

Come, come, don't maunder any longer,
Time tests the weaker and the stronger;
And we, without procrastination,
Must set, you know, to our vocation.   80

293

O goodness; won't you find it pleasant
To own the positive and present;
To see yourself like people round,
And feel your feet upon the ground!

Little Bo Peep, she lost her sheep!

Dipsychus

Peace, peace! I come.

(*Exeunt ambo*)

EPILOGUE

'I DON'T very well understand what it's all about,' said my uncle. 'I won't say I didn't drop into a doze while the young man was drivelling through his later soliloquies. But there was a great deal that was unmeaning, vague, and involved; and what was most plain was least decent and least moral.'

'Dear sir,' said I, 'says the proverb—"Needs must when the devil drives"; and if the devil is to speak—'

'Well,' said my uncle, 'why should he? Nobody asked him. Not that he didn't say much which, if only it hadn't been for the way he said it, and that it was he who said it, would have been sensible 10 enough.'

'But, sir,' said I, 'perhaps he wasn't a devil after all. That's the beauty of the poem; nobody can say. You see, dear sir, the thing which it is attempted to represent is the conflict between the tender conscience and the world. Now, the over-tender conscience will, of course, exaggerate the wickedness of the world; and the Spirit in my poem may be merely the hypothesis or subjective imagination, formed—'

'Oh, for goodness' sake, my dear boy,' interrupted my uncle, 'don't go into the theory of it. If you're wrong in it, it makes bad 20 worse; if you're right, you may be a critic, but you can't be a poet.

And then you know very well I don't understand all those new words. But as for that, I quite agree that consciences are often much too tender in your generation—schoolboys' consciences, too! As my old friend the Canon says of the Westminster students, "They're all so pious." It's all Arnold's doing; he spoilt the public schools.'

'My dear uncle,' said I, 'how can so venerable a sexagenarian utter so juvenile a paradox? How often have I not heard you lament the idleness and listlessness, the boorishness and vulgar tyranny, the brutish manners alike, and minds—' 30

'Ah!' said my uncle, 'I may have fallen in occasionally with the talk of the day; but at seventy one begins to see clearer into the bottom of one's mind. In middle life one says so many things in the way of business. Not that I mean to say that the old schools were perfect, any more than we old boys that were there. But whatever else they were or did, they certainly were in harmony with the world, and they certainly did not disqualify the country's youth for after-life and the country's service.'

'But, my dear sir, this bringing the schools of the country into harmony with public opinion is exactly—' 40

'Don't interrupt me with public opinion, my dear nephew; you'll quote me a leading article next. "Young men must be young men," as the worthy head of your college said to me touching a case of rustication. "My dear sir," answered I, "I only wish to heaven they would be; but as for my own nephews, they seem to me a sort of hobbadi-hoy cherub, too big to be innocent, and too simple for anything else. They're full of the notion of the world being so wicked, and of their taking a higher line, as they call it. I only fear they'll never take any at all." What is the true purpose of education? Simply to make plain to the young understanding the laws of the 50 life they will have to enter. For example—that lying won't do, thieving still less; that idleness will get punished; that if they are cowards, the whole world will be against them; that if they will have their own way, they must fight for it. Etc. etc. As for the conscience, mamma, I take it—such as mammas are now-a-days, at any rate— has probably set that a-going fast enough already. What a blessing to see her good little child come back a brave young devil-may-care!'

'Exactly, my dear sir. As if at twelve or fourteen a roundabout boy, with his three meals a day inside him, is likely to be over-troubled with scruples.' 60

'Put him through a course of confirmation and sacraments, backed up with sermons and private admonitions, and what is much the same as auricular confession, and really, my dear nephew, I can't answer for it but he mayn't turn out as great a goose as you—pardon me—*were* about the age of eighteen or nineteen.'

'But to have passed *through* that, my dear sir! surely that can be no harm.'

'I don't know. Your constitutions don't seem to recover it, quite. We did without these foolish measles well enough in my time.'

'Westminster had its Cowper, my dear sir; other schools theirs 70 also, mute and inglorious, but surely not few.'

'Ah, ah! the beginning of troubles—'

'You see, my dear sir, you must not refer it to Arnold, at all at all. Anything that Arnold did in this direction—'

'Why, my dear boy, how often have I not heard from you, how he used to attack offences, not as offences—the right view—against discipline, but as sin, heinous guilt, I don't know what beside! Why didn't he flog them and hold his tongue? Flog them he did, but why preach?'

'If he did err in this way, sir, which I hardly think, I ascribe it to 80 the spirit of the time. The real cause of the evil you complain of, which to a certain extent I admit, was, I take it, the religious movement of the last century, beginning with Wesleyanism, and culminating at last in Puseyism. This over-excitation of the religious sense, resulting in this irrational, almost animal irritability of conscience, was, in many ways, as foreign to Arnold as it is proper to—'

'Well, well, my dear nephew, if you like to make a theory of it, pray write it out for yourself nicely in full; but your poor old uncle does not like theories, and is moreover sadly sleepy.'

'Good night, dear uncle, good night. Only let me say you six 90 more verses.'

NOTES

The sources of the text of the poems, printed or manuscript, are described in § II of the Introduction.

AMBARVALIA

Ambarvalia was published in January 1849 and was a joint production by Clough and his friend Thomas Burbidge. Clough's part, the first sixty-four pages, was reissued in 1850 as a separate volume. He proposed to exclude about one-third of them from the collected edition of his poems which he had prepared for publication in America before he died (see Introduction, p. vii). He had also provided titles for some of them. The poems were written at Oxford, between 1839 and 1847. They are printed here in the order in which they appeared in *Ambarvalia*, without the later titles, but with some corrections made by Clough.

'The human spirits saw I on a day' (*p.* 1)

C. wrote THROUGH A GLASS DARKLY in a marked copy of *1850*. His posthumous editors gave it a different title: THE QUESTIONING SPIRIT.

'Ah, what is love' (*p.* 2) and 'I give thee joy!' (*p.* 3)

Both omitted in *1862, 1863, 1869*. C.'s suggested titles were FLET NOCTEM and IN FAITH, NOTHING WAVERING.

'When panting sighs' (*p.* 4)

Title LOVE AND REASON inserted *1869*. There are longer versions of the poem in the MSS.

SIC ITUR (*p.* 7)

Title (not in *Amb.*) supplied by C.

COMMEMORATION SONNETS (*p.* 7)

Omitted *1862, 1863, 1869*. The occasion was the visit of the King of Saxony to receive a degree at the Oxford Encaenia in June 1844.

'Come back again my olden heart' (*p.* 9)

Title THE HIGHER COURAGE inserted *1869*.

'When soft September' (*p.* 11)

Title WRITTEN ON A BRIDGE inserted *1869*.

'Oh, ask not what is love' (*p.* 11)

Omitted *1862, 1863, 1869*.

NOTES

'Light words they were' (*p.* 12)
Title A PROTEST inserted *1869*.

'With graceful seat' (*p.* 13)
Omitted *1862*, *1863*, *1869*. C.'s suggested title was CONTEMPLATOR.

WHEN ISRAEL CAME OUT OF EGYPT (*p.* 16)
Title changed to THE NEW SINAI *1862*, *1863*, *1869*.

'Why should I say I see the things I see not' (*p.* 21)
First 28 lines omitted *1862*, *1863*, restored, and title THE MUSIC OF THE WORLD AND OF THE SOUL inserted, *1869*.

'Sweet streamlet bason' (*p.* 23)
Title A RIVER POOL inserted *1869*.

'Away, haunt thou not me' (*p.* 24)
Title IN A LECTURE ROOM inserted *1862*, *1863*, *1869*.

'My wind is turned to bitter north' (*p.* 24)
Title A SONG OF AUTUMN inserted *1869*.

'Look you, my simple friend' (*p.* 25)
Omitted *1862*, *1863*, *1869*. C.'s suggested title THE POET.

'Thought may well be ever ranging' (*p.* 26)
C.'s suggested title DUTY-LOVE, but LOVE NOT DUTY inserted *1869*.

'Duty—that's to say complying' (*p.* 27)
Title DUTY inserted *1869*.

'BLANK MISGIVINGS . . .' (*p.* 28)
Sections I and IV omitted *1862*, *1863*, restored *1869*. Section X printed as a separate poem, *1862*, *1863*, *1869* and title τὸ καλόν inserted *1869*.

ALCAICS (*p.* 35)
Omitted *1862*, *1863*, restored *1869*. An exercise in a classical metre written before the *Bothie*.

ὁ θεὸς μετὰ σοῦ (*p.* 38) (ho theos meta sou)
There are three MSS., which contain, altogether, thirty-eight lines not included by C. in his final version.

'Ἐπὶ Δάτμῳ (*p.* 39)

Omitted *1862*, *1863*, restored *1869*.

'Is it true, ye gods' (*p.* 43)

Omitted *1862*, *1863*, restored, and title WEN GOTT BETRÜGT IST WOHL BE-
TROGEN inserted, *1869*.

SHORTER POEMS

NEARLY all these poems were published in one or more of the posthumous editions, from C.'s MSS. Some had been selected by him for inclusion in the collected edition which he was planning with C. E. Norton (see Introduction, p. vii). Eight of them appeared for the first time in the Oxford edition of 1951. The poems are here printed in chronological order of composition, as far as is known or surmised.

The first eight were written between 1839 and 1847, while C. was at Oxford, and belong to the same period as *Ambarvalia*. Nos. 9–38 were written after he resigned his Oxford Fellowship in 1848 and before he sailed for America in 1852. The remaining poems were written in 1852 and 1853, some on the voyage across the Atlantic, some in America, and two or three, perhaps, just before he left England or soon after he got back.

As in the case of the *Ambarvalia* poems, a number of titles which have no known MS. authority were inserted by the posthumous editors, and are noted below.

1. Not in *1862*, *1863*. Title THE THREAD OF TRUTH inserted *1869*.
2. Not in *1862*, *1863*. Title THE SHADY LANE inserted *1869*.
3. Not in *1862*, *1863*. Title REVIVAL inserted 1869.
4. Not in *1862*, *1863*. Title *WIRKUNG IN DER FERNE* inserted 1869.
5, 6, 7. First published *1951*.
12. The MS. originally contained an opening section of 10 lines, but the leaf containing them was cut off the main folder, perhaps by C. himself, and the lines were omitted in *1869* and in *1951*. They are as follows:

> So while the blear-eyed pimp beside me walked,
> And talked,
> For instance, of the beautiful danseuse,
> And 'Eccellenza sure must see, if he would choose'
> Or of the lady in the green silk there,
> Who passes by and bows with minx's air,
> Or of the little thing not quite fifteen,
> Sicilian-born who surely should be seen.
> So while the blear-eyed pimp beside me walked
> And talked, and I too with fit answer talked,

13. The last four lines were printed for the first time in *1951*.
14. Title THROUGH A GLASS DARKLY inserted *1869*.
16. There were at least six MSS. of this famous poem, the earliest a rough draft in a notebook used by C. when he was in Rome in 1849 during its siege and capture by the French. It has long been assumed that it first appeared in print in *1862*, but it was in fact published in an American art journal, *The Crayon*, in 1855 (the discovery was reported by F. G. Townsend in *Publications of the Modern Language Association of America*, vol. lxvii, p. 1191, December 1952).

The *1951* text, here reprinted, differs significantly in two places from *1862* and all other previous editions. In them l. 4 reads 'And as things have been they remain', but all the MSS., and *The Crayon*, have '. . . have been, things remain'. In previous editions, and in *The Crayon*, l. 12 reads 'Comes silent, flooding in, the main', but the MSS. have 'Came, silent, . . .'
There is a discussion of the text by A. L. P. Norrington in *Essays . . . presented to Sir Humphrey Milford* (O.U.P. 1948), written without knowledge of the publication in *The Crayon*.

17. The first thirty-four lines were omitted in *1862* and subsequent editions and first printed, from the MS., in *1951*. Title AT ROME inserted (for ll. 35–88) in *1869*.

19. Title *ITE DOMUM SATURAE, VENIT HESPERUS* inserted *1862, 1863, 1869*.

20. First published *1951*.

21. First published in *Putnam's Magazine*, 1854, and subsequently in *1862*, etc. The poem was written in August 1850 and the last two lines of the first and last stanzas echo Tennyson's *In Memoriam*, published in the same year.

23. First published *1951*.

24. Title WITH WHOM IS NO VARIABLENESS, NEITHER SHADOW OF TURNING inserted *1869*.

25, 26. First published *1951*.

27. Not in *1862, 1863*. Title ἀνεμώλια (anemolia, 'windy words') inserted *1869*.

28, 29. Not in *1862, 1863*.

32. Title AH! YET CONSIDER IT AGAIN inserted *1869*.

33. Title WHAT WENT YE OUT FOR TO SEE? inserted *1869*.

34. First published in *Putnam's Magazine*, 1853. Not in *1862*. Title PERCHÈ PENSA? PENSANDO S'INVECCHIA inserted *1869*.

35. Not in *1862, 1863*. Title IN THE DEPTHS inserted *1869*.

36. Not in *1862*.

37. Not in *1862, 1863*. Title IN STRATIS VIARUM inserted *1869*.

38. Title IN A LONDON SQUARE inserted *1869*.

39. First published in *Fraser's Magazine*, 1853. Not in *1862, 1863*.

40–52. Printed in a group in *1869* with the general title SONGS IN ABSENCE, and with the footnote 'These songs were composed either during the writer's voyage across the Atlantic in 1852, or during his residence in America'. Nos. 40, 41, 46, 50, and 51 are not in *1862, 1863*.

53. Not in *1863*. Title COLUMBUS inserted *1869*.

54. First published 1951.

55. Title TO A SLEEPING CHILD inserted *1862, 1863, 1869*.

56. First published in *Putnam's Magazine*, 1853.

57. First published in *Putnam's Magazine*, 1853. Not in *1862*. Title πάντα ῥεῖ— οὐδὲν μένει (panta rhei, ouden menei, 'everything is in flux, nothing stays still') inserted *1869*.

58. Title THE STREAM OF LIFE inserted *1869*.

59. Not in *1862, 1863*. Title SHADOW AND LIGHT inserted *1869*.

60. Not in *1862, 1863*.

62. Not in *1862, 1863*. Title ELEGIACS inserted *1869*.

63. Not in *1862, 1863*.

THE BOTHIE OF TOBER-NA-VUOLICH

THE *Bothie* was written at great speed in the autumn of 1848, probably in less than six weeks, sent straight to the printers, and published in December. An American edition appeared in 1849. It had this dedication: 'My long-vacation pupils will I hope allow me to inscribe this trifle to them, and will not, I trust, be displeased if in a fiction, purely fiction, they are here and there reminded of times we enjoyed together.' Its 1848 title was *The Bothie of Toper-na-Fuosich*, but no sooner had the poem been published than C. was told that the name had an unseemly meaning. 'You remember Toper na Fuosich, in the map', he wrote to Tom Arnold in New Zealand on 24 February 1849, 'on Loch Ericht—and how I made out afterwards that Dallungart was the present name. Good reason why! For now that . . . I have published the name to all the drawing rooms and boudoirs (of course) of all the world—What think you?—It turns out, they tell me, to mean what Horace calls "teterrima belli causa" . . . in the boat on Loch Ericht I asked the boatman 1st where it was, and 2nd what it meant. He replied, the bairds' well, which I could not understand. Did he mean the *bairns'* well? homunculorum fons et origo.' A new name was accordingly chosen at random by C. and substituted in *1862*. It is not certain, however, that the information given to C. in 1849 was correct. The Gaelic may have meant nothing worse than 'the well of the frightful (*or* bearded) woman'. The present editor was once told that there was a hamlet in the west of England whose name, 'St. Paul's Epistle', was originally 'bull's pizzle'. Countrymen will have their jokes.

The text printed after C.'s death differed in more than title. He had begun to revise the poem in 1859, and a copy of the 1848 edition has been preserved with C.'s corrections in it, almost all of which were carried out in *1862*. In addition to verbal changes, about 200 lines were omitted (about twenty-five of them were restored in 1863), and about ten new lines added. Our text follows *1863*, and is thus nearly 200 lines shorter than *1848*. A few of the lines omitted are printed below.

II

Before l. 51

> I was too awkward, too shy, a great deal, be assured, for advances,
> Shyly I shambled away, stopping oft, but afraid of returning,
> Shambled obliquely away, with furtive occasional sidelook,
> Long, though listless no more, in my awkward hobbadiboyhood.
> Still, though a new thing was in me, though vernal emotion, the secret,
> Yes, amid prurient talk, the unimparted mysterious secret
> Long, the growing distress, and celled-up dishonour of boyhood,
> Recognised now took its place, a relation, oh bliss! unto others;

1848

V

110–13 A longer version of this passage occurs in a MS. which seems to be an early draft of Cantos I–III:

> Nay then but is not the Useful alone the Beautiful truly?
> She that is handy is handsome; good dairymaids must be goodlooking,
> So but the butter be nice, the ancles are sure to be taper,
> So but the cream cheese white, far whiter the hands that produced it,
> So but the bed be well made, who made it is worthy to fill it,
> Proof of the pudding the eating, and proof of the girl be the pudding.

IX

Before l. 40

> But they will marry, have husbands, and children, and guests, and households—
> Are there then so many trades for a man, for women one only,
> First to look out for a husband and then to preside at his table?
> Learning to dance, then dancing, then breeding, and entertaining?
> Breeding and rearing of children at any rate the poor do
> Easier, say the doctors, and better, with all their slaving.
> How many, too, disappointed, not being this, can be nothing!
> How many more are spoilt for wives by the means to become so,
> Spoilt for wives and mothers, and every thing else moreover!

1848

AMOURS DE VOYAGE

WRITTEN in 1849, when C. was spending three months in Rome. There are three versions: (i) an early draft in two notebooks, with alternative or additional lines in other MSS., considerably longer than the printed versions; (ii) the version printed in the *Atlantic Monthly* (*A.M.*) in 1858; (iii) the posthumous version of *1862*, containing further revisions and sixty-four lines longer than *A.M.*

Some of the lines in the early draft, omitted in *A.M.* and *1862*, are printed below.

CANTO I

After l. 50

> Flippant all this and absurd, and doubtless your host of exclaimants,
> Goethe included, are right, but till I admire, I shall cavil.
> Admiration I doubt not is due; and indeed after sitting
> In the Pantheon two hours, I thought I had got a sensation,
> But as you know very well if one sat in a ditch for two hours
> One could contrive to imagine great things about Earth and Water.
> So though I lie on my back and adore the Sistine frescos
> Till the Custode returns the fifth time; I cannot be certain.
> Great is learning indeed, but safer a deal is Nature
> Great is Antiquity truly, but I, if I am small, *am* small.

After l. 167

> No thou stately Pantheon, thou art not Christian, canst not
> Alter, improve, and embellish, and do what they will to thee, be so!
> No, my dear Eustace, how rapid soever the sequence of service
> However warm the extatics of that too devotional damsel
> However fervent the kisses impressed on the daub of a Virgin
> However many the altars and however pious the pictures,
> However glibly the priest pitter patters the Ave Maria,
> I,—somehow,—could not manage, Our Father which are in Heaven!

After l. 204

> Hoping still for the possible tin yet to come. Oh, doubtless
> Fairly descended; past question; yet of all things I least like
> These poor younger sons that make their money in commerce.
> These who ascend to the work are respectable, those who inherit
> More so, they do it, one thinks, as duty at once and pleasure;
> These men take to it simply and solely to make their fortunes.
> And they lose the morale of their order, and, like the Spartans
> In the old books, losing that can never attain to another.
> What can a poor devil do who would honestly earn him his victuals?
> What can he do, you ask! why, of course, go into the Army,
> Or which is better, it may be, the Navy! But fighting is over,

And the industrial age not of gold but of well-endorsed paper
Slowly, but certainly, Io Triumphe; Huzza; Hallelujah;
Slowly advances but surely with 'PEACE' on a Calico banner.
Well, take orders like you! and truly the rectory parlour
Is not untempting; alack! but our foolish people of England
Is in these last days turned so theology-sick that one could not
Possibly now settle down in a peaceful Arcadian parish,
But one were forced to attend and receive one's clerical Meetings.
And gradatim be steeped in professional tan; sit bound, and
Feel the insidious moistures come oozing in! be stuck to
Listen while gravely paraded the obsoletest of follies
Try on their modern costumes; take a part; get angry, and quarrel,
Vex one's friends and oneself, and in fine to prevent worse evil
Turn (the more popular course) Evangelical, or, the refined one,
Puseyite!—Ah but indeed my ladylike priests and deacons,
Ah but indeed indeed my lofty Tractarian friends, it
Is odd to see *you* at last condescending to be religious.
Oh, but democracy makes sad inroads here! Your fathers
Managed these things much better—this matter of Church and Religion.
Oh! they gave it their proper support! Of course!—but did not
Trust me for that reason ever forget what was due to their station:
Lent it their names as was fit, but maintained, above all, their position.
Sometimes consented to wear too its honours; accepted with grace its
Offices, charges, emoluments, place and appurtenant income,
Put on its lawn and its purple; but lived—superior to them.
Yes, as you say, took its money, performed its perfunctory functions
Patronized it—as the Arts and the Lying-in Hospitals; kept it
Up—with the Chace and the Turf and the other great Institutions
Not to be lightly abandoned—but *You*—you go and believe it!
Wish to obey,—to learn,—to realize—make efficacious:
Ah,—but are you not quitting the pale of a Sacreder Church, yea
Rudely, profanely, the Voice of an older Antiquity scorning
Laying-waste pillars and walls and with axes and hammers destroying
All the cedar-work choice of a yet more auguster religion?
Perverts, renegades mere, from a great esoteric belief, a
Vast Eleusinian system of lady-and-gentleman doctrine,
With its own careful tradition, its pure Apostolic succession
Reaching far back in a clear though a delicate line through the ages
With its own Martyrs and Saints, its kingly and queenly Confessors,
Saints of high breeding and Martyrs of self-sustaining composure.
Ah, for I fear me this faith, if you come to your realizations,
Scarce will submit to alliance—with vulgar New Testament doings.
No as a younger son and bound to be not overnice I
Could, I believe, endure much, but hardly the *Cloth*. The *Pulpit*,
After a season, perhaps, with those glorious Anglican fathers
Sterne and our own Sydney Smith for exemplars in style and in matter;
Sermons in time no doubt, but scarcely the Clerical Meetings.
Public Offices then! but to beg one is fairly ashamed, and
Dig one cannot; or else, not to name Californian diggings,
There is the Cape to be dug with the Vines and occasional Caffres,
Snowy Canadian woods, penitential Australian acres
And the Phlegraean fields, far famed, of the Cannibal islands.

Digging's a thing to be learnt, but begging comes easier somehow
And the dear country appears to consider us still worth the feeding.
Eat one must, one thinks, and drink, and assuredly dress, and
If God will one is smit with a fancy for one of one's equals,
Marry; and have small children; who in their turn must likewise,
Eat and drink and be drest younger sons of younger brothers.
Starving meanwhile is a quiet and most inexpensive process;
I for my part now and then could all but incline to prefer it!

CANTO II

After l. 27

When with the guilt of a single ill-deed a most suffering race have
Rid them of three heavy century loads of confusion and wrong—But
What is the good of my talking? Yet Politics I will confess it,
Yes, my political friends, I recant and acknowledge, have something
Generous—something organic Creative and Art-like in them;
Something at some great times which a man forgetting all else and
Casting to moles and to bats his idols of thought and self knowledge,
Losing his soul for the gospel, with joy could embrace and could die in—
Could as it were with quick fingers extinguish the light in the chamber,
Enter the great bridal bed of the combat and conflict of men, and
Know not, nor ask, whether morning should ever return to awake him.
This is delusion, of course, as the rest; but delusions are nobler
When they apply to great numbers, when not to ourselves; and always
What is creative is good and the purpose of Nature. For which cause
I with the fervent apostle acknowledging gifts without number
Gifts of tongues and of ologies, governments, helps and healings,
Show you yet a more excellent Way. For now abideth—
Politics, Art, and Love, these three, and of these the greatest
Is—but I am not the Shepherd Idaean to settle the question—
Politics, Art, and Love, and the greatest of these is the purest.

After l. 248

When God makes a great Man he intends all others to crush him:
Pharaoh indeed, it is true, didn't put down Moses, but then that
Happened in barbarous times ere Polity rose to perfection
Ere the World had known bankers, and funds, and representation.
Rise up therefore ye Kings, and ye, ye Presidents! bring forth
Bayonet, mortar and bomb, and that patent tool the soldier!
Murder and mangle and waste and establish order. But meantime
Honour to lofty Speech and the Voice of the godlike spirit;
Yea—*though* journals write and ministers make explanations,
Spite of the able Débats, and the Eloquent Odillon-Barrot,
Honour yet to the Tongue, and the Pen of the Ready Writer,
Honour to speech and great honour to thee, thou noble Mazzini!—
Rise up therefore ye Kings and ye, ye Presidents—Ah, but
What is the use of all this? let me sing the song of the shopman
And my last word be like his: let me shout, with the chorus of journals,
O happy Englishmen we! that so truly can quote from Lucretius
Suave mari magno—how pleasant indeed in a tempest

Safe from the window to watch and behold the great trouble of others.
O blessed government ours, blessed Empire of Purse and Policeman,
Fortunate islands of Order, Utopia of—breeches-pockets,
O happy England, and oh great glory of self-laudation.

CANTO III

The following two extra letters are in the early draft:

CLAUDE TO EUSTACE

Curious things are whales. I speak apropos of the Triton.
Curious, Nature's strife in the waters first, in the air, in
This kind, that, to work up to her limit of organization.
Curious also the thought of Creation, embodied most purely
As I have seen it at last on the roof of the Sistine Chapel,
Man taking shape by the Act of the thought of the absolute thinker.
  Meanwhile notice, my brother, in Genesis, chapter the 1st, how
He who made great whales and the like, on the previous mornings
Says, let the Earth bring forth, let the Waters produce and so on
But on the day so momentous for you and for me, on a sudden
Alters his word to the form, Let Us make man in our Image.
Lo, Inspiration discerns the Creative and Germinant Methods,
And from Immediate Act thus discriminates Natural Process.
Curious surely this fact and I only this moment observed it.
Not that I trust it; tho' doubtless in some old Papa you may find it,
I do not trust it; but you who have got to expound us the Scripture,
Weekly or is it *bi*-weekly? might manage a sermon about it.
I for the pulpit unlicensed in humble and laical function
Must for my commoner wear, for my week-day and work-day thinking
Suffer my soul to relapse to the faith of the lady in Tancred,
First we were nothing, and then we were something, and then something else, and
Something succeeding to that, and so to the nth; which is not
Human Nature, I guess; but, say, the divine Ideal:
No, *we* stand with the brutes at the other side of the series
With an huge gap between, unfillable-up, an hiatus
Valde deflendus indeed betwixt the ideals and reals
Those descendent from God and these from Nothing ascendent.
What we are we know in a fashion, but what we shall be
Or more correctly to speak what will be to us succeeding
That we must leave I suppose to our Mother the tail-eraser;
Only on Sundays of course remembering still to remember
Far away over the gap with a term or two before him
Out of sight, and alas out of mind, the Divine Ideal.
  What will you say to all this? will you smile or be vexed and be solemn?
Is it in earnest? you hope not; and yet if in jest, is it better?
Well—we must try all things and hold fast that which is—proper.

CLAUDE TO EUSTACE

Oh you are perfectly right to scorn these sceptical follies.
And you *will* properly scorn them, I see you; will call them affected
False and assumed, or to use my own favorite word, factitious.

It was an effort, my friend, most futile, I shall not repeat it
Truly I cannot sustain it, to write in my old flippant manner.
    No, I am not, you may trust me in any true sense a Sceptic,
Not in the highest things a Sceptic, however I seem so.
Look you, most people accepting, as Time or Locality, Birth or
Education suggests, some *particular* things, are therefore
Credited largely for faith, heaven help us, in *things in general.*
I who sincerely believe, as I fancy, in *things in general,*
That is, in God, you know, am a sceptic forsooth, as I do not
Make-up instanter my mind to believe in your *things in particular.*
I am, believe me, at bottom nor sceptic nor unbeliever,
Misbeliever perhaps, as I go the wrong way about it;
So it would seem; yet rather account me an over-believer
Young and romantic; perhaps as you say too a little bit cracky.

CANTO V

The following extra letter from Eustace to Claude is in the early draft, before
letter ii:

No I didn't think much of your sceptical letters. Far from it.
No: but believe me my friend God walks a great orb above us
All that we look on and see is illumined by His light only:
Why should a man shut his shutters in daylight, to follow the flickering
Infinitesimal ray of his own petty halfpenny candle?
Yes, I do scorn as you say, your sceptical vein: for, I know, it
Cannot endure the test of a single good minute of Action.
Action involves belief. *In*action such stuff as you sent me.
Act and all will be clear; the Laws of Action are God's laws:
What they entail to our Minds, God's gift and prime revelation,
This is His world, you know, and He didn't make Man to cheat him.
Yet I could venture to say too that even if life be delusion,
'Tis a delusion of God, and we need not fear to accept it.
But I am greatly rejoicing to think of you now as at Florence.
Happy, ere this, in the presence of something that's better than Tibur.

DIPSYCHUS

Dipsychus was first published in *Letters and Remains of Arthur Hugh Clough* printed for private circulation in 1865. Mrs. Clough then thought it 'too unfinished to be published among his poems', but it was subsequently included in the collected editions of 1869 and thereafter. The poem was begun during a visit to Venice in 1850. In the first draft the speakers are 'Mephisto' and 'Faustulus', but in the later drafts became 'Dipsychus' ('double-minded', the man 'in two minds') and 'The Spirit'.

His fiancée came across the MSS. while Clough was in America in 1852, and wrote to him to ask if she might read them. 'Please don't read Dipsychus yet', he wrote back, 'I wish particularly not. You shall see it sometime—but not now, please.' He had copied three short extracts—less than thirty lines in all—into a notebook of fair copies of unpublished poems which he had given to Blanche Smith before he sailed to America, and at the end of his life he wrote out a longer version of 'As I sat at the café, I said to myself' (Scene IV) in a notebook containing parts of *Mari Magno*. Apart from this, he seems to have put the poem aside, unfinished, after 1851. Eight extracts were printed in *1862*, and two more in *1863*—about 300 lines in all. They were all printed as part of *Dipsychus* in 1865, but 'O let me love my love unto myself alone' was again printed separately (as well as within *Dipsychus*) and in a longer version, with the title THE HIDDEN LOVE, in 1869.

In constructing her text Mrs. Clough not only used the methods of combination and choice which the state of the MSS. forces upon an editor if a coherent text is aimed at, but also omitted many lines and one entire scene. The text of the Oxford edition of 1951, here reprinted, is based on a fresh examination of the MSS., and is longer by nearly 400 lines.

SCENE IIA. The whole of this scene was omitted by Mrs. Clough, except for Dipsychus' opening speech ('O moon and stars forgive'), which she printed as the ending of Scene II. The MS. in which it occurs seems to have been C.'s second revision. He omitted it in his third (and last) revision, but the general plan of the poem is clearer if the scene is retained. The 1951 editors printed a selection of lines intended to preserve the general sense and the best of the verse. The missing lines are printed below:

Dipsychus
O hateful, hateful, hateful To the Hotel!

Spirit
Pooh, what the devil! what's the harm?
I merely bid you take her arm.

NOTES

Dipsychus

And I half yielded! O unthinking I!
O weak weak fool! O God how quietly
Out of our better into our worse selves
Out of a true world which our reason knew
Into a false world which our fancy makes
We pass and never know—O weak weak fool.

Spirit

Well, if you don't wish, why, you don't.
Leave it! but that's just what you won't.
Come now! how many times per diem
Are you not hankering to try 'em
    [*Here follow ll. 1–11 of our text, D. speaking.*]
O were it that vile questioner that loves
To thrust his fingers into right and wrong
And before proof knows nothing—or the fear
Of being behind the world—which is, the wicked.
    [*Here follow ll. 12–19 of our text, S. speaking.*]
With the high amatory-poetic
My temper's no way sympathetic;
To play your pretty woman's fool
I hold but fit for boys from school
    [*Here follow ll. 20–41 of our text*]

Dipsychus

Strange talk, strange words. Ah me, I cannot say.
Could I believe it even of us men
That once the young exuberance drawn off
The liquor would run clear; that once appeased
The vile inquisitive wish, brute appetite fed,
The very void that ebbing flood had left
From purer sources would be now refilled;
That to rank weeds of rainy spring mowed off
Would a green wholesome aftermath succeed
That the empty garnished tenement of the soul
Would not behold the seven replace the one:
Could I indeed as of some men I might
Think this of maidens also. But I know;
Not as the male is, is the female, Eve
Was moulded not as Adam.

Spirit

                    Stuff!
The women like it; that's enough.

Dipsychus

Could I believe, as of a man I might,
So a good girl from weary workday hours
And from the long monotony of toil
Might safely purchase these wild intervals,
And from that banquet rise refreshed, and wake

310

And shake her locks and as before go forth
Invigorated, unvitiate to the task
But no it is not so.

Spirit

                    That may be true
It is uncommon, though some do.
In married life you sometimes find
Proceedings something of the kind.

Dipsychus

No, no, apart from pressure of the world
And yearning sensibilities of soul,
The swallowed dram entails the drunkard's curse
Of burnings ever new; and the coy girl
Turns to the flagrant woman of the street,
Ogling for hirers, horrible to see.

Spirit

That is the high moral way of talking
I'm well aware about street-walking.

Dipsychus

Hungering but without appetite; athirst
From impotence; no humblest feeling left
Of all that once too rank exuberance.
No kindly longing, no sly coyness now
Not e'en the elastic appetence of lust
Not a poor petal hanging to that stalk
Where thousands once were redolent and rich.
Look, she would fain allure; but she is cold
The ripe lips paled, the frolick pulses stilled,
The quick eye dead, the once fair flushing cheek
Flaccid under its paint; the once heaving bosom—
Ask not!—for oh, the sweet bloom of desire
In hot fruition's pawey fingers turns
To dullness and the deadly spreading spot
Of rottenness inevitably soon
That while we hold, we hate—Sweet Peace! no more!

Spirit

Fiddle di diddle, fal lal lal!
By candlelight they are pas mal;
Better and worse of course there are,—
Star differs (with the price) from star.
        [*Here follow ll. 42–45 of our text, D. speaking.*]
Could I think cherry lips and chubby cheeks
That seem to exist express for such fond play,
Hold in suppression nought to come; o'ershell
No lurking virtuality of more—
        [*Here follow ll. 46–58 of our text, S. speaking.*]
Still I must urge, that though tis sad

311

Tis sure, once gone, for good or bad
The prize whose loss we are deploring
Is physically past restoring:
C'en est fait. Nor can God's own self
As Coleridge on the dusty shelf
Says in his wicked Omniana
Renew to Ina frail or Ana
The once rent hymenis membrana.
So that it needs consideration
By what more moral occupation
To support this vast population?

Dipsychus

Could I believe that purity were not
Lodged somewhere, precious pearl, e'en underneath
The hardest coarsest outside: could I think
That any heart in woman's bosom set
By tenderness o'ermastering mean desire,
Faithfulness, love, were unredeemable.
Or could I think it sufferable in me
For my poor pleasure's sake to superadd
One possible finger's pressure to the weight
That turns, and grinds as in a fierce machine
This hapless kind, these pariahs of the sex—

Spirit

Well; people talk—their sentimentality.
Meantime, as by some sad fatality
Mortality is still mortality;
Nor has corruption, spite of facility,
And doctrines of perfectibility
Yet put on incorruptibility,
As women are and the world goes
They're not so badly off—who knows?
They die, as we do in the end;
They marry; or they—superintend:
Or Sidney Herberts sometimes rise,
And send them out to colonize.
        [*Here follow ll. 59–78 of our text*]

Dipsychus

Shyness. Tis but another word for shame;
And that for Sacred Instinct. Off ill thoughts!
Tis holy ground your foot has stepped upon.

Spirit

Ho, Virtue quotha! trust who knows;
There's not a girl that by us goes
But mightn't have you if she chose:
No doubt but you would give her trouble;
But then you'd pay her for it double.

312

DIPSYCHUS

By Jove—if I were but a lass,
I'd soon see what I'd bring to pass.
[*Here follow ll. 79–end of our text*]

SCENE IV

3–34, 236–45, 280–7, and 302–5 were printed separately, with the title IN A
GONDOLA, in *1863*.

43–54 copied by C. into his 1852 notebook.

63 ff. Compare *A. de V*. iii. 173 ff.

82–98. Printed separately, *1863*. There are several MS. versions, two of them
separate from the main *Dipsychus* MSS., and a longer version, constructed from
more than one MS., was printed separately with the title THE HIDDEN LOVE in
1869.

102–21. One MS. contains the following two extra verses, printed in 1865
and thereafter.

> Oh yes, my pensive youth, abstain:
> And any empty sick sensation,
> Remember, anything like pain
> Is only your imagination.

> Trust me, I've read your German sage
> To far more purpose e'er than you did;
> You find it in his wisest page,
> Whom God deludes is well deluded.

122–7. Printed separately, *1862, 1863*.

130–95. A revised version with some verses omitted and others added, and
longer by thirty-six lines, was written by C. in a notebook containing parts of
Mari Magno, with the title SPECTATOR AB EXTRA. This version was printed as
a separate poem in *1862* and *1863*, but not in later editions. It contains the
following section headed 'Le Diner':

II

Le Diner

> Come along, 'tis the time, ten or more minutes past,
> And he who came first had to wait for the last;
> The oysters ere this had been in and been out;
> Whilst I have been sitting and thinking about
> How pleasant it is to have money, heigh-ho!
> How pleasant it is to have money.

> A clear soup with eggs; *voilà tout*; of the fish
> The *filets de sole* are a moderate dish
> *À la Orly*, but you're for red mullet, you say:
> By the gods of good fare, who can question to-day
> How pleasant it is to have money, heigh-ho!
> How pleasant it is to have money.

313

After oysters, sauterne; then sherry; champagne;
Ere one bottle goes, comes another again;
Fly up, thou bold cork, to the ceiling above,
And tell to our ears in the sound that they love
  How pleasant it is to have money, heigh-ho!
  How pleasant it is to have money.

I've the simplest of palates; absurd it may be,
But I almost could dine on a *poulet-au-riz*,
Fish and soup and omelette and that—but the deuce—
There were to be woodcocks, and not *Charlotte Russe!*
  So pleasant it is to have money, heigh-ho!
  So pleasant it is to have money.

Your chablis is acid, away with the hock,
Give me the pure juice of the purple médoc:
St. Péray is exquisite; but, if you please,
Some burgundy just before tasting the cheese.
  So pleasant it is to have money, heigh-ho!
  So pleasant it is to have money.

As for that, pass the bottle, and d——n the expense,
I've seen it observed by a writer of sense,
That the labouring classes could scarce live a day,
If people like us didn't eat, drink, and pay.
  So useful it is to have money, heigh-ho!
  So useful it is to have money.

One ought to be grateful, I quite apprehend,
Having dinners and suppers and plenty to spend,
And so suppose now, while the things go away,
By way of a grace we all stand up and say
  How pleasant it is to have money, heigh-ho!
  How pleasant it is to have money.

204–23. Printed separately, *1862, 1863*.

SCENE V

154–85. Printed separately, *1862, 1863*.
197–200. Copied by C. into his 1852 Notebook with the title 'The Lido', and printed separately, *1862, 1863*.

SCENE IX

160–84. Printed separately, with X, 164–70 and XI, 87–104, 199–213, *1862, 1863*.

SCENE X

72–84. Printed separately with the title IN THE PIAZZA AT NIGHT, *1862, 1863*, together with V, 197–200, the two extracts grouped under the heading *AT VENICE*.

72. All editions before *1951* print 'in her rest', but the MSS. have 'on her nest' (cf. I, 6, where the posthumous editors made a similar alteration from 'nesting' to 'resting').

SCENE XII

9–31. Printed separately, *1862*, *1863*.

SCENE XIII

65. The complete text, from Ephesians vi. 12, is *tous cosmocratoras tou skotous tou aionos toutou*, 'the rulers of the darkness of this world' (see l. 68, 'you dropt a word').

INDEX OF FIRST LINES

INDEX OF FIRST LINES

INDEX OF FIRST LINES

REPRINTED LITHOGRAPHICALLY IN GREAT BRITAIN
AT THE UNIVERSITY PRESS, OXFORD
BY VIVIAN RIDLER
PRINTER TO THE UNIVERSITY